ECONOMIC ANALYSES OF FINANCIAL CRISES

To

my children Irit, Shira, Gail, Jonathan, David

my wife Celia

and my parents Hana and Hayeem Levy

Economic Analyses of Financial Crises

AMNON LEVY-LIVERMORE

Routledge
Taylor & Francis Group
LONDON AND NEW YORK

First published 1995 by Ashgate Publishing

Reissued 2018 by Routledge
2 Park Square, Milton Park, Abingdon, Oxon OX14 4RN
711 Third Avenue, New York, NY 10017, USA

Routledge is an imprint of the Taylor & Francis Group, an informa business

A Library of Congress record exists under LC control number : 95078263

Typeset by Robert Hood
Department of Economics
University of Wollongong
Australia

ISBN 13: 978-1-138-31190-9 (hbk)
ISBN 13: 978-0-429-45854-5 (ebk)

Contents

Figures

Tables

Acknowledgements

I wish to express my deepest gratitude to Robert Hood for his fine editing, advice, patience and support throughout the countless revisions of the manuscript.

I also wish to thank the co-authors of some of the chapters for letting me include the outcomes of our collaborative research in this volume. Six chapters of the book have been co-authored by the following friends and colleagues: Khorshed Chowdhury (Chapters 4, 7, 9 and 10), Eithan Hochman (Chapter 5), Moshe Justman (Chapter 5), Ran Bar-Niv (Chapter 3), Lillian Cheung (Chapter 4), Charles Harvie (Chapter 4) and Edgar Wilson (Chapter 9). Although I have been the initiator, chief investigator and the first author of these chapters, the collaboration of the above-mentioned co-authors has contributed considerably to the quality of the book.

I am indebted to D.P. Chaudhri for background and data provision on cereal production in Punjab, which enabled the analysis in Chapter 7.

I am also indebted to Christopher Adam and the participants of the Twelfth Economic Theory Workshop hosted by the University of Tasmania for comments on the geometrical interpretation of the analytical results of Chapters 1 and 2.

Last but not least, I am grateful to Iris Firstman, Hillel Vardey, Mark Freeman and Mai Ball for dedicated research assistance.

Preface

This book is a collection of fifteen essays on causes and implications of financial problems in three different economic organizations — corporations, semi-cooperative and non-cooperative farming communities, and sovereign states. Correspondingly, these essays are arranged in three distinct parts. The first part of the book deals with corporate insolvency and bankruptcy and includes four chapters. Chapters 1 and 2 highlight conceptually the nexus of interactions among financial, industrial and macroeconomic factors determining the Pareto optimal date in which the claimants of an insolvent firm stop collaborating and force the firm into liquidation. The analysis is conducted within a framework in which the firm's managers are profit maximizers; the firm's claimants have different priority in liquidation and unbiased expectations about their net returns from continuation, but variances that are proportional to the length of the continuation period, and maximize their expected utility from those net returns. The Pareto optimal period of continuation of the firm's operation is found by maximizing the stockholder's expected utility from the net returns from continuation while maintaining the bondholder's utility level equal to that under immediate liquidation. The solution to this problem displays the effects of the firm's initial assets and liabilities and their rates of depreciation and accumulation, the claimants' rates of time preference and attitudes toward risk, the firm's expected profits and macroeconomic and industrial conditions on the optimal continuation period of the firm's operation and liquidation timing. Chapter 3 provides additional theoretical and empirical insights into the relationships between the likelihood of corporate bankruptcy and macroeconomic conditions. The theoretical part hypothesizes that fluctuations in aggregate income and price level adversely affect the well-being of the business sector and links the likelihood of firm failure to the structural parameters of an aggregate demand and supply model governing business cycles. The empirical findings indicate that the annual rate of bankruptcy in the United States is positively correlated with the variances of the GNP and the GNP deflator and negatively correlated with the covariance of these variables. Using a unique dataset on industry bankruptcy rates in Australia, Chapter 4 explores the potential relationships among backruptcy rates in Australia's major industries within the framework of cointegration tests and simultaneous-equation systems. The results lend support to the existence of relationships between the bankruptcy rate in the building and construction industry and the bankruptcy rate in the finance and property industry, as well as between the bankruptcy rate in the manufacturing industry and the bankruptcy rate in the transport, storage and communication industry.

Farming, perhaps more than many other occupations, is a very risky business. The second part of the book deals with risk-sharing and risk-spreading behaviour in two polar agricultural systems. Chapters 5 and 6 highlight the problems that might arise from financial cooperation by referring to the recent experience of the Israeli semi-cooperative agricultural sector. Financial cooperation, through credit sharing and co-signing of debts, was a source of strength for Israel's semi-cooperative villages (*moshavim*) in the early decades of their development. Such cooperation, however, entails a potential 'free-rider' problem when farmers' borrowings are uncoordinated, and recent events in Israel have demonstrated the severe implications it can have. Chapters 5 and 6 present two complementary ways of modelling the externalities generated by financial cooperation, and tests their effects on borrowing and investment behaviour. While the empirical analysis in Chapter 5 focuses on the role of the 'free-rider' problem at the micro level, Chapter 6 estimates the effect of such a negative externality in the more aggregate level. Simulation results indicate that the potential instability of financial cooperation is aggravated when the *moshav* population is heterogeneous. In contrast, Chapter 7 deals with traditional farming communities and organizations, and studies the existence of a risk-spreading behaviour in that sector. In particular, this chapter investigates the applicability of a well-known portfolio selection method in explaining farm-resource allocation in developing countries during the green-revolution period. The effects of yield variation, price expectation, risk aversion and money illusion on farm-land allocation in India's most agriculturally advanced state, Punjab, are estimated and tested within a Markowitzian mean-variance framework.

During the 1970s and 1980s, the external debts of many developing countries grew at an unprecedented rate and became one of the most sensitive and explosive issues in international affairs. The third part of the book deals with the causes and implications of sovereign external debt and insolvency with special reference to the cases of the developing countries in Latin America, Asia and the Pacific and Sub-Saharan Africa. This part comprises Chapter 8 to Chapter 14. Chapter 8 provides an overview of the external debt problem and its evolution during the 1970s and 1980s. Chapter 9 attempts to resolve the controversy about the cause-and-effect relationship between external debt and economic slowdown by conducting Granger causality tests with data on twenty-nine highly indebted developing countries in four distinct geographical regions. The results of these tests are mixed and imply that there is no general coherent relationship between external debt and economic slowdown. They therefore suggest that the design of a recovery policy should consider the case of each developing country separately. The results also suggest that the recovery policy should be based on the country's interrelationships between its GNP and external debt and should incorporate the effects of other intervening macroeconomic variables within an integrative system. In view of these conclusions, Chapter 10 estimates the nexus of inter-relationships between public and private external debts accumulation, capital accumulation and production within a simultaneous equation system using panel data on highly indebted developing countries clustered into three distinct regions: Latin-America, Asia-Pacific and Sub-Saharan Africa. The estimation results indicate that the full effects of the public and private external debts on GNP are small and of an opposite sign, whereas an increase in the GNP level raises substantially the public and private external debts. These findings support the Bulow-Rogoff proposition that the external debts of developing countries are not a primary cause of economic slowdown. They also indicate the important role of intervening socio-economic factors, such as industrial structure, terms of trade, population size and income inequality, in the determination of the GNP level and the accumulation of capital and external debts.

In addition to investigating the cause-and-effect relationship between external debt and economic growth, the third part is also concerned with the possibility of negative externalities in the international credit market and with the issues of repudiation, reputation, secondary-market prices and restructuring. Chapter 11 analyses both conceptually and empirically the effects of three types of externalities on the individual developing country's cost of credit and borrowing behaviour. The first type is the adverse effect of the aggregate borrowing level of the rest of the countries on the interest rate charged on credit extended to a particular country. The second is the group reputation problem. That is, the relatively high level of indebtedness of some countries and their problems to service their external debts might adversely affect the reputation of the developing countries as a whole and reduce their financial credibility. A third type of externality might evolve from uncertainty about the borrowing levels of countries competing in the international credit markets and the associated costs of risk bearing for the individual country. The estimation results of the interest-rate equations and the credit-demand equations confirm the significant role of these externalities in the three distinct developing regions of Latin America, Sub-Saharan Africa, and Asia-Pacific. Chapter 12 studies the relationship between the secondary-market price of sovereign debts and the possibility of repudiation and retaliation. Using the distinction between 'good' and 'bad' states of world, the debtor countries optimal repudiation rate, as well as the creditor's optimal retaliation and reservation price for any repudiation rate are analysed under the assumption that the debtor and creditor are risk averse and expected-utility maximizers. Matching both debtor and creditor's considerations, the chapter presents and discusses the properties of the equilibrium repudiation and retaliation rates and the equilibrium secondary-market price of a sovereign debt. Chapter 13 analyzes further the interaction between a creditor and an indebted sovereign and identifies and describes the possible Nash equilibria in mixed and pure strategies within the framework of a 'one-shot game'. The payoffs of the game include reputation gains and losses for the players as their present behaviour might affect their future payoffs from dealing with other lenders or borrowers in the international credit market. The analysis indicates that both the creditor and the indebted sovereign should prefer a Nash equilibrium in pure strategies to the Nash equilibrium in mixed strategies. It also shows that the possibility of any strategy combination being a Nash equilibrium in pure strategies depends on the trustworthy reputation gains and losses for the players, as well as on the size of the indebted country's external debt and asset holding abroad.

Chapter 14 analyses the optimal accumulation of capital stock, external debt and reputation by incorporating explicitly the inclination of a sovereign country to service its external liabilities and the adverse effects of not meeting foreign loans' commitments on the country's trustworthy reputation. Repudiation and loss of reputation might limit the country's access to international markets of credit, consumer and capital goods; and subsequently might raise the average cost of servicing the country's future external liabilities, deteriorate the terms of trade with the rest of the world and accelerate the depreciation of capital stock. By assuming that the probability of default increases with the debt-service burden, Chapter 15 shows that the set of admissible rescheduling schemes of a sovereign debt to a private creditor can be depicted by a U-shaped curve in the plane spanned by the renegotiated annual debt repayment and the renegotiated length of the repayment period. By classifying creditors and debtors by risk and time preference, this chapter also analyzes the choice of a rescheduling scheme from this set and the likelihood of agreement for eighty-one possible combinations of creditors and debtors.

Amnon Levy
May 1995

Part 1

CORPORATE INSOLVENCY AND BANKRUPTCY

1 Continuation and liquidation timing: A Pareto optimal approach

This chapter derives analytically the Pareto optimal date at which the claimants of an insolvent firm stop collaborating and force the firm into liquidation. The analysis indicates that the greater difference between the stockholder's discounting rate and the bondholder's discounting rate, the longer the continuation period of the insolvent firm's operation.

1.1 Introduction

Though financial distress is a necessary condition for bankruptcy, it is not a sufficient one. It has been argued by Bulow and Shoven (1978) that the criterion for bankruptcy is a positive gain to the coalition of the firm's claimants from immediate liquidation and hence a firm's operation might be liquidated (continued) even when its going-concern value exceeds (is below) its liquidation value. Using a similar analytical framework, White (1980) has further examined the social-efficiency properties of alternative priority rules in liquidation, including the 'me–first' rule, and has concluded that those rules are not socially efficient, except under very strong assumptions about the payment to the bondholder and the interest rates on bonds. In contrast, Ang and Chua (1980) have stressed the important role of the 'me–first' rule in bankruptcy–liquidation decision. They have argued that as long as the firm's claimants are value maximisers and the 'me–first' rule is not violated the liquidation of a firm in a financial distress should take place when the firm's liquidation value exceeds its going-concern value, no matter what coalitions of the firm's claimants are formed.

In all of these pioneering studies of the liquidation decision, as well as in the more modern game-theoretic ones (e.g., Aghion, Hart and Moore, 1992, and White, 1994), the outcomes have a zero–one characteristic, i.e., either an immediate liquidation of the firm, or a continuation of its operation. The length of the continuation period has not been analysed. As in the 'real option' approach to investment decision under uncertainty (e.g., Dixit and Pindyck, 1994, and Hubbard, 1994), a possible justification for ignoring that aspect is that new information is accumulated as time progresses and therefore it might be sub-optimal to determine the duration of the insolvent firm's continued operation in advance. However, when alternatives are time-dependent and span more than a single period, high-priority claimants need to know in advance the length of the period in which their collaboration with low-priority claimants in continuing the insolvent firm's operation is required. This information is essential for identifying the alternatives given up and assessing compensation for the forgone income and excessive risk bearing. It is also essential for loan restructuring. Hence, it is important to study this neglected issue.

The conceptual analysis of the continuation period and liquidation timing developed in this chapter refers to a financially distressed firm whose future operating profits are random. The structure of the industry in which the firm operates and the sources of uncertainty will be described in detail in Chapter 2. In order to simplify the mathematical analysis, the definition of the firm's claimants includes a stockholder and a bondholder (or any other lender) only. Both claimants have unbiased expectations about the firm's future operating profits; but may differ with regard to the degree of absolute risk aversion, assessment of the level of uncertainty involved in the firm's future operation and priority on the firm's liquidation proceeds. It is assumed that the financial crisis arises from the firm's current inability to pay back the bond value which matures in the present period. In liquidation, bond principal claim and interest payments are paid first. It is also assumed that the firm's immediate liquidation value is at least as large as the firm's liabilities. Due to uncertainty about future returns from continuation and the existence of alternatives, the bondholder (or any other lender), unless sufficiently compensated, is not willing to extend the bond (or loan) maturity period and calls for an immediate liquidation; whereas the stockholder considers backing the firm as long as the expected returns from doing so sufficiently exceed the costs of keeping the firm solvent. These costs consist of the costs of risk bearing and the compensation payments required for keeping the bondholder at least as well off as under immediate liquidation while extending the bond's maturity period. Of course, when these costs exceed the stockholder's expected returns from continuation, the stockholder also prefers an immediate liquidation of the firm's assets. Thus, an interior solution to the problem of optimal liquidation time exists when the net returns to the stockholder from continuation are non-negative.

Along these lines the chapter continues as follows. The second section describes the claimants' returns from continuation. The third section presents the claimants' evaluations of those net returns and the collaboration decision problem. The fourth section derives the optimal collaboration period and the condition for immediate liquidation. The fifth section displays and interprets geometrically the optimal collaboration period under various assumptions about the claimants' rates of time preference.

1.2 Claimants' returns from continuation

The conceptual framework uses the following notations:

T	=	the firm's liquidation date;
t	=	a continuous time index, $0 \leq t \leq T$;
S_0	=	the liquidation value of the firm's productive assets at $t = 0$;
B_0	=	the bond (or any other liabilities) claim against the firm at $t = 0$;
$\pi(t)$	=	the firm's operating profit at t;
δ	=	a fixed rate of depreciation of the firm's productive assets;
i	=	the bond's contracted interest rate;
γ	=	the bondholder's subjective discounting rate;
ρ	=	the stockholder's subjective discounting rate;

C = the present value of the compensation payment to the bondholder for continuation to T;

$y_s(T)$ = the (random) present value of the net returns to the stockholder from continuation to T; and

$y_b(T)$ = the (random) present value of the net returns to the bondholder from continuation to T.

The collaboration period (0,T) is determined by a consensus reached by the firm's claimants. It is assumed, for simplicity, that the sale price of the firm's productive assets remains the same over time and that there is no income tax. In this case, the present expected value of the net returns to the stockholder from keeping the firm solvent during the time interval (0,T) is the sum of the discounted operating profits, minus the depreciation costs, plus the salvage value of the firm's assets, minus the liabilities at the end of the period and minus the compensation payment to the bondholder:

$$E[y_s(T)] = \int_0^T e^{-\rho t} \{E[\pi(t)] - \delta S_0\} dt + S_0 - B_0 e^{(i-\rho)T} - C. \qquad (1)$$

The first and the second terms on the right-hand side of equation 1 are constructed under the assumption that, due to its financial difficulties, the firm's net investment is zero. The third term on the right-hand side of equation 1 reflects the assumption that in a case of continuation the firm receives a grace period (0,T). That is, the interest on bond is accumulated and paid at T. The firm's liabilities are discounted by the stockholder's subjective rate, ρ. Cash or other liquid assets, are not included in equation 1. Their inclusion will not change the analysis considerably. It is assumed in the following that the firm's expected instantaneous profit remains the same as time progresses. Thus, the discounted expected value of the net returns to the stockholder from keeping the firm solvent during the time interval (0, T) can be equivalently rendered as

$$E[y_s(T)] = \frac{1}{\rho} [E(\pi) - \delta S_0](1 - e^{-\rho T}) + S_0 - B_0 e^{(i-\rho)T} - C. \qquad (2)$$

Correspondingly, the present value of the expected net returns to the bondholder from continuation are

$$E[y_b(T)] = B_0 e^{(i-\gamma)T} + C. \tag{3}$$

Here, the first term on the right-hand side indicates the value of the principal and the accumulated interest discounted by the bondholder's rate of return on the alternative transaction; and the second term on the right-hand side represents the value of the compensation received by the bondholder for continuation to T.

It is assumed that the claimants' expectations about their net returns from continuation are unbiased, but reflect, naturally, increased uncertainty as the collaboration period expands. More specifically, the claimants' expected net returns from continuation to T, $y_s^e(T)$ and $y_b^e(T)$, are assumed to be normally distributed with means equal to the theoretical values presented by equation 2 and equation 3, and with variances proportional to the collaboration period, $\sigma_s^2 T$ and $\sigma_b^2 T$, respectively. This is equivalent to arguing that the expected net returns to the stockholder and bondholder from continuation to T can be approximated by Wiener processes (Brownian motion).

1.3 Claimants' preferences and the collaboration decision problem

It is postulated that both claimants maximize expected utility and that their preferences on the expected net returns can be represented by utility functions which, in order to simplify the mathematical analysis, reflect constant degrees of absolute risk aversion R_s and R_b, respectively:

$$U_j(y_j^e(T)) = 1 - \exp\{-R_j y_j^e(T)\} \text{ for } j = s, b. \tag{4}$$

With this specification of U, the expected utility functions can be displayed as

$$E(U_j) = 1 - \int_{-\infty}^{\infty} \exp\{-R_j y_j^e(T)\}\, \phi_j(y_j^e(T))\, dy_j^e(T) = 1 - m(-R_j) \text{ for } j = s, b \tag{5}$$

where ϕ_j is the density-probability function of $y_j^e(T)$ and m is its moment-generating function. Given that $y_j^e(T)$ is normally distributed, we obtain

$$E(U_j) = 1 - \exp\{-R_j E[y_j^e(T)] + 0.5\, R_j^2 \sigma_j^2 T\} \text{ for } j = s, b. \tag{6}$$

Unless sufficiently compensated, the bondholder prefers an immediate liquidation (i.e., T = 0) upon continuation of the firm's operation. Thus, the Pareto optimal collaboration period can be found by specifying the stockholder's decision problem as

$$\max_T E[U_s(y_s^e(T))]$$

subject to

$$E[U_b(y_b^e(T))] = E[U_b(y_b^e(0))]. \tag{7}$$

The above constraint reflects the compensation payment, C, required in order to keep the bondholder at least as well off as under immediate liquidation. In view of equations 6 and 3, this constraint can be rendered as

$$R_b[B_0 e^{(i-\gamma)T} + C] - 0.5 R_b^2 \sigma_b^2 T = R_b B_0 \tag{8}$$

and consequently,

$$C = B_0[1 - e^{(i-\gamma)T}] + 0.5\, R_b\, \sigma_b^2 T. \tag{9}$$

That is, in order to postpone the liquidation of the firm to T, the bondholder should be paid the forgone interest differential between his alternative financial investment and the firm's bond plus the costs of risk bearing, which are equal to the product of the perceived level of uncertainty associated with his net returns from continuation to T and his degree of absolute risk aversion.

Summing up, the Pareto optimal collaboration period can be found by solving the stockholder decision problem

$$\max_{T} \{1 - \exp\{-R_s E[y_s(T)] + 0.5 R_s{}^2 \sigma_s{}^2 T\}\}$$

where $E[y_s(T)]$ is given by equation 2 and C by equation 9.

1.4 Optimal collaboration period and the condition for immediate liquidation

Since maximizing $\{1-\exp\{-R_s E[y_s(T)]+0.5R_s{}^2\sigma_s{}^2T\}\}$ is equivalent to maximizing the risk-deducted expected return from continuation to the stockholder $\{E[y_s(T)]-0.5R_s\sigma_s{}^2T\}$, the Pareto optimal collaboration period (T^o) should satisfy the first-order condition

$$[E(\pi) - \delta S_0]e^{-\rho T^o} = [(i-\rho)e^{(i-\rho)T^o} + (\gamma - i)e^{(i-\gamma)T^o}]B_0 + 0.5(R_b\sigma_b^2 + R_s\sigma_s^2) \tag{10}$$

and the second-order condition

$$H = -\rho\,[E(\pi)-\delta S_0]\,e^{-\rho T^o} - (i-\rho)^2 B_0 e^{(i-\rho)T^o} + (i-\gamma)^2 B_0 e^{(i-\rho)T^o} < 0. \tag{11}$$

Furthermore, by setting T^o to be equal to zero in equation 10 we obtain that the condition for immediate liquidation is:

$$E(\pi) - \delta S_0 = (\gamma - \rho)B_0 + 0.5(R_b\sigma_b^2 + R_s\sigma_s^2). \tag{12}$$

That is, the financially distressed firm should be immediately forced into liquidation if the expected profit after depreciation obtained from an infinitesimal continuation of the firm's operation (the term on the left-hand side) is just equal to the cost of doing so in terms of the forgone interest on the alternative financial investment for the bondholder, discounted by the stockholder rate of time preference, and the risk bearing for both claimants. Of course, immediate liquidation is also optimal when the expected profit gained from infinitesimal continuation is overweighed by the costs.

1.5 Geometrical interpretation of the solution under various assumptions about the claimants' rates of time preference

The left-hand side of equation 10 indicates the marginal benefit from continuation (MBFC) to the stockholder, whereas the right-hand side is the marginal cost of continuation (MCOC). The slope of the MBFC curve in the T-$ plane is given by the first term on the left-hand side of inequality 11:

$$\frac{dMBFC}{dT} = -\rho[E(\pi) - \delta S_0]e^{-\rho T} \tag{13}$$

In the following we consider the non-trivial case where the expected instantaneous profit after depreciation, $E(\pi) - \delta S_0$, is positive and hence the MBFC curve is downward sloping.

Similarly, the slope of the MCOC curve in the T-$ plane is equal to the sum of the second and third terms on the left-hand side of the second-order condition 11, and hence

$$\frac{dMCOC}{dT} \gtreqless 0 \text{ as } \frac{i-\rho}{i-\gamma} \gtreqless e^{(\rho-\gamma)T} \tag{14}$$

or, equivalently,

$$\frac{dMCOC}{dT} \gtreqless 0 \text{ as } \gamma \gtreqless \rho. \tag{15}$$

That is, if the bondholder' rate of time preference is greater than, equal to, or smaller than the stockholder's rate of time preference, the MCOC curve is upward-sloping, flat, or downward-sloping, respectively, as displayed by Figures 1.1a to 1.1d. These figures have been drawn under the assumption that the expected instantaneous profit after depreciation (i.e., the left-hand side of equation 12 and the intercept of the MBFC curve) exceeds the instantaneous costs of continuation (i.e., the right-hand side of equation 12 and the intercept of the MCOC curve). As argued earlier, under the alternative assumption that the expected instantaneous profit after depreciation is equal to, or smaller than, the instantaneous costs of continuation, the stockholder prefers an immediate liquidation of the firm.

Figures 1.1a to 1.1d indicate that the smaller the discrepancy between the bondholder's and the stockholder's rates of time preference, the longer the period of collaboration. This period can even be infinite when ρ is sufficiently larger than γ so that the MCOC curve is downward-sloping and lies entirely below the MBFC curve. This conclusion is valid as long as ρ is held constant while γ is lowered and moderates the slope of the MCOC curve as we move from Figure 1.1a to Figure 1.1d. The underlying rationale is that γ represents the bondholder's opportunity costs, and hence the lower γ, the smaller the compensation payment required for keeping the bondholder as well off as under immediate liquidation and, subsequently, the longer the period of continuation desired by the stockholder.

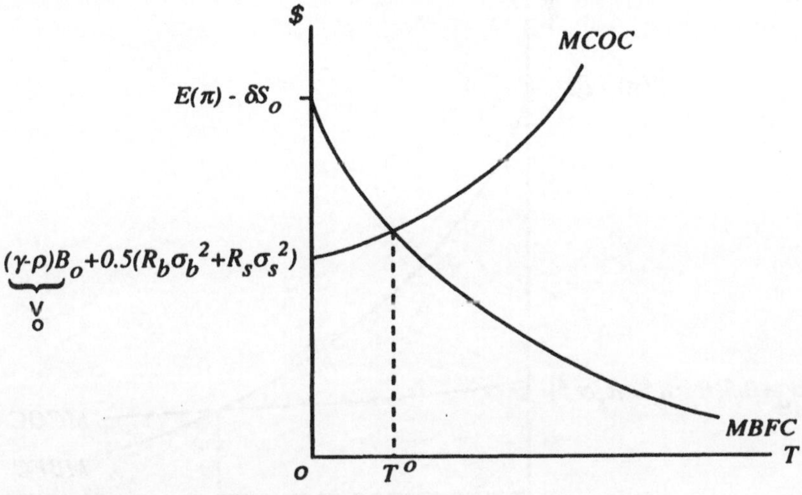

Figure 1.1a The collaboration period when $\gamma > \rho$

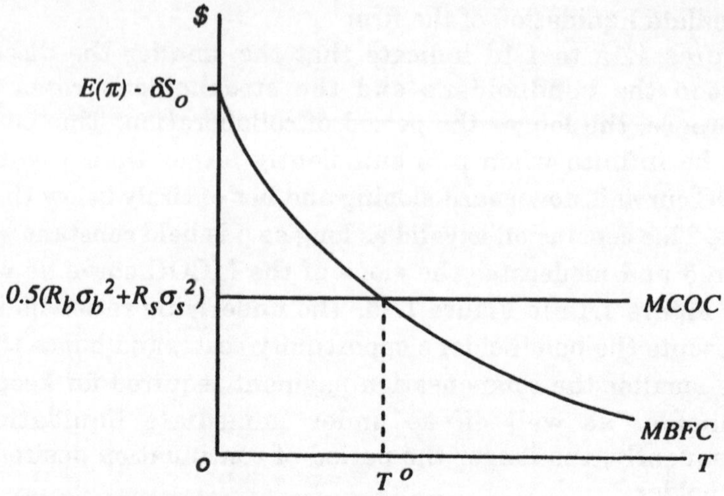

Figure 1.1b The collaboration period when $\gamma = \rho$

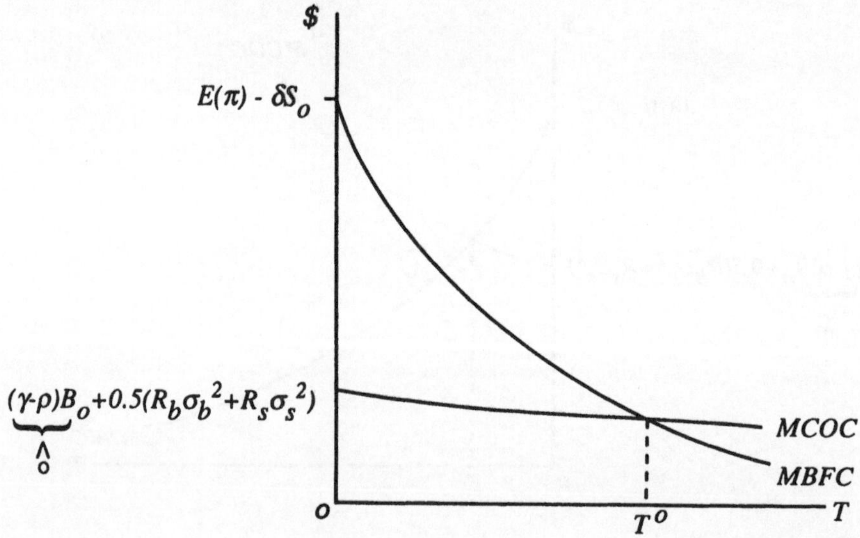

Figure 1.1c $\gamma < \rho$, finite collaboration period

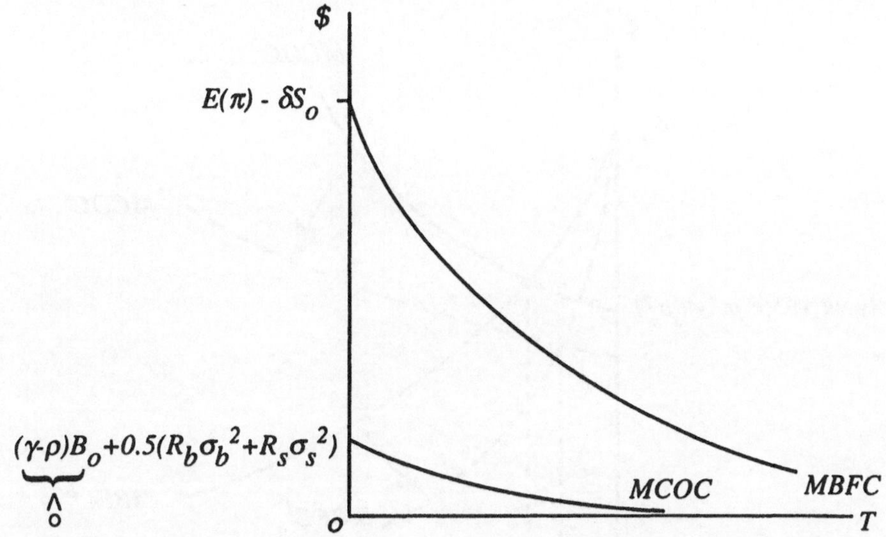

Figure 1.1d $\gamma \ll \rho$**, infinite collaboration period**

It is important to note, however, that if we also allow ρ to rise within the open unit interval (0,1) the MCOC curve is flattened and shifted downward as the discounted compensation costs diminish, whereas the MBFC curve is steepened and tilted toward the origin as the discounted expected future profit diminishes. Thus, the net effect of an hypothetical rise in the stockholder's rate of time preference on the collaboration period is not clear, *a priori*, as displayed by Figure 1.2a and Figure 1.2b.

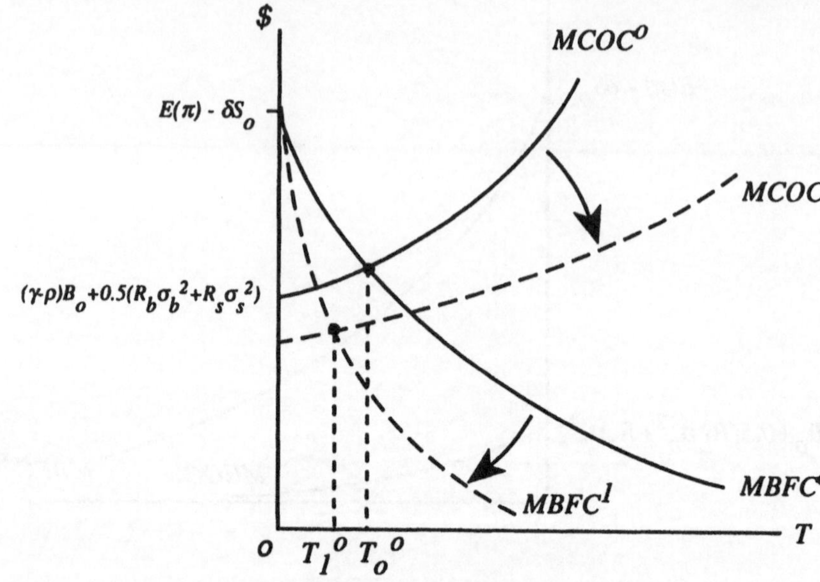

Figure 1.2a A rise in ρ shortens T^o

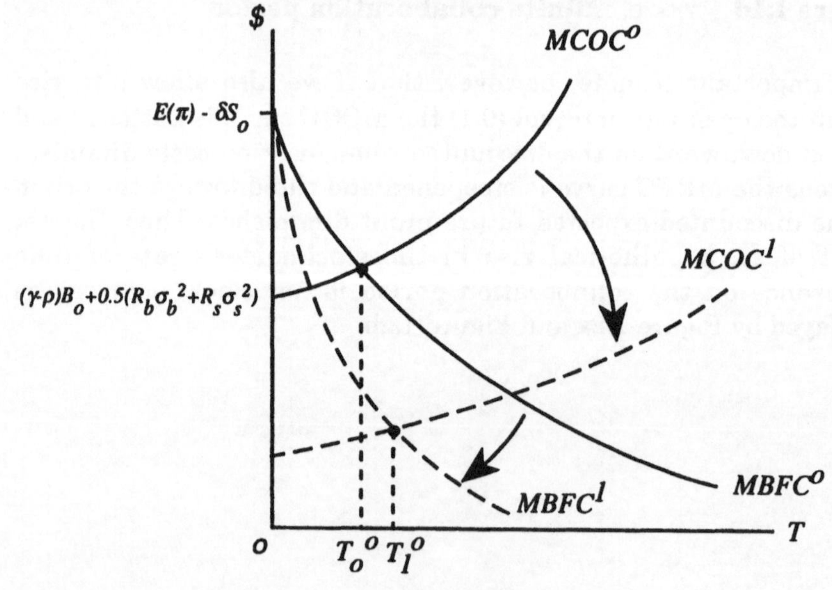

Figure 1.2b A rise in ρ lengthens T^o

References

Aghion, P., Hart, O. and Moore, J. (1992), 'The Economics of bankruptcy Reform', *Journal of Law, Economics, & Organization*, vol. 8, pp. 523–46.

Ang, J.S. and Chua, J.H. (1980), 'Coalition, the Me-First Rule, and the Liquidation Decision', *The Bell Journal of Economics*, vol. 11, no. 1, pp. 355–9.

Bulow, J. and Shoven, J. (1978), 'The Bankruptcy Decision', *The Bell Journal of Economics*, vol. 9, no. 2, pp. 437–56.

Dixit, A.K. and Pindyck, R.S. (1994), *Investment under Uncertainty*, Princeton University Press, Princeton.

Hubbard, G.R. (1994), 'Investment Under Uncertainty: Keeping One's Options Open', *Journal of Economic Literature*, vol. XXXII, pp. 1816–31.

White, M.J. (1980), 'Public Policy Toward bankruptcy: Me-First and Other Priority Rules', *The Bell Journal of Economics*, vol. 11, no. 2, pp. 550–64.

—— (1994), 'Corporate Bankruptcy as a Filtering Device: Chapter 11 Reorganizations and Out-of-Court Debt Restructurings', *Journal of Law, Economics, & Organization*, vol. 10, no. 2, pp. 268–95.

2 The effects of financial, industrial and macroeconomic factors on the continuation and liquidation timing

This chapter completes the previous chapter's analysis by deriving the effects of the firm's initial liabilities, liquidation value, capital depreciation rate, contracted interest rate, uncertainty, expected profit, aggregate consumer price and income volatility, demand elasticity, and industry's concentration level on the claimants' decision regarding the liquidation date of an insolvent firm.

Due to the mathematical complexity of the necessary condition for maximum expected utility for the insolvent firm's claimants from continuation, a closed-form solution to the Pareto optimal collaboration period cannot be obtained. Nevertheless, the effects of financial, industrial and macroeconomic factors on the continuation period of the insolvent firm's operation can be analyzed by comparative statics of equation 10 from Chapter 1 and consideration of the second-order condition 11 as displayed by the mathematical appendix at the end of this chapter. These effects are summarized in the following sections.

2.1 Effect of the firm's initial liabilities B_0

Proposition 1: If the bondholder's time-preference rate exceeds the stockholder's time-preference rate (i.e., $\gamma > \rho$), the greater the firm's initial liabilities the shorter the collaboration period. In contrast, if the stockholder's rate of time preference exceeds the bondholder's rate of time preference, the greater the firm's initial liabilities the longer the collaboration period. If, however, both claimants have the same rate of time preference, the collaboration period is not affected by the firm's initial liabilities.

The geometrical interpretation of this proposition is as follows. When $\gamma < \rho$, the MCOC is upward-sloping. In which case, a rise in B_0 steepens the MCOC curve and shifts it upward and therefore reduces T^o as displayed in Figure 2.1a. When $\gamma < \rho$, the MCOC is downward-sloping. In which case, a rise in B_0 steepens the MCOC curve and shifts it downward and therefore increases T^o a s displayed in Figure 2.1b. However, when $\gamma = \rho$, the MCOC curve is flat and its location is not affected by the size of B_0.

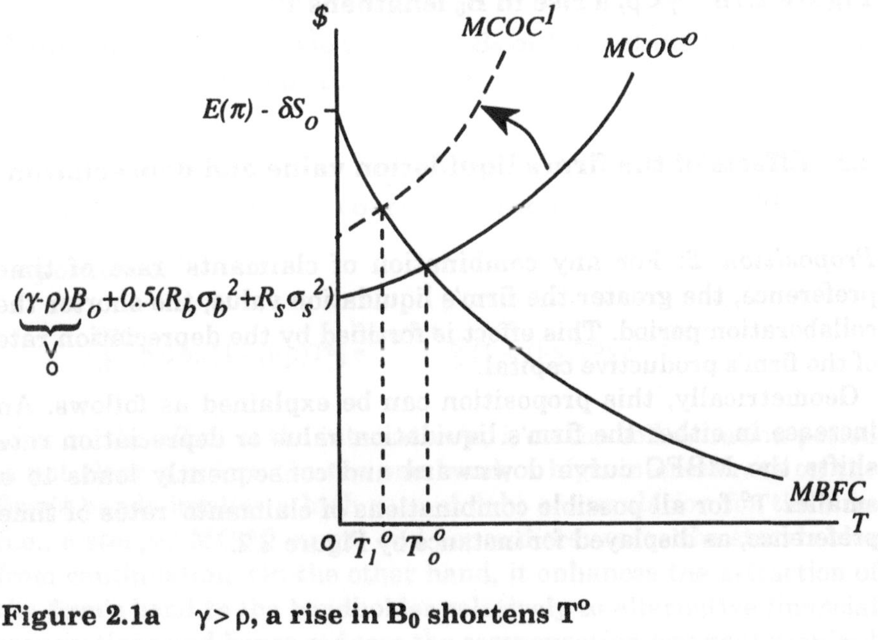

Figure 2.1a $\gamma > \rho$**, a rise in** B_0 **shortens** T^o

2.4 Effect of uncertainty

Proposition 4: If both claimants are risk averse, then for any combination of claimants' rate of time preference the greater the level of uncertainty about the claimants' net returns from continuation, the shorter the collaboration period.

The underlying rationale of this proposition is that an increase in the level of uncertainty about the net returns raises the costs of risk bearing to the stockholder and hence moderates his or her inclination for continuation. Moreover, an increase in the costs of risk bearing to the bondholder raises the compensation payment in a case of continuation for keeping the bondholder as well off as under immediate liquidation and thereby shortens the collaboration period. Geometrically, an increase in the costs of risk bearing shifts the MCOC curve upward and hence shortens the period of collaboration for any combination of claimants' rate of time preference, as displayed for instance by Figure 2.3.

Figure 2.3 **$\gamma > \rho$, a rise in the uncertainty level shortens the collaboration period**

2.5 Effect of the firm's expected profit

Proposition 5: For any combination of claimants' rates of time preference, the larger the firm's expected instantaneous profit the longer the collaboration period.

The underlying rationale of this proposition is straightforward. A more optimistic outlook for the firm's instantaneous profit leads to a larger marginal benefit from continuation of the firm operation and hence lengthens the collaboration period for any combination of the claimants' rates of time preference. Geometrically, despite steepening the MBFC curve, an increase in $E(\pi)$ shifts that curve upward, as displayed for instance by Figure 2.4.

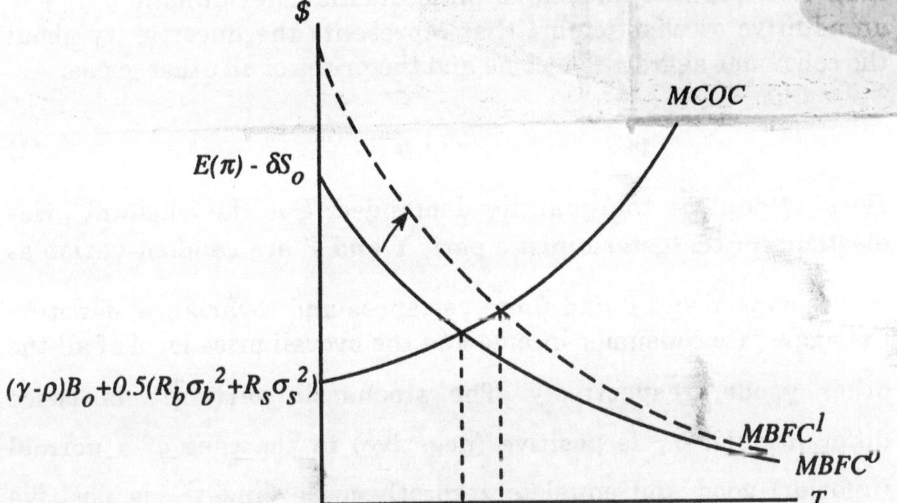

Figure 2.4 $\gamma > \rho$, a rise in the expected instantaneous profit lengthens the collaboration period

2.6 Effects of industrial and macroeconomic conditions

As indicated earlier, the firm's expected profits are a key factor in the determination of the net returns to the stockholders from continuation and hence in the determination of the length of the collaboration period. These expected profits might be affected by the industrial and global economic environment in which the firm operates. This section explores the possible effects of industrial and macroeconomic conditions on the liquidation decision and timing. It is assumed that the firm operates in a Cournot-Nash equilibrium where all firms are expected profit maximisers, take their competitors' supply as given (i.e., zero conjectural variation), and have an identical and constant marginal cost of production (i.e., $mc_n(q_n) = mc$ for all q_n and for every $n = 1,...,N$). However, these firms are different with regard to their financial (debt-equity) structure.

It is assumed further that the inverse demand function for the industry's product consists of an isoelastic deterministic part and an additive stochastic part that represents the uncertainty about the consumer aggregate income and the prices of all other goods:

$$p(Q, Y, P) = Q^{-1/\xi} + \tilde{\mathbf{p}}\,(P, Y). \tag{1}$$

Here, Q denotes the quantity demanded; ξ is the constant price elasticity of the deterministic part; Y and P are random variables with means $\bar{Y}$ and $\bar{P}$ and finite variances and covariance, denoting the aggregate consumer income and the overall price level of all the other goods, respectively. The stochastic part, $\tilde{\mathbf{p}}$, is twice differentiable; $\tilde{\mathbf{p}}_Y$ is positive (negative) in the case of a normal (inferior) good and equal to zero otherwise; and $\tilde{\mathbf{p}}_p$ is positive (negative) when the industry's product is essentially a substitute (complementary) to the rest of the goods and zero otherwise. In order to introduce the effects of variations in the macroeconomic factors Y and P on the bankruptcy decision, a second-order Taylor approximation of the inverse demand function at the means' point $(\bar{Y}, \bar{P})$ is considered:

$$p(Q, Y, P) \cong Q^{-1/\xi} + \tilde{\mathbf{p}}_Y(Y - \bar{Y}) + \tilde{\mathbf{p}}_P(P - \bar{P}) + 0.5\tilde{\mathbf{p}}_{YY}(Y - \bar{Y})^2$$
$$+ 0.5\tilde{\mathbf{p}}_{PP}(P - \bar{P})^2 + 0.5\tilde{\mathbf{p}}_{YP}(Y - \bar{Y})(P - \bar{P}). \tag{2}$$

It is postulated that the firms' expected profit-maximization problem is

$$\max_{q_n} E\{[p(Q, Y, P) - mc]q_n\}$$

subject to

$$Q = \sum_{n'=1}^{N} q_{n'} \ . \tag{3}$$

The solution of this problem yields the Cournot-Nash expected product price

$$E(p^*) = \frac{1}{1 - 1/\xi N}\{mc - 0.5[\tilde{p}_{YY}Var(Y) + \tilde{p}_{PP}Var(P) + \tilde{p}_{YP}Cov(Y, P)]\} \tag{4}$$

as is shown in the Appendix.

The firm's expected instantaneous profit is given by

$$E[\pi(t)]_n = E[(p^* - mc)\ q_n^*] \tag{5}$$

and by recalling equation 4 and that q_n^* is a chosen quantity and all of the firms have an identical production operation, the individual firm's expected instantaneous profit can be expressed further as:

$$E[\pi(t)]_n = \frac{Q^*}{N}[E(p^*)-mc] = \frac{mcQ^*}{N(\xi N-1)} - \frac{0.5\xi Q^*}{\xi N-1}[\tilde{p}_{YY}Var(Y) + \tilde{p}_{PP}Var(P) + \tilde{p}_{YP}Cov(Y, P)] \tag{6}$$

where Q^* is the industry's volume of sales. *A priori*, the signs of the second derivatives of $\tilde{p}$ and Cov(Y, P) are unknown and hence the effects of uncertainty about the macroeconomic conditions, as well as the effects of the degree of industry concentration and price elasticity, on the firm's expected operating profit are not clear. When the overall effect of aggregate income and consumer price volatility on the industry product price (i.e., $\tilde{p}_{YY}Var(Y) + \tilde{p}_{PP}Var(P)$ +

$\tilde{p}_{YP}Cov(Y, P)$) is negative (positive) the expected profit is greater (smaller) than that under certainty ($mcQ^*/N(\xi N-1)$). The discrepancy between the two decreases with the level of the price elasticity and the number of producers. Note further that the assumption of time-invariant expected profit underlying the transition from equation 1 to equation 2 in Chapter 1 requires that the industry's structure (e.g., number of rival firms, marginal cost of production and demand elasticity), as well as the functional form of $\tilde{p}$ and the variances and covariance of Y and P, are perceived to remain the same over time.

The effects of the industrial and macroeconomic conditions on the collaboration period can now be obtained by virtue of equation 10 from Chapter 1 and equation 6. They are summarized by the following three propositions whose proofs are given in the Appendix.

Proposition 6 (The effects of aggregate price and income volatility):

$\frac{dT^o}{dVar(Y)} \gtreqless 0$ as $\tilde{p}_{YY} \lesseqgtr 0$, $\frac{dT^o}{dVar(P)} \gtreqless 0$ as $\tilde{p}_{PP} \lesseqgtr 0$, and $\frac{dT^o}{dCov(Y,P)} \gtreqless 0$ as $\tilde{p}_{YP} \lesseqgtr 0$.

This proposition indicates that the effects of the aggregate consumer price and income volatility crucially depend upon the signs of the second derivatives of the inverse demand function's stochastic part. If the marginal effect of income on the firm's product price (i.e., the extent of being a normal good) rises (diminishes) with Y, the higher the volatility of aggregate income, the shorter (longer) the optimal continuation period of the firm's operation. If the marginal effect of the aggregate consumer price on the firm's product price (i.e., the substitution effect) increases (diminishes) with P, the higher the volatility of the consumer price level, the shorter (longer) the optimal collaboration period. Finally, if the extent of being a normal good is positively (adversely) affected by a rise in the aggregate consumer price level, the larger the correlation between the aggregate income level and the consumer price level, the shorter (longer) the optimal collaboration period.

Proposition 7 (The effect of the price elasticity of the demand for the firm's product):

$$\frac{dT^o}{d\xi} \gtreqless 0 \text{ as } 0.5[\,\tilde{\mathbf{p}}_{YY}\mathrm{Var}(Y) + \tilde{\mathbf{p}}_{PP}\mathrm{Var}(P) + \tilde{\mathbf{p}}_{YP}\mathrm{Cov}(Y,P)] \gtreqless mc.$$

This proposition indicates that if the effect of the aggregate consumer income and price volatility on the expected price of the insolvent firm's product is greater (smaller) than the firm's marginal cost of production, the more elastic the demand for the firm's product, the longer (shorter) the optimal continuation period of the firm's operation.

Proposition 8 (The effect of the industry's level of concentration):

$$\frac{dT^o}{d\left(\frac{1}{N}\right)} \gtreqless 0 \text{ as } mc \gtreqless 0.5[\tilde{\mathbf{p}}_{YY}\mathrm{Var}(Y)+\tilde{\mathbf{p}}_{PP}\mathrm{Var}(P)+\tilde{\mathbf{p}}_{YP}\mathrm{Cov}(Y,P)][\xi^2 N/(2\xi N-1)].$$

This proposition indicates that if the firm's marginal costs of production are larger (smaller) than the effect of the aggregate consumer income and price volatility on the expected price of the insolvent firm's product adjusted to the industry size and demand elasticity, the more concentrated the industry, the longer (shorter) the optimal continuation period of the firm's operation.

Appendix

Proof of Proposition 1: Assuming that all other things remain the same, the total differential of the necessary condition 10 from Chapter 1 with respect to B_0 and T^o implies

$$\frac{dT^o}{dB_0} = \frac{(1-\rho)\, e^{(i-\rho)T^o} - (i-\gamma)\, e^{(i-\gamma)T^o}}{H}$$

and since $H < 0$, $\frac{dT^o}{dB_0} \gtreqless 0$ as $i \lesseqgtr r + (i-g)\, e^{(r-g)T^o}$.

Proof of Proposition 2: Assuming that all other things remain the same, the total differential of the necessary condition 10 with respect to S_0 and T^o implies

$$\frac{dT^o}{dS_0} = \frac{\delta e^{-\rho T^o}}{H} < 0$$

since $H < 0$.

Proof of Proposition 3: Assuming that all other things remain the same, the total differential of the necessary condition 10 with respect to i and T^o implies:

$$\frac{dT^o}{di} = \frac{\left\{ [1 - (i-\rho)T^o]e^{(i-\rho)T^o} - [1+(i-\gamma)T^o]e^{(i-\gamma)T^o} \right\} B_0}{H}$$

and since $H < 0$,

$$\frac{dT^o}{di} \gtreqless 0 \text{ as } [1 - (i-\rho)T^o]\, e^{(i-\rho)T^o} \lesseqgtr [1 + (i-\gamma)T^o]\, e^{(i-\gamma)T^o}.$$

Proof of Proposition 4: Assuming that all other things remain the same and $H < 0$, the total differential of the necessary condition 10 with respect to $0.5R_s\sigma_s^2$ and T^o implies

$$\frac{dT^o}{d(0.5R_s\sigma_s^2)} = \frac{1}{H} < 0$$

and similarly,

$$\frac{dT^o}{d(0.5R_b\sigma_b^2)} = \frac{1}{H} < 0.$$

Proof of Proposition 5: Assuming that all other things remain the same, the total differential of the necessary condition 10 with respect to $E(\pi)$ and T^o implies

$$\frac{dT^o}{dE(\pi)} = \frac{-e^{-\rho T^o}}{H} > 0$$

since $H < 0$.

The Solution to the Firm's Expected Profit-Maximization Problem

Given the second-order Taylor approximation of the inverse demand function, the firm's objective function can be displayed as

$$\max_{q_n} E\{[Q^{-1/\xi} + \tilde{p}_Y(Y - \bar{Y}) + \tilde{p}_P(P - \bar{P}) + 0.5\,\tilde{p}_{YY}(Y - \bar{Y})^2$$

$$+ 0.5\,\tilde{p}_{PP}(P - \bar{P})^2 + 0.5\,\tilde{p}_{YP}(Y - \bar{Y})(P - \bar{P}) - mc]\,q_n\}.$$

Taking the expectation of the objective function and recalling that

the choice variable q_n is deterministic and that $E(Y-\bar{Y})=0=E(P - \bar{P})$, the objective function can be expressed further as

$$\max_{q_n} \{Q^{-1/\xi} q_n + 0.5[\,\tilde{p}_{YY}Var(Y) + \tilde{p}_{PP}Var(P) +$$

$$\tilde{p}_{YP}Cov(Y,P)]q_n - mc\,q_n\}.$$

The first-order condition for maximum is

$$-(1/\xi)Q^{*-1/\xi}\,q_n^*/Q^* + Q^{*-1/\xi} - mc + 0.5[\tilde{p}_{YY}Var(Y) + \tilde{p}_{YY}Var(P) + \tilde{p}_{YP}Cov(Y,P)] = 0$$

and since $Q^{*-1/\xi} = E(p^*)$ and $q_n^*/Q^* = 1/N$ (all firms have identical production operation)

$$E(p^*) = \frac{1}{1 - 1/\xi N}\{mc - 0.5[\tilde{p}_{YY}Var(Y) + \tilde{p}_{PP}Var(P) + \tilde{p}_{YP}Cov(Y,P)]\}.$$

Proof of Proposition 6: By virtue of proposition 5 and equation 6

$$\frac{dT^o}{dVar(Y)} = \frac{dT^o}{dE(\pi)}\frac{dE(\pi)}{dVar(Y)} = -\frac{0.5\xi Q^*}{\xi N - 1}\frac{dT^o}{dE(\pi)}\tilde{p}_{YY} \gtreqless 0 \text{ as } \tilde{p}_{YY} \lesseqgtr 0,$$

$$\frac{dT^o}{dVar(P)} = \frac{dT^o}{dE(\pi)}\frac{dE(\pi)}{dVar(P)} = -\frac{0.5\xi Q^*}{\xi N - 1}\frac{dT^o}{dE(\pi)}\tilde{p}_{PP} \gtreqless 0 \text{ as } \tilde{p}_{pp} \lesseqgtr 0,$$

and

$$\frac{dT^o}{dCov(Y,P)} = \frac{dT^o}{dE(\pi)}\frac{dE(\pi)}{dCov(Y,P)} = -\frac{0.5\xi Q^*}{\xi N - 1}\frac{dT^o}{dE(\pi)}\tilde{p}_{YP} \gtreqless 0 \text{ as } \tilde{p}_{YP} \lesseqgtr 0 .$$

Proof of Proposition 7: By virtue of proposition 5 and equation 6

$$\frac{dT^o}{d\xi} = \frac{Q^*\left\{mc - 0.5\left[\tilde{p}_{YY}Var(Y) + \tilde{p}_{PP}Var(P) + \tilde{p}_{YP}cov(Y,P)\right]\right\}e^{-\rho T^o}}{(\xi N - 1)^2 H}$$

and since $H < 0$,

$$\frac{dT^o}{d\xi} \gtreqless 0 \text{ as } 0.5\left[\tilde{p}_{YY}Var(Y) + \tilde{p}_{PP}Var(P) + \tilde{p}_{YP}Cov(Y,P)\right] \gtreqless mc.$$

Proof of Proposition 8: By virtue of proposition 5 and equation 6

$$\frac{dT^o}{dN} = \frac{Q^*\{(2\xi N - 1)mc - 0.5\xi^2 N^2[\tilde{p}_{YY}Var(Y) + \tilde{p}_{PP}Var(P) + \tilde{p}_{YP}cov(Y,P)]\}e^{-\rho T^o}}{N^2(\xi N - 1)^2 H}$$

and recalling that $H < 0$,

$$\frac{dT^o}{d\left(\frac{1}{N}\right)} \gtreqless 0 \text{ as } mc \gtreqless 0.5[\tilde{p}_{YY}Var(Y) + \tilde{p}_{PP}Var(P) + \tilde{p}_{YP}Cov(Y,P)][\xi^2 N/(2\xi N - 1)].$$

3 Macroeconomic aspects of firm bankruptcy analysis

Co-authored by Ran Bar-Niv

This chapter provides theoretical and empirical insights into the relationships between the probability of corporate bankruptcy and macroeconomic factors. The theoretical part hypothesizes that fluctuations in aggregate income and price level adversely affect the well-being of the business sector and links the likelihood of firm failure to structural parameters governing the business cycles. Our empirical findings for the United States indicate that the annual rate of bankruptcy is positively correlated with the variances of the GNP and the GNP deflator and negatively correlated with the covariance of these variables.

3.1 Introduction

The purpose of this chapter is to explore relationships between corporate bankruptcy and fundamental macroeconomic aspects. Research in the field of bankruptcies among firms has focused primarily on microeconomic analyses which emphasize financial aspects in explaining and predicting business failures. Stiglitz

Reprinted with permission from the *Journal of Macroeconomics* 9, 1987, 407–416, with some modifications.

(1972, 1975) has shown that market valuation of a firm is a decreasing function of its debt-equity ratio when there is a finite probability of bankruptcy, when bondholders have unambiguously more pessimistic expectations of the firm's prospects than stockholders, and when both are risk neutral. Using the Modigliani-Miller arbitrage argument, Stapleton (1975) has argued that leverage cannot reduce the value of the firm. Bulow and Shoven (1978) have assumed that the criterion for bankruptcy is the positive gain from immediate liquidation to the coalition of claimants with negotiating power, and they derive the conditions under which bankruptcy occurs where there are three asymmetrical classes of claimants on the firm's assets and income flows. Munch and Smallwood (1980) have found that minimum capital requirements appear to reduce insolvency, but other forms of regulations do not have the desired effects.

Although business failure is essentially a microeconomic phenomenon reflecting a particular firm's situation, the probability of this outcome is likely to be influenced by the overall performance of the economy that defines the environment in which firms operate. In contrast to the extensive microeconomic literature, the linkage between insolvency and macroeconomic theory appears to have attracted little attention. The study of business cycles or variations in aggregate economic variables can further enhance understanding of the determinants of the probability of firm failure. In particular, fluctuations in national income affect the demand for the firm's products, unless it is income inelastic, and, in the case of a normal (inferior) good, lead to lower (higher) demand in downturns and higher (lower) demand in upturns. Altman (1971) has found that the corporate failure rate in America is negatively correlated with changes in the GNP, stock prices, and money supply; and that slowdowns in economic activity increase the failure rate. Stiglitz (1992) has argued, in turn, that an economic downturn can be amplified by the reduction in bank lending activity caused by regular customers going bankrupt. Fluctuations in prices might also affect a firm's net cash flow when payments and receipts are not fully linked to relevant price indices.

Along the lines of this rationale, this chapter continues with a theoretical analysis that links the underlying macroeconomic factors determining the nature of fluctuations in aggregate economic variables with the probability of business failures. In order to provide the analysis with a wide and profound theoretical basis, the Dornbusch-Fischer (1978) macroeconomic model is used as a benchmark. The reduced form of this model, incorporating the adaptive expectations' hypothesis, is presented in Section 3.2 by a system of first-order difference equations, and is then solved for the case of conjugate complex roots displaying oscillations in the aggregate variables. The probability of firm failure is discussed on the basis of the properties of the derived business cycles. Section 3.3 estimates the effects of variations of aggregate variables on the annual rate of bankruptcy in post-Second World War United States. The estimations' results are statistically significant and confirm *a priori* expectations that the annual rate of bankruptcy rises with the variances of the real GNP and the GNP deflator. The results also indicate that the annual rate of bankruptcy declines with the covariance of these variables.

3.2 Business cycles and insolvency

The well-known (closed economy) model of Dornbusch and Fischer (1978) is a macroeconomic structure which is capable of generating cyclical fluctuations in major aggregate variables such as income and inflation rate. In this model the aggregate supply is represented by the expectations-augmented Phillips curve

$$\pi = \pi^* + \delta(Y - Y_p),\ \delta > 0, \tag{1}$$

the aggregate demand by the time differential of the solution to the IS–LM system

$$Y = Y_{-1} + \gamma\alpha + \phi(m - \pi),\ \gamma, \phi > 0, \tag{2}$$

and the public's expectations about the rate of inflation are assumed to be adaptive

$$\pi^* = \frac{\beta}{1 - (1 - \beta)L}\pi_{-1},\ 0 < \beta < 1. \tag{3}$$

(Cagan, 1956; and Friedman, 1956.) Here Y is the current level of output; Y_p is the potential level of output; π is the actual inflation rate; π^* is the expected inflation rate; α is the increase in the autonomous expenditures; m is the growth rate of the nominal money stock; δ is a positive parameter reflecting the short-run trade-off, on the supply side, between inflation and GNP gap; γ is the fiscal multiplier; ϕ is the monetary multiplier; β is the inflationary expectations correction coefficient; and L is the lag operator. By substituting equation 3 for π^* in equation 1, the above macroeconomic structure can be displayed by the following first-order difference equation system:

$$\begin{bmatrix} \pi \\ Y \end{bmatrix} - \frac{1}{1+\delta\phi} \begin{bmatrix} 1 & \delta\beta \\ -\phi & 1+\delta\phi(1-\beta) \end{bmatrix} \begin{bmatrix} \pi_{-1} \\ Y_{-1} \end{bmatrix}$$

$$= \frac{1}{1+\delta\phi} \begin{bmatrix} \delta(\gamma\alpha + \phi m - \beta Y_p) \\ \delta\phi\beta Y_p + \gamma\alpha + \phi m \end{bmatrix}. \qquad (4)$$

Fluctuations in Y and π arise from changes in the monetary and fiscal policy instruments m and α, respectively, and from changes in potential output Y_p, which activate forces embedded in the system. The solution to equation 4 displays oscillations of the aggregate variables when $[4\beta/(1-\beta)^2] > \delta\phi$, in which case the eigenvalues of the state-transition matrix are a complex conjugate pair. In the other case, the system converges to steady state along a nonspiral trajectory. The deviations of Y and π from their steady-state levels at any point of time t are given for the case where the eigenvalues of the state-transition matrix in equation 4 are a complex conjugate pair by

$$\begin{bmatrix} \pi_t - m \\ Y_t - Y_p \end{bmatrix} = \begin{bmatrix} b_1 \\ b_2 \end{bmatrix} \left(\frac{1}{1+\delta\phi} \right)^{0.5t} \cos(\psi + \theta t) \qquad (5)$$

where θ (expressed in radians) is the amplitude of the complex roots satisfying the equality

$$\text{tg}\theta = \left\{ \frac{4(1 + \delta\phi)}{[2 + \delta\phi(1 - \beta)]^2} - 1 \right\}^{0.5} \tag{6}$$

and the parameters b_1, b_2, and ψ are determined by the initial conditions.

Equations 4 and 5 show that the fluctuations of Y and π, which follow changes in the government's policy instruments and potential output, are amplified by the modulus of the complex roots

$$r = \frac{1}{1 + \delta\phi}, \tag{7}$$

and by the parameters, b_1 and b_2. The latter are directly connected to Δm, Δa and ΔY_p. Equation 5 also implies that the length of each business cycle is given by[1]

$$\ell = \frac{2\pi}{\theta}. \tag{8}$$

We assume that the probability of firm failure during a given period increases with the intensity of the fluctuations of Y and π (i.e., with Δm, $\Delta \alpha$, and ΔY_p, and with the modulus) and decreases with the time interval between successive troughs (i.e., the cycle length). The underlying rationale is that the greater and more frequent the fluctuations of GNP, the more drastic and frequent the changes in the demand for a firm's product. Moreover, when payments and receipts are not automatically linked to an overall price index, a firm's net cash-flow is increasingly sensitive to fluctuations in the rate of inflation. Managing a firm, it is suggested, bears a strong analogy to sailing in rough seas where the magnitude and frequency of the waves, as well as the boat's characteristics and crew's skills, are the determinants of survival.

Equations 6, 7, and 8 depict the relationships connecting the modulus and cycle length to the structural parameters δ, ϕ, and β, which represent the trade-off on the supply side between inflation and GNP gap, the monetary multiplier, and the expectations correction coefficient, respectively. These parameters may vary across economic periods and countries in correspondence to differences in the social, cultural, institutional, and political structures. For instance, δ is related to the degree of concentration of the labour markets and to the productivity of labour; ϕ to the propensity to consume (which in turn is affected by the availability of consumer credit and by the nature of the taxes and transfers' systems and the like), the sensitivity of the private investment to interest rate, the velocity of money, and the population's liquidity preferences; and β to the level of education and the technology of communication and data processing. In particular, these equations indicate the important role of the degree (β) to which the public modifies its expectations about the rate of inflation. The probability of bankruptcy increases with β due to higher frequency of the fluctuations in GNP and inflation rate. Furthermore, for sufficiently small values of β, an increment in either the monetary multiplier of the inflation-GNP gap trade-off lowers the frequency of the fluctuations of the aggregate variables as well as their magnitude (i.e., lengthens the cycles and decreases the modulus) and hence reduces the likelihood of insolvency. These results and the direct relationship between the monetary multiplier and the Keynesian multiplier imply, for example, that policy measures and institutional developments which moderate the Keynesian multiplier may affect the business sector's stability in one direction or another, according to the intensity of the public inflationary expectations' modification.

When we modify the macroeconomic system by introducing additive random disturbances in the aggregate supply equation 1 and the aggregate demand equation 2 and incorporating the hypothesis that the public inflationary expectations are rather rational, we find that a greater monetary multiplier does not necessarily lead to larger variations of output and inflation rate. In fact, for a sufficiently small ratio between the variances of the disturbances in the aggregate supply and demand schedules, the greater the effectiveness of the monetary policy, the lower the likelihood of firm failure. Furthermore, the smaller the effectiveness of monetary policy, the more likely that an increment in the inflation-output trade-off reduces the probability of insolvency.

3.3 Testing the underlying hypothesis

Our empirical analysis tests the chapter's basic hypothesis of direct relationship between the probability of bankruptcy and variations in the aggregate variables by estimating the parameters of the annual bankruptcy rate regression equation. The underlying rationale is that the probability of firm failure increases with fluctuations in the demand for the firm's product, and that the latter in turn are intensified by variation in the public purchasing power. Our regression analysis also takes into account the effects of possible lags between payment and receipts on the firm's net cash flow by including a measure of variation in the overall price level. It considers further the effect of covariation of these factors. Finally, the inclusion of the time index (t) on the right-hand side of the regression equation allows testing the existence of a trend. In this regard, one may expect that, *ceteris paribus*, due to the increasing number of federal and state regulations on firm operation and improvements in managerial systems and methods, the rate of bankruptcy declines as time progresses.

The estimation of bankruptcy rate regression equation parameters is carried out with post-Second World War US time-series data on the number of bankruptcies per ten thousand firms (Dun and Bradstreet, 1984) and on the real GNP in 1972 dollars (billion) and the GNP deflator, GNPD (Gordon, 1984). The best estimation results, as regards level of significance and goodness of fit, are obtained with the semilog specification:

$$\exp\{BR_t\} = \alpha_0 + \alpha_1\,[\mathrm{var(GNP)}]_t + \alpha_2[\mathrm{var(GNPD)}]_t + \alpha_3\,[\mathrm{cov(GNP,GNPD)}]_t + \alpha_4 t + u_t, \tag{9}$$

where *BR* is the annual number of bankruptcies per ten thousand firms; α_0, α_1, α_2, α_3, and α_4 are unknown parameters; and *u* is a random disturbance which we assume to be independently and identically distributed. The variances and the covariance of the real GNP and the GNP deflator are computed with quarterly observations of the real GNP and the GNPD according to formulae which capture the variations of these variables before and during the time of bankruptcy:

$$[\text{var(GNP)}]_t = \frac{1}{J} \sum_{j=0}^{J} (GNP_{t-j} - \overline{GNP})^2 \qquad (10)$$

$$[\text{var(GNP)}]_t = \frac{1}{J} \sum_{j=0}^{J} (GNPD_{t-j} - \overline{GNPD})^2 \ ; \qquad (11)$$

$$[\text{cov(GNP,GNPD)}]_t = \frac{1}{J} \sum_{j=0}^{J} (GNP_{t-j} - \overline{GNP})\ (GNPD_{t-j} - \overline{GNPD}); \qquad (12)$$

where $\overline{GNP}$ and $\overline{GNPD}$ are the averages of the real GNP and the GNP deflator, respectively, for the period started *J* quarters before the end of year *t*.

The ordinary least squares (OLS) estimates for four reasonable choices of *J* (twelve, sixteen, twenty, and twenty-four quarters), which also lead to better estimation results, are summarized in Table 3.1.

Table 3.1
OLS estimates of the parameters of the bankruptcy rate equation

Explanatory variable	Value of J: 12 quarters	16 quarters	20 quarters	24 quarters
Var(GNP)	0.2669 *E* + 36 (1.11)	0.3609 *e* + 35 (3.08)	0.1997 *E* + 35 (2.09)	0.1399*E* + 35 (2.09)
Var(GNPD)	0.1115 *E* + 36 (2.97)	0.1242 *E* + 37 (6.26)	0.1218 *E* + 37 (6.51)	0.1378 *E* + 37 (7.54)
Cov(GNP, GNPD)	-0.3603 *E* + 36 (2.03)	-0.4436 *E* + 36 (3.08)	-0.3280 *E* + 36 (4.03)	-0.3398 *E* + 36 (5.07)
t (trend)	-0.3719 *E* + 36 (0.19)	-0.1154 *E* + 37 (0.81)	-0.1933 *E* + 37 (1.37)	-0.2164 *E* + 37 (1.61)
R^2	0.375	0.685	0.725	0.786
F	4.19	14.69	17.20	22.94
Durbin-Watson statistic	1.84	1.54	1.73	1.12

* The sample period is 1947–82 and the *t*-ratios are in parentheses.

These estimation results are statistically significant and very robust with regard to the choice of J. The estimates of α_1 and α_2 confirm a priori expectations that the annual rate of bankruptcy in post-Second World War US increases with the degrees of dispersion of the real GNP and the GNP deflator. The results also indicate that the annual rate of bankruptcy declines with the covariance of these aggregate variables. This implies further that, all other things being equal, in periods where the real GNP and the GNP deflator proceed in the same direction, the probability of firm failure is lower than in periods where they go in opposite directions. Finally, as expected, the estimated trend is negative but statistically insignificant. Note that its level of significance increases with J and reaches a peak (12 per cent) when J is equal to twenty-four quarters.

3.4 Conclusion

This chapter examines the effects of fluctuations of macroeconomic variables on the firm's prospects of failure. The empirical analysis indicates that variations of GNP and GNP deflator increase the probability of bankruptcy but the covariance of these variables moderates the probability of bankruptcy. It was also found that there is no significant trend in the rate of bankruptcy. The theoretical analysis of business cycles suggests further that the probability of firm failure increases with the intensity with which the public modifies its inflationary expectations (β) and that for sufficiently small values of β the likelihood of bankruptcy declines with the monetary multiplier and the inflation-output gap trade-off.

Notes

1. Due to its deterministic character, the model presents cyclical symmetries and regularities, which might be viewed as a point of weakness. Mitchell (1927) and Keynes (1936) have believed that business cycles are asymmetric, consisting of brief and severe downturns and longer and more gradual upturns. This belief was supported recently by Neftci (1984), who has examined the behaviour of the unemployment rate in the US.

However, Delong and Summers (1984), who have calculated the coefficient of skewness of the distribution of GNP growth rates and industrial production growth rates for the US, Japan, West Germany, the UK, and France at various time intervals, have concluded that symmetry is insignificant and probably not a phenomenon of first-order importance in understanding business cycles.

References

Altman, E.I. (1971), *Corporate Bankruptcy in America*, Heath Lexington Books, Lexington, Mass.

Bulow, J.I. and Shoven, J.B. (1978), 'The Bankruptcy Decision', *The Bell Journal of Economics,* vol. 9 (Autumn), pp. 437–55.

Cagan, P. (1956), 'The Monetary Dynamics of Hyperinflation', in Friedman, M. (ed.), *Studies in the Quantity Theory of Money*, University of Chicago Press, Chicago.

Delong, B.J. and Summers, L.H. (1984), 'Are Business Cycles Symmetric?', Discussion Paper no. 1076, Harvard Institute of Economic Research.

Dornbusch, R. and Fischer, S. (1978), *Macroeconomics,* 2nd ed., McGraw-Hill, New York.

Dun and Bradstreet, *The Business Record* (1984).

Friedman, M. (1956), *A Theory of the Consumption Function*, Princeton University Press, Princeton.

Gordon, R.J. (1984), *Macroeconomics*, 3rd ed., Little and Brown, Boston.

Keynes, J.M. (1936), *The General Theory of Employment, Interest and Money*, Macmillan, London.

Mitchell, W.C. (1927), *Business Cycles: The Problem and Its Setting*, NBER, New York.

Munch, P. and Smallwood, D.E. (1980), 'Solvency Regulation in the Property-Liability Insurance Industry: Empirical Evidence', *The Bell Journal of Economics*, vol. 11 (Spring), pp. 261–79.

Neftci, S.N. (1984), 'Are Economic Time-Series Asymmetric Over the Business Cycle?', *Journal of Political Economy*, vol. 42 (April), pp. 307–28.

Stapleton, R.C. (1975), 'Some Aspects of the Pure Theory of Corporate Finance: Bankruptcies and Take-Overs: Comment', *The Bell Journal of Economics*, vol. 6 (Autumn), pp. 708–10.

Stiglitz, J.E. (1972), 'Some Aspects of Pure Theory and Corporate Finance: Bankruptcy and Turnovers', *The Bell Journal of Economics*, vol. 3 (Autumn), pp. 458–83.

—— (1992), 'Capital Markets and Economic Fluctuations in Capitalist Economies' (Alfred Marshall lecture), *European Economic Review*, vol. 36, pp. 269–306.

—— (1975), 'Some Aspects of Pure Theory and Corporate Finance: Bankruptcy and Turnovers: Reply', *The Bell Journal of Economics*, vol. 6 (Autumn), pp. 711–4.

4 Interindustry linkages and business bankruptcy rates: Evidence from Australia

Co-authored by Lillian Cheung, Khorshed Chowdhury and Charles Harvie

This chapter explores the potential relationships among bankruptcy rates in Australia's major industries during the observed period 1973–1991 within the framework of cointegration tests and simultaneous-equation systems. The empirical findings obtained from national and cross-state observations lend support to the existence of relationships between the bankruptcy rate in the building and construction industry and the bankruptcy rate in the finance and property industry as well as between the bankruptcy rate in the manufacturing industry and the bankruptcy rate in the transport, storage and communication industry.

4.1 Introduction

As indicated in the previous chapters, although business bankruptcy in itself is essentially a microeconomic process, it is likely to be affected by the economic environment in which a firm operates. These aggregate and interindustry effects have attracted little attention by researchers in the field of corporate bankruptcy. Most of the empirical studies in this field have dealt with the microeconomic aspects of bankruptcy. In particular, financial ratios have been used to predict failure of firms within the context of Beaver's (1966) univariate approach which has been broadened and improved upon by Altman, Haldeman and Narayanan (1977), Ohlson (1980), Zavgren (1983 and 1985) and Johensen and Melicher (1994). A major empirical study on predicting corporate bankruptcy in Australia with financial ratios has been conducted by Castagna and Matolcsy (1981). Altman and Izan (1983) have also investigated factors associated with corporate distress in Australia and developed a business-failure classification which can be applicable to a number of industry groups.

In spite of the analytical improvements and modifications that have led to a fairly high predictive ability, all the above-mentioned studies have exhibited a common feature of limiting the set of variables explaining business failure to financial characteristics. That is, they have implicitly assumed that bankrupt firms can be distinguished entirely by their financial characteristics and independently from the surrounding global economic environment. Only a few studies, most notably Altman (1971, 1980), have focused on the effects of macroeconomic factors and the business cycle on business bankruptcy. Chapter 3 complemented these studies with some findings for the United States and Chapter 2 also stressed the importance of industry-specific conditions.

In an attempt to incorporate more aggregate aspects into the empirical study of business failure, this chapter tests the existence of inter-industry linkages with regards to business bankruptcy. The underlying rationale is that a high rate of business failure in a given industry might have a considerable effect on the rest of the economy. On the one hand, a slowdown in the economic activity in an industry might reduce the demand for production inputs produced by other industries as well as the demand for their products as the level of unemployment rises and aggregate consumer income declines. On the other hand, if labour mobility is possible and requires only low costs of adjustment, a high rate of business failure in one industry might lower the wage rate in other industries and subsequently reduce their production costs. Thus, the net effect of a rise in the bankruptcy rate in one industry on other industries is not clear *a-priori*.

In particular, this chapter explores the potential relationships among bankruptcy rates in Australia's major industries; namely, primary production, mining and quarrying, manufacturing, building and construction, transport, storage and communication and finance and property; during the period 1973–1991 for which data on business bankruptcy by industry are available. This period was a very significant one to a country such as Australia which depends on the export of coal, wheat and other primary goods, as it includes the oil crises of the 1970s, the American ban on the export of cereals to the Soviet Union that followed the invasion of Afghanistan, and the oil glut of the mid 1980s. To the best of our knowledge, such a database is not available for any other economy. Hence, the use of the Australian data provides a unique opportunity for analyzing interindustry bankruptcy linkages.

The analysis of the potential effect of inter-industry linkages on the bankruptcy rates in Australia is organized as follows. A brief description of the data sources and the evolution of the rates of bankruptcy in the aforementioned industries during the observed period, as well as the statistical correlations among these rates, is provided in section 4.2. This description is followed by unit-root tests that check whether the time-series of the industry bankruptcy rates satisfy the nonstationary requirement for performing cointegration tests. Section 4.3 describes the cointegration tests and their results. Section 4.4 complements the evidence of long-run relationships provided by the cointegration tests by estimating possible relationships between industry bankruptcy rates within a framework of simultaneous and dynamic equations.

4.2 Industry bankruptcy rates' trajectories and their properties

The industry bankruptcy rates displayed in Figure 4.1 are computed as the ratio of the number of business bankruptcies in an industry (available from the Bankruptcy Act 1966 Annual Reports 1972/73 to 1990/91) to the total number of businesses in that industry (approximated by the total number of business taxpayers as recorded in the Department of Taxation's Annual Taxation Statistics, 1972/73 to 1990/91). Figure 4.1 shows that the rate of

Figure 4.1 Bankruptcy rates in Australia by industry (1973–1991)

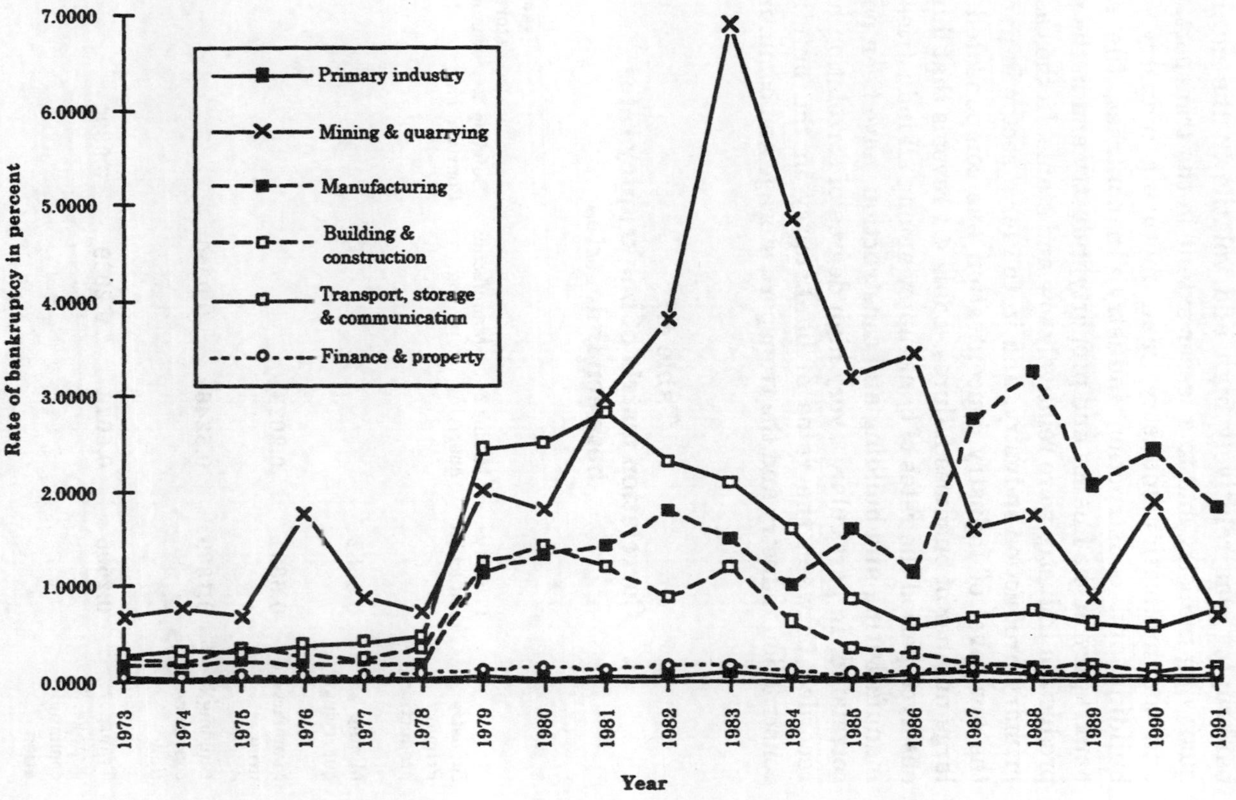

bankruptcy was relatively high and volatile in the mining and quarrying industry and to a lesser extent in the transport, storage and communication industry, manufacturing industry and the building and construction industry. In contrast, the rates of bankruptcy in the finance and property industry and in the primary production industry were relatively low and stable. In the case of the primary production industry, and in the farm sector in particular, the low level of industry concentration has compensated for the large number of business failures. Table 4.1 reveals that during the observed period the rates of bankruptcy among all industries, except manufacturing and building and construction, have been positively correlated. In particular, a very high degree of correlation has been recorded between the rates of bankruptcy in the building and construction industry and the transport, storage and communication

Table 4.1
Correlation matrix of bankruptcy rates between industries

Industry	Primary production	Mining & quarrying	Manufacturing	Building & Construction	Transport, storage & communication
Primary production					
Mining & quarrying	0.5582				
Manufacturing	0.6891	0.2023			
Building & construction	0.1339	0.5246	–0.0350		
Transport, storage & communication	0.2535	0.5676	0.2089	0.9390	
Finance & property	0.6771	0.6504	0.4775	0.7080	0.7864

industry. This table also indicates that the rate of bankruptcy in the finance and property industry has been positively and highly correlated with the bankruptcy rates in the other industries and that the rate of bankruptcy in the manufacturing industry has been highly correlated with that in the primary production industry.

As indicated in the introduction, it is essential to check the nature of the industry bankruptcy rate time series ($IBR_1,\ldots,IBR_6$) before proceeding with the cointegration tests. If these time-series are nonstationary, the Engle-Granger two-step method of cointegration can be employed for testing long-run relationships between industry bankruptcy rates. A basic approach for testing whether a time series is nonstationary has been developed by Dickey and Fuller (1981). According to their approach, two forms of regression equations can be specified for any given industry bankruptcy rate:

$$\Delta IBR_t = \alpha_0 + \alpha_1 IBR_{t-1} + \sum_{j=1}^{p} \gamma_j \Delta IBR_{t-j} + \varepsilon_t \quad (1)$$

and

$$\Delta IBR_t = \alpha_0 + \alpha_1 IBR_{t-1} + \alpha_2 t + \sum_{j=1}^{p} \gamma_j \Delta IBR_{t-j} + \varepsilon_t \quad (2)$$

where ε_t is assumed to be a Gaussian white noise. The difference between these two specifications is that the latter includes a time-trend variable. When $\alpha_1=0$, the time series IBR_t is nonstationary. The corresponding F-tests are computed under three different null hypotheses, namely $\phi_1(H_0\text{: } \alpha_0= \alpha_1=0)$, $\phi_2(H_0\text{: } \alpha_0= \alpha_1= \alpha_2=0)$ and $\phi_3(H_0\text{: } \alpha_1= \alpha_2=0)$. The test associated with ϕ_2 can be viewed as the most comprehensive one as the test equation has both a constant term and a trend on top of the autoregressive terms. This unit-root test has been modified by Phillips (1987) and Perron (1988) who used non-parametric correction for serial correlation rather than including lags. In their method the unit-root tests are computed from the aforementioned Dickey-Fuller regression equations with p equal to zero, and the statistics are then transformed to remove the effects of serial correlation.

The Phillips-Perron unit-root test results for each of the time series of the industry bankruptcy rates (as obtained by SHAZAM version 7.0) are summarized in Table 4.2 below. The number of lags has been selected by Akaike (AIC) information criterion. The tests of the null hypotheses ϕ_1, ϕ_2 and ϕ_3 indicate that the time series of industry bankruptcy rates are all nonstationary.

Table 4.2
Results of Phillips-Perron unit-root tests

Variables	*Phillips-Perron test statistic*			
	No. of lags	ϕ_1	ϕ_2	ϕ_3
IBR_1	2	2.245	1.934	2.900
IBR_2	1	1.380	0.934	1.401
IBR_3	4	1.348	2.307	2.916
IBR_4	1	1.146	1.100	1.646
IBR_5	1	1.241	0.947	1.402
IBR_6	1	1.960	1.238	1.839

4.3 Cointegration test results

Following Engle and Granger (1987), the test for evidence of long-run relationships between the nonstationary industry bankruptcy rates is based on two alternative forms of the cointegrating regression equations as regards the inclusion or exclusion of a trend. Let i and j denote industry indexes, then the cointegration regression equation can be expressed as:

$$IBR_{it} = b_0 + \sum_{j \neq i}^{K} b_j IBR_{jt} + u_{it} , \qquad (3)$$

or

$$IBR_{it} = \beta_0 + \beta_1 t + \sum_{j \neq i}^{K} \beta_j IBR_{jt} + u_{it} \qquad (4)$$

where K≤6. In this context, a test for no cointegration is given by a test for a unit root in the estimated residuals. The Phillips-Perron test results are summarized in Table 4.3 and Table 4.4. While the former table presents the test results for long-run relationships between industry bankruptcy rates within a multivariate model, the latter displays the test results for long-run relationships between industry bankruptcy rates for pairs of industries.

Table 4.3
Engle-Granger cointegration test within a multivariate model

Dependent variable	Explanatory variable	Phillips-Perron test statistic No. of lags	z-test	τ-test
IBR_1	IBR_2, IBR_3, IBR_4, IBR_5, IBR_6	1	−20.980	5.500*
	t, IBR_2, IBR_3, IBR_4, IBR_5, IBR_6	1	−21.212	5.270*
IBR_2	IBR_1, IBR_3, IBR_4, IBR_5, IBR_6	1	−11.287	−2.762
	t, IBR_1, IBR_3, IBR_4, IBR_5, $IBR6_2$	1	−12.466	−2.796
IBR_3	IBR_1, IBR_2, IBR_4, IBR_5, IBR_6	4	−17.093	−4.212
	t, IBR_1, IBR_2, IBR_4, IBR_5, IBR_6	4	−17.311	5.341*
IBR_4	IBR_1, IBR_2, IBR_3, IBR_5, IBR_6	2	−21.238	6.673*
	t, IBR_1, IBR_2, IBR_3, IBR_5, IBR_6	2	−19.859	6.256*
IBR_5	IBR_1, IBR_2, IBR_3, IBR_4, IBR_6	2	−23.033	7.323*
	T, IBR_1, IBR_2, IBR_3, IBR_4, IBR_6	2	−22.661	7.380*
IBR_2,	IBR_1, IBR_2, IBR_3, IBR_4, IBR_5	4	−23.817	9.082*
	T, IBR_1, IBR_2, IBR_3, IBR_4, IBR_5	4	−23.376	8.792*

* An asterisk denotes the presence of a cointegrating relationship.

In general, the multivariate cointegration-test results support the proposition of long-run relationships among all the industry rates of bankruptcy except that of the mining and quarrying sector. In particular, the pairwise cointegration tests indicate a possible long-run relationship between the rates of bankruptcy in the manufacturing sector and finance and property sector as well as a long-run relationship between the rates of bankruptcy in the building and construction sector and the transport, storage and communication sector for which a very high positive correlation had been recorded (0.9390).

Table 4.4
Engle-Granger cointegration test for pairs of industries

Dependent variable	Explanatory variable	Phillips-Perron test statistic No. of lags	z-test	τ-test
IBR_1	IBR_2	2	−9.141	−2.393
IBR_1	t, IBR_2	2	−11.852	−2.915
IBR_1	IBR_3	2	−11.408	−2.747
IBR_1	t, IBR_3	2	−11.741	−2.899
IBR_1	IBR_4	2	−7.640	−2.167
IBR_1	t, IBR_4	2	−11.559	−2.701
IBR_1	IBR_5	2	−8.072	−2.226
IBR_1	t, IBR_5	2	−11.628	−2.716
IBR_1	IBR_6	1	−10.110	−2.608
IBR_1	t, IBR_6	1	−14.356	−3.330
IBR_2	IBR_3	1	−5.627	−1.716
IBR_2	t, IBR_3	1	−5.239	−1.586
IBR_2	IBR_4	1	−6.021	−1.844
IBR_2	t, IBR_4	1	−6.950	−1.856
IBR_2	IBR_5	1	−7.473	−2.047
IBR_2	t, IBR_5	1	−7.823	−2.016
IBR_2	IBR_6	4	−10.750	−2.721
IBR_2	t, IBR_6	4	−10.729	−2.694
IBR_3	IBR_4	4	−4.013	−1.635
IBR_3	t, IBR_4	4	−10.314	−3.259
IBR_3	IBR_5	4	−3.690	−1.483
IBR_3	t, IBR_5	4	−10.460	−3.213
IBR_3	IBR_6	1	−3.426	−1.332
IBR_3	t, IBR_6	1	−15.919	3.615*
IBR_4	IBR_5	2	−11.495	−2.832
IBR_4	t, IBR_5	2	−19.409	7.414*
IBR_4	IBR_6	1	−6.951	−2.000
IBR_4	t, IBR_6	1	−12.634	−2.988
IBR_5	IBR_6	1	−10.405	−2.641
IBR_5	t, IBR_6	1	−12.536	−2.983

* An asterisk denotes the presence of a cointegrating relationship.

4.4 Simultaneous-equation results and conclusion

In view of the cointegration-test results, it is sensible to explore further the relationship between the rates of bankruptcy in the manufacturing sector and finance and property sector and the relationship between the rates of bankruptcy in the building and construction sector and the transport, storage and communication sector within a framework of simultaneous equations. In addition to the simultaneity aspects each equation includes a lag of the dependent variable in order to test whether the reduced excess production capacity in an industry exceeds inertia; i.e., whether a high bankruptcy rate in any given year is associated with a lower bankruptcy rate in the following year. The inclusion of these lags also makes the simultaneous-equation systems identifiable. The estimated systems also incorporate the potential effect of the interest rate on bankruptcy rates. If at all, it is expected that the effect of this variable would be most noticeable in the building and construction industry, where, in addition to a hike in production costs, a rise in the interest rate might lower the demand for new houses and apartments substantially as the costs of servicing home loans increase. The interest rate employed in the analysis is the interest rate on ninety-day discounted bank bills. Since there is a considerable time differential between insolvency and the juridical declaration of bankruptcy, it is more appropriate to consider a one-year lag of the interest rate rather than the current one.

It is important to note that in spite of being unique, the Australia-wide time series of annual observations on industry bankruptcy rates is not sufficiently large to yield statistically significant estimation results. Therefore, the systems were also estimated with cross-state and time-series observations. Moreover, since the states of Australia differ in their economic and business transaction volume, a three-stage least squares estimation procedure has also been applied to the cross-state and time-series database where each observation is weighted by the square root of the relevant state's (or territory's) aggregate product share in the national gross domestic product. The three-stage least squares (3SLS) estimation results with nation-wide observations and with unweighted and weighted pooled cross-state and time-series observations with (model 1) and without (model 2) the interest rate are summarized in Table 4.5 for the manufacturing industry and the finance and property industry and in Table 4.6 for the building and construction industry and the transport, storage and communication industry.

With the exception of model 1, when estimated with national observations, the 3SLS estimation results for the building and construction and the transport, storage and communication industries indicate that the effect of the rate of bankruptcy in the building and construction industry on the rate of bankruptcy in the transport, storage and communication industry is significantly different from zero and substantial — a one per cent rise in the rate of bankruptcy in the former industry is likely to increase the rate of bankruptcy in the latter by 1.243 to 1.432 per cent. In contrast, a reciprocal effect is not found to be statistically significant. The estimation results with weighted cross-state and time-series observations reveal further a statistically significant inertia effect in both the building and construction industry and the transport, storage and communication industry. They also indicate that low rates of bankruptcy in the building and construction industry is associated with relatively high interest rates. This seemingly surprising result can be reconciled by the hikes of the interest rate during upturns in economic activity, which, to a certain extent, are engineered by the Reserve Bank of Australia in order to suppress inflationary pressures in boom periods.

The estimation results for the manufacturing and the finance and property industries indicate that only when unweighted cross-state and time-series observations are employed is there evidence that the effect of the rate of bankruptcy in the manufacturing industry on the current rate of bankruptcy in the finance and property industry is significantly different from zero and that a rise of one per cent in the rate of bankruptcy in the former industry is likely to raise the rate of bankruptcy in the latter by 0.015–0.16 percentage points. The effect of the rate of bankruptcy in the finance and property industry on the rate of bankruptcy in the manufacturing industry was found to be statistically insignificant for every specification of the database. Note further that statistically significant and substantial inertia effects have been found for both industries with all three data-sets employed. Finally, the estimation results obtained from cross-state and time-series observations indicate further that a rise in the interest rate is likely to increase the rate of

Table 4.5

3SLS estimates of the manufacturing industry and the finance & property industry bankruptcy rates equation system*

Explanatory Variables	Estimation Results with Nation-wide Time-Series Observations				Pooled Cross-States Time-Series Observations				Pooled and Weighted Cross-State Time-Series Observations			
	MODEL 1		MODEL 2		MODEL 1		MODEL 2		MODEL 1		MODEL 2	
	$IBR3_t$	$IBR6_t$	$IBR3_t$	$IBR6_t$	$IBR3_t$	$IBR6_t$	$IBR3_t$	$IBR6_t$	$IBR3_t$	$IBR6_t$	$IBR3_t$	$IBR6_t$
Constant	-0.006 (-1.202)	-0.001 (-0.752)	0.001 (0.267)	3.67E-04 (1.760)	-0.005 (-0.524)	0.001 (2.242)	0.004 (0.554)	0.001 (4.118)	-0.001 (-1.114)	8.13E-05 (1.420)	0.001 (2.275)	8.01E-05 (2.925)
$IBR3_t$		-0.056 (-1.165)		-0.012 (-0.731)		0.016 (3.271)		0.015 (3.522)		0.008 (0.488)		0.007 (0.695)
$IBR6_t$	3.751 (0.872)		0.711 (4.734)		0.636 (6.198)		0.658 (6.460)		0.477 (4.988)		0.610 (6.736)	
$IBR3_{t-1}$	0.492 (2.517)		3.920 (0.879)		0.935 (0.114)		2.365 (0.290)		1.719 (0.624)		0.776 (0.267)	
$IBR6_{t-1}$		0.894 (2.413)		0.781 (3.063)		0.235 (.2307)		0.231 (2.280)		0.421 (4.048)		0.422 (4.263)
Interest $Rate_{t-1}$	0.001 (1.436)	7.26E-04 (1.267)			0.001 (1.732)	-1.48E-05 (-0.474)			1.69E-04 (2.935)	-1.42E-07 (-0.022)		

**The t-ratios are indicated in the parentheses.*

Table 4.6

3SLS estimates of the building & construction industry and the transport, storage & communication industry bankruptcy rates equation system*

Explanatory Variables	Estimation Results with Nation-wide Time-Series Observations				Pooled Cross-States Time-Series Observations				Pooled and Weighted Cross-State Time-Series Observations			
	MODEL 1		MODEL 2		MODEL 1		MODEL 2		MODEL 1		MODEL 2	
	$IBR4_t$	$IBR5_t$	$IBR4_t$	$IBR5_t$	$IBR4_t$	$IBR5_t$	$IBR4_t$	$IBR5_t$	$IBR4_t$	$IBR5_t$	$IBR4_t$	$IBR5_t$
Constant	0.002	-0.008	0.001	0.001	0.003	0.010	0.003	0.007	3.89E-04	-6.69E-05	1.39E-04	1.42E-04
	(1.372)	(-0.622)	(0.419)	(0.880)	(0.619)	(1.585)	(0.404)	(2.949)	(2.299)	(-0.222)	(1.337)	(1.560)
$IBR4_t$		2.630		1.329		1.243		1.293		1.432		1.372
		(1.147)		(2.595)		(2.455)		(2.722)		(5.992)		(6.711)
$IBR5_t$	0.667		-0.123		0.058		-0.152		0.111		-0.004	
	(1.046)		(-0.1102)		(0.176)		(-0.203)		(0.667)		(-0.020)	
$IBR4_{t-1}$	-0.304		0.977		0.697		0.939		0.615		0.811	
	(-0.294)		(0.538)		(0.384)		(1.080)		(2.166)		(2.347)	
$IBR5_{t-1}$		-0.222		0.310		0.124		0.100		0.287		0.312
		(-0.242)		(1.551)		(0.666)		(0.581)		(3.061)		(3.903)
Interest $Rate_{t-1}$	-2.78E-04	0.001			-2.04E-04	-3.79E-04			-2.61E-05	1.82E-05		
	(-1.773)	(0.730)			(-1.029)	(-0.532)			(-1.967)	(0.752)		

**The t-ratios are indicated in the parentheses.*

bankruptcy in the manufacturing industry but not the rate of bankruptcy in the finance and property industry. Moreover, the insignificant effect of the manufacturing industry's bankruptcy rate on the finance and property industry's bankruptcy rate implies that the adverse effect of a rise in the interest rate on the manufacturing industry is not transmitted to the finance and property industry.

References

Altman, E.I. (1971), *Corporate Bankruptcy in America*, Lexington, Mass: Heath Lexington Books.

Altman, E.I., R.G. Haldeman, and P. Narayanan (1977), 'ZETA Analysis: A New Model to Identify Bankruptcy Risk of Corporations', *Journal of Banking and Finance*, vol. 1, pp. 29–54.

Altman, E.I., and H.Y. Izan, 'Identifying Corporate Distress in Australia: An Industry Relative Analysis', Working Paper 83-103, Australian Graduate School of Management, University of New South Wales, August 1983.

Beaver, W.H. (1966), 'Financial Ratios as Predictors of Failure', Empirical Research in Accounting: Selected Studies. Supplement, *Journal of Accounting Research*, vol. 4, pp. 71–111.

Castagna, A.D., and S.P. Matolcsy (1981), 'The Prediction of Corporate Failure: Testing the Australian Experience', *Australian Journal of Management*, June, pp. 23–50.

Dickey, D.A. and W.A. Fuller (1981), 'Likelihood Ration Statistics for Autoregressive Time Series with a Unit Root', *Econometrica*, vol. 49, pp. 1057–72.

Engle, R.F. and C.W. Granger (1987), 'Cointegration and Error Correction: Representation, Estimation and Testing', *Econometrica*, vol. 55, pp. 251–76.

Johensen, T., and R.W. Melicher (1994), 'Predicting Corporate Bankruptcy and Financial Distress: Information Value Added by Multinomial Logit Models', *Journal of Economics and Business*, vol. 46, pp. 269–86.

Ohlson, J.A. (1980), 'Financial Ratios and the Probabilistic Prediction of Bankruptcy', *Journal of Accounting Research*, vol. 18, pp. 109–31.

Perron, P. (1988), 'Trends and Random Walks in Macroeconomic Time Series', *Journal of Economic Dynamics and Control*, vol. 12, pp. 297–332.

Phillips, P.C.B. (1987), 'Time Series Regression with a Unit Root', *Econometrica*, vol. 55, pp. 277–301.

SHAZAM User's Reference manual, Version 7.0, McGraw-Hill Book Co., 1993.

Zavgren, C.V. (1985), 'Assessing the Vulnerability to Failure of American Industrial Firms: A Logistic Analysis', *Journal of Business Finance and Accounting*, pp. 19–44.

Part 2
RISK SHARING, RISK SPREADING AND INSOLVENCY IN AGRICULTURE

5 The implications of financial cooperation in Israel's semi-cooperative villages

Co-authored by Moshe Justman and Eithan Hochman

Financial cooperation, through credit sharing and co-signing of debts, was a source of strength for Israel's semi-cooperative moshavim in the early decades of their development. But such cooperation entails a potential 'free-rider' problem when farmers' borrowings are uncoordinated, and recent events in Israel have demonstrated the severe implications it can have. This chapter presents a theoretical analysis of the externalities generated by financial cooperation, and tests its conclusions empirically using Israeli data. Simulation results indicate that the potential instability of financial cooperation is aggravated when the moshav population is heterogeneous.

5.1 Introduction

This chapter deals with certain financial externalities embedded in a cooperative organization. These externalities arise when the cooperative acts as an association of individuals seeking to further

---

Reprinted with permission of the *Journal of Development Economics*, vol. 30, 1989, pp. 25–46, with some modifications.

their individual interests rather than to achieve a common goal. Specifically, it focuses on the implications of financial cooperation among farmers, in the context of Israel's semi-cooperative villages — *moshavim*.

The relevance of these implications goes beyond the Israeli case. Farmers' cooperatives play an important role in many developing countries and often include elements of financial cooperation. Indeed, where institutional arrangements limit the use of land as collateral, credit sharing may be essential in making loans available to small farmers. In any event, financial cooperation can exploit economies of scale and risk sharing to lower the cost of capital for cooperative members and reduce their administrative costs.

However, as we shall show in this chapter, such cooperative arrangements may also lead to a 'free-rider' problem characteristic of price pooling. That is, if debt behaviour is uncoordinated, farmers will not take into account the collective effect of their accumulated debt on the terms of their credit, and consequently leverage their farms more than is optimal. Moreover, uncoordinated financial cooperation obliges the farmer to predict the debt accumulation of other cooperative members when planning for the future. This introduces an added measure of uncertainty which, given a natural aversion to risk, will discourage investment in productive capacity. Finally, if cooperative members are heterogeneous in their attitudes to bearing debt, uncoordinated credit behaviour may undermine the stability of the cooperative. In the absence of non-market constraints, 'debt-prone' members may find it to their advantage to increase their leverage ratio indefinitely, while 'debt-averse' members share the consequences and react by cutting back the scope of their productive activity. This erodes the moral basis for cooperation and undermines its organizational stability.[1]

In the specific context of Israel's moshavim, which we consider in the present chapter, the financial cooperative is the chief tunnel through which members obtain credit. It functions as a risk pool in which all cooperative members share the same credit terms and guarantee each other's loans. We take this to imply that the cost of credit to the individual farmstead is an increasing function of the overall leverage of the cooperative; and that the farmstead's resale value is a decreasing function of aggregate leverage. This chapter explores the implications of this assumption for farmers' investment and borrowing behaviour in both a theoretical and an empirical context.

We present a brief background survey of cooperation in the moshavim in section 5.2. Then, in section 5.3, we develop a conceptual framework and formal analysis of the individual farm's demand for credit and investment, based on the assumption that each farmholder seeks to maximize individual expected utility from present consumption and the resale value of the farm. This yields a system of simultaneous equations of investment and borrowing behaviour. In section 5.4 we compare the individually optimal behaviour indicated by these equations, with a coordinated joint optimum. Section 5.5 presents empirical estimates of their reduced form, using data on over three hundred farms in five moshavim. These estimation results are used, in section 5.6, to simulate the path of investment and borrowing of individual farms over time, highlighting differences in the typical behaviour of three generations of farmers. The chapter ends with some concluding remarks on the inherent difficulties of financial cooperation, in section 5.7.

5.2 Background

The *moshav* (singular of *moshavim*) is a cooperative village consisting of 40 to 100 small family farms, each endowed with a land and water allotment of equal size. The moshav's members farm individually, but market part of their produce collectively, and share a common source of inputs and credit provided by a purchasing organization. The cooperative in the moshav also acts as an intermediary between its members and external financial institutions. In doing so, it maintains the principle of collective responsibility for members debts through mutual co-signing.

The first moshav was founded in 1921. Since then more than 300 moshavim have been established. In the early stages of Israel's development, they played a critical role in providing agricultural goods for the general population, in establishing sovereignty over the country's peripheral regions, and in absorbing many of the immigrants who came as refugees after the declaration of independence of the State of Israel. In those pioneer years, the cooperative organization of the moshav carried substantial benefits for small farmholders, allowing them to exploit opportunities for scale economies by sharing agricultural equipment; through collective purchasing and marketing; and in credit sharing. Moreover, the implicit and mutual undertaking of moshav members to help each other in difficult times proved invaluable in the early years, allowing many of the moshavim to grow and prosper while maintaining an egalitarian framework.

In the last five years, however, many of the less established moshavim have experienced severe financial difficulties and sunk into large debts. This is reflected in Table 5.1, which describes the distribution and composition of debt and real interest rates paid on short-term liabilities in three moshavim which have given us direct access to their ledgers.

The average debt in each of these three moshavim is about two to five times its members' aggregate average annual earnings. This and the very high real interest rates on short-term liabilities (credit extended by the purchasing organizations), coupled with the large shares of short-term liabilities, raise doubts about the ability of these cooperatives to withstand the financial crisis they are experiencing.

There are exogenous reasons for these serious difficulties: government cuts in subsidies and support for the agricultural sector; a decline in the profitability of exports due to adverse changes in international exchange rates and an overvalued domestic currency; uncertainty and confusion which arose from Israel's very high and accelerating rate of inflation; and very high real interest rates. But there are significant endogenous reasons too. Informed observers generally agree that in the period in question many moshav farmers over-extended themselves, taking on debt that generated exorbitant interest charges which they could only repay with great difficulty, if at all; and some moshavim appear to have channelled too large a portion of their financial resources to consumption — most visibly housing.[2]

These phenomena cannot be entirely attributed to the moshav's cooperative structure. Cobweb effects, a common source of exaggerated fluctuations in agricultural capacity, were probably also at work, and many moshavim suffer from inadequate accounting systems which severely hamper their business

Table 5.1
Debt and real interest rates in three moshavim, September 1985

Statistical summary of the debt distribution among the moshav's members

Moshav	Shape	Mean ($)	Median ($)	Mode ($)	Std. dev. ($)
M1	lognormal	24,216	18,778	22,825	18,529
M2	lognormal	12,967	11,463	10,316	6,271
M3	lognormal	8,385	6,553	6,000	6,000

Moshav	*Ratio of short-term liabilities to total liabilities*	*Real interest rate paid on short-term liabilities*
M1	0.96	34.6%
M2	0.97	19.1%
M3	1.00	50.4%

judgement. But the 'free-rider' effect, which we outlined above, is a very serious part of the problem and a matter of great practical concern, calling into question the viability of the special blend of cooperation and individualism embodied in the moshav. A few moshavim have responded by disbanding their financial cooperatives, and more and more successful moshav farmers are showing increasing concern about their own efforts being undermined by the imprudent or irresponsible borrowing of some of their fellow cooperative members.

These difficulties seem to indicate a basic inconsistency between financial cooperation as practised on the moshav and the uncoordinated maximization of individual utility by its members. It has become much more evident in recent years because exogenously difficult financial conditions have made credit terms more sensitive to credit-worthiness, and because the increased imminence of insolvency has meant that the market's valuation of the individual farmstead must take more careful account of the financial soundness of other members of the cooperative to which it belongs.

In the early years of moshav settlement, a high degree of social cohesion and homogeneity among moshav members, and the strong influence of nation-wide institutions of which the moshavim were a part, assured a large measure of, at least, tacit coordination of borrowing behaviour. But over time social cohesion and homogeneity have eroded considerably and national institutions no longer play the role that might have been expected of them. The type of financial cooperation practised by the moshav demands an institutional answer to the 'free-rider' problem which it raises. A comprehensive treatment of these institutional issues is, however, beyond the scope of the present chapter.[3]

5.3 Model of the individual member's borrowing and investment behaviour

In modelling the individual moshav member's borrowing and investment behaviour we assume that each moshav farmer seeks to further his individual interest and neglects other effects of his decisions on the group as a whole. The conceptual model assumes maximization of expected utility, and incorporates the effect of the moshav's overall financial position on the cost of credit for the single farm and on its resale value. The first effect stems from the moshav's principle of sharing collective financial services, and the second from the moshav's principle of mutual responsibility for members' debts.

The symbols used in the subsequent analysis are:

D_{-1i}, D_i = the debt of the i-th farm household at the beginning and at the end of the period (year), respectively;

K_{-1i}, K_i = the stock of capital (in purchasing prices) in the i-th farm household at the beginning and at the end of the period, respectively, including agricultural equipment, buildings and land;

d_i = the credit extended to the i-th unit during the period ($d_i = D_i - D_{-1i}$);

I_i = the i-th unit's net investment in productive capital during the period (K_i - K_{-1i}), equal to gross investment as we ignore depreciation;

y_i = the financial resources available to the i-th unit during the period;

c_i = the prospective consumption expenditures of the i-th farm household during the period;

S_i = the prospective resale value of the i-th farm at the end of the period;

u_i = the utility function of the i-th farm household;

R_i = the i-th farm household's absolute degree of risk aversion;

ρ_i = the i-th farm household's subjective discounting factor;

$(MD/MK)_{-1}$ = the moshav's ratio of debt to capital (leverage at the beginning of the period); and

r = the interest rate charged by the purchasing organization on credit extended to the moshav.

The common pool of credit provided by the input-purchasing organization to the moshav implies that the interest rate paid by the individual farm is that which is set by the input-purchasing organization for the moshav as a whole, and reflects the moshav's financial position rather than that of the single unit. This externality is introduced in the model via the assumption that the interest rate is identical for all the moshav's members and rises with the moshav's leverage, a widely accepted indicator of corporate financial health (e.g., Stiglitz, 1972, 1975 and Zusman, 1983).

We assume that each i-th member is aware of this financial common-pool externality, is fully informed about the moshav's last period total closing debt, has correctly observed the stock of capital in the moshav at the end of the last period, and naively expects the moshav's current leverage to deviate from its last period value by a zero mean term ε:

$$(MD/MK)_i^{\text{expected}} = (MD/MK)_{-1} + \varepsilon_i. \qquad (1)$$

The 'free-rider' phenomenon is introduced here through the individual member's belief that this current borrowing and investment decisions have a negligible effect on the cooperative's financial position and leverage. This belief is consistent with the small size of the individual farm and the large number of cooperative members. It implies non-strategic interaction among moshav members. The random term ε_i represents the effect of imperfect information about the rest of the moshav members' current borrowing and investment on the individual member's expectations regarding the cooperative's financial position. The more uncertain the individual member is about the other member's borrowing and investment, the greater the variance (σ_i^2) he attaches to the distribution of ε_i.

First-hand familiarity with three of the five moshavim included in the subsequent empirical analysis (M1, M2 and M3) strongly supports this hypothesis of naive expectations vis-á-vis alternative hypotheses such as rational expectations or perfect foresight. In general, the members of these moshavim underestimated the current level of the moshav's debt; and the common reaction to new reports of closing balances was astonishment. Since time-series observations are not available, the naive expectations hypothesis could not be tested against the possible alternative hypothesis that the members' expectations about the moshav's current leverage are adaptive or higher order autoregressive.

We assume that the (stochastic) interest rate which the i-th member of the moshav expects to pay on his debt balance is an increasing linear function of the moshav's prospective leverage ratio as he perceived it:[4]

$$r_i = \alpha_0 + \alpha_1[(MD/MK)_{-1} + \varepsilon_i], \tag{2}$$

where α_0 and α_1 are positive parameters. They reflect the moshav's scale of operation and reputation, as well as supply conditions in the credit market — all of which affect the cooperative's bargaining power in obtaining credit.

The financial resources available to the i-th farm household (y_i) are composed of its income from farming and the credit extended by the purchasing organization (d_i). Part of this credit, $ø_i d_i$, is spent on buying perishable production inputs (e.g., water, fertilizers, pesticides, livestock feeding material, energy) and the rest, $(1 - ø_i)d_i$, is directed to consumption, investment in productive capital and interest payments. Hence, the i-th member's financial resources satisfy the equation:

$$y(K_i,d_i) = F(K_i,\o_i d_i) + (1 - \o_i)d_i, \tag{3}$$

where F denotes the income (valued added) from the farm. We assume that F increases with capital and perishable inputs and is concave, and that the marginal product of capital increases with the quantity of the perishable inputs. That is:

$$\frac{\partial y}{\partial K_i}, \frac{\partial y}{\partial d_i} > 0, \frac{\partial^2 y}{\partial K_i^2}, \frac{d^2 y}{\partial d_i^2} < 0 \text{ and } \frac{\partial^2 y}{\partial K_i \partial_i d} > 0.$$

For simplicity's sake, and since the analysis focuses on the financial aspects of moshav cooperation rather than on its production aspects, the income for farming, F, is considered here to be non-stochastic. However, the inclusion of an additive random term independent of the inputs (K_i and $\o d_i$) would not change the results of the analysis substantially.

By equations (2) and (3), the i-th farm household's prospective consumption can be rendered as

$$c_i = y(K_i, d_i) - I_i - \{\alpha_0 + \alpha_1[(MD/MK)_{-1} + \varepsilon_i]\}(D_{-1i} + d_i), \tag{4}$$

where the third term on the right-hand side is the interest payment. The level of uncertainty associated with this payment is proportional to the farm's total debt.

Consistent with Stiglitz' (1972, 1975) argument that the market valuation of a firm is inversely related to its leverage and with the assertion that potential buyers of farms in the moshav are aware of the cooperative's rule of mutual responsibility for members' debts enforced by the practice of mutual co-signing, the farm's resale value at the end of the period as perceived by the i-th member is specified as a linearly decreasing function of the cooperative's prospective leverage:

$$S_i = \{\beta_0 - \beta_1[(MD/MK)_{-1} + \varepsilon_i]\} K_i - D_i, \tag{5}$$

where β_0 and β_1 are positive parameters. The stronger the cooperative's commitment to the principle of mutual responsibility, the greater is β_1. The level of uncertainty associated with the farm's resale value is proportional to its capital stock. This specification captures the second source of externalities affecting the cooperative's operation.

Equations 2 and 5 illustrate the 'free-rider' problem as a case of pooling input prices. Due to the large number and small size of member farms, the assumption of price-taking behaviour by all members is reasonable, and the externalities are similar to pecuniary externalities occurring in competitive markets.

It is postulated that each individual member determines his current credit and investment requirements by maximizing his expected utility from present consumption and the farm's subjectively discounted end-of-period resale value, i.e., by maximizing $E[u_i(c_i + \rho_i S_i)]$. Assuming for tractability a constant absolute degree of risk aversion, R_i, and that the error term, in the moshav's prospective leverage, ε_i, is a Gaussian variate having zero mean and finite variance σ_i^2, this is equivalent to maximizing $[E(c_i + \rho_i S_i) - 0.5R_i \operatorname{var}(c_i + \rho_i S_i)]$.[5]

Recalling equations 4 and 5 and taking the mean and variance of the prospective consumption and the discounted resale value, the i-th member's decision problem can be rendered as

$$\max_{(d_i, I_i)} \{V_i = y(K_i, d_i) - I_i - [\alpha_0 + \alpha_1(MD/MK)_{-1}](D_{-1i} + d_i)$$

$$+ \rho_i[\beta_0 - \beta_1(MD/MK)_{-1}]K_i - \rho_i D_i$$

$$- 0.5R_i\sigma_i^2[\alpha_1^2(D_{-1i} + d_i)^2 + \rho_i^2\beta_1^2K_i^2]\}. \tag{6}$$

Note that $D_i \equiv D_{-1i} + d_i$ and $K_i \equiv K_{-1i} + I_i$ and hence the necessary conditions for a maximum V_i are:

$$\frac{\partial V_i}{\partial d_i} = \frac{\partial y(K_i^*, d_i^*)}{\partial d_i} - [\alpha_0 + \alpha_1(MD/MK)_{-1}]$$

$$- \alpha_1^2 R_i \sigma_i^2 (D_{-1i} + d_i^*) - \rho_i = 0, \tag{7a}$$

$$\frac{\partial V_i}{\partial I_i} = \frac{\partial y(K_i^*, d_i^*)}{\partial I_i} - \rho_i[\beta_0 - \beta_1(MD/MK)_{-1}]$$

$$- 1 - \rho_i^2\beta_1^2 R_i\sigma_i^2(K_{-1i} + I_i^*) = 0. \tag{7b}$$

They indicate that the i-th member chooses d_i by equating the marginal contribution of borrowing with its marginal cost, comprising interest charges, increased risk, and a decline in the farm's resale value. Simultaneously and interdependently, he chooses I_i by equating the marginal contribution of capital from increased farm income and resale value with the marginal cost of investment, including the purchase price of capital (numéraire) and the increase in risk.

The necessary conditions 7a and 7b define a non-linear system of simultaneous equation. To fix ideas and motivate the subsequent empirical analysis this system is linearized by considering the second-order Taylor polynomial of $y(K_i, d_i)$ at $(K_{-1i}, 0)$. The mathematical appendix presents the reduced form A.4 of the resultant system in matrix notation, and demonstrate that V_i has a (local) maximum at the critical point (d_i^*, I_i^*). By differentiating the reduced form A.4 and taking into account the second-order conditions A.5–A.7 for maximum expected utility, the full (direct plus indirect) effects of the predetermined variables $(MD/MK)_{-1}$, D_{-1i} and K_{-1i} on the individual members' borrowing and investment are obtained:

$$\frac{\partial d_i^*}{\partial (MD/MK)_{-1}} = -\left(\alpha_1 H_{22} + \rho_i\beta_1 \frac{\partial^2 y}{\partial K\, \partial d}\right) \Big/ \det H < 0, \tag{8a}$$

$$\frac{\partial d_i^*}{\partial D_{-1i}} = -\alpha_i^2 R_i \sigma_i^2 H_{22} \Big/ \det H < 0, \tag{8b}$$

$$\frac{\partial d_i^*}{\partial K_{-1i}} = \rho_i^2\beta_1^2 R_i \sigma_i^2 \frac{\partial^2 y}{\partial K \partial d} \Big/ \det H < 0, \tag{8c}$$

$$\frac{\partial I_i^*}{\partial (MD/MK)_{-1}} = -\left(\alpha_1 \frac{\partial^2 y}{\partial K \partial d} + \rho_i\beta_1 H_{11}\right) \Big/ \det H < 0, \tag{8d}$$

$$\frac{\partial I_i^*}{\partial D_{-1i}} = -\alpha_i^2 R_i \sigma_i^2 \frac{\partial^2 y}{\partial K \partial d} \Big/ \det H < 0, \tag{8e}$$

$$\frac{\partial I_i^*}{\partial K_{-1i}} = -\rho_i^2 \beta_i^2 R_i \sigma_i^2 H_{11} \Big/ \det H < 0, \tag{8f}$$

where H denotes the Hessian of V_i and H_{11} and H_{22} its principal minors. As shown by 8a to 8f, the full effect of each of the predetermined variables is to reduce the amount of money borrowed and the investment in capital stock.

The underlying economic intuition stems from the necessary conditions 7a and 7b. Thus, an increase in $(MD/MK)_{-1}$, *ceteris paribus*, reduces d_i directly through the increase in the mean of the prospective interest rate. It also reduces d_i indirectly through its adverse effect on the prospective resale price of capital, which dampens the demand for capital. Given our previous assumption that the marginal product of perishable inputs (ϕd_i) increases with capital ($\partial^2 y/\partial K \partial d > 0$), this implies that the net benefit from borrowing decreases, and thus, too, the amount of money borrowed.

Similarly, the direct effect of an increase in $(MD/MK)_{-1}$ on the individual member's investment is negative due to the decrease in the prospective resale price of capital stock. And the indirect effect of $(MD/MK)_{-1}$ on I_i is also negative: an increase in $(MD/MK)_{-1}$ raises the mean of the prospective interest rate and therefore decreases the demand for credit. Given our assumption that $(\partial^2 y/\partial K\, \partial d) > 0$, this implies that the net benefit from investment decreases, and consequently so does the additional capital stock demanded.

An increase in the individual member's initial debt (D_{-1i}), *ceteris paribus*, reduces his demand for credit due to the higher cost of risk bearing from the increased variance of the perceived interest payments. Furthermore, the decline in the individual member's borrowing in turn reduces the marginal product of capital and thus the net benefit from investment, therefore decreasing the individual member's investment in capital stock.

Similarly, an increase in the individual farm's initial capital stock (K_{-1i}), *ceteris paribus*, reduces the current investment due to the higher cost of risk bearing from the increased variance of the farm's perceived discounted resale value. Furthermore, in the vicinity of the optimum the decrease in the individual member's investment reduces the marginal product of perishable inputs and thus the net benefit from money borrowed to finance the purchasing of these inputs. Therefore, an increase in K_{-1i} also reduces the individual member's borrowing.

Note that the variances of the prospective interest payments and the perceived discounted resale value of the farm increase with the perceived level of uncertainty about the cooperative's financial position (σ_i^2), which in turn rises with the lack of information about the current borrowing and investment of the rest of the moshav's members. Thus, the less informed the i-th member is about the other member's borrowing and investment (i.e., the greater σ_i^2), the stronger the effects of D_{-1i} and K_{-1i} on his current borrowing and investment. These effects are amplified further by the i-th member's degree by absolute risk aversion (R_i). They vanish under a jointly coordinated operation of the cooperative as such conduct ensures full information about the cooperative's leverage. They also vanish for a risk-neutral person ($R_i = 0$). This is because the effects of D_{-1i} and K_{-1i} on d_i and I_i are generated through the variances of the interest payments and the farm's perceived resale value, and the costs of risk bearing for a risk-neutral person are nil.

5.4 Comparison with a coordinated joint optimum

The type of financial cooperation described in the previous section gives rise to individual behaviour which is likely to diverge from a joint optimum of moshav members coordinating their credit demands. Our analysis suggests three distinct sources for such a divergence. Two of these can be examined within a standard comparative statics framework with identical farmers. The first is the usual pecuniary externality that results when individual moshav members act as price takers regarding the cost of credit, though the moshav as a whole faces an upward sloping credit supply function. The second is a spurious measure of uncertainty with regard to interest charges and farm resale values stemming from the farmer's dependence on an uncoordinated credit pool. A third source of divergence (which we shall demonstrate in section 6, through simulation) arises when members of the same moshav have heterogeneous attitudes to debt, leading 'debt-prone' members to expand at the expense of 'debt-averse' members. Such a development path carries the seeds of instability.

Consider the case of a moshav with identical members (i.e., having the same production technologies, initial endowments, utility functions, etc.) and assume that the members of the moshav coordinate their investment and borrowing activities so as to maximize the objective function of the representative member:

$$V = y(K,d)_{-1} - I - [\alpha_0 + \alpha_1(D/K)]D + \rho[(\beta_0 - \beta_1(D/K))K - D]. \qquad (9)$$

Note that this differs from equation 6 in that the moshav's leverage ratio, which the individual farmer takes as exogenous in the uncoordinated case, equals the leverage ratio of the representative farmer; and this leverage ratio is deterministic, eliminating the element of risk aversion reflected in the final term of equation 6.

Recalling that $D=D_{-1}+d$ and $K=K_{-1} + I$, the partial derivation of V with respect to I and d yields the following first-order conditions:

$$\partial V/\partial d = \partial y/\partial d - [\alpha_0 + \alpha_1(D/K)] - \alpha_1(D/K) - \rho - \beta_1\rho = 0 \qquad (10a)$$

$$\partial V/\partial I = \partial y/\partial K - 1 + \alpha_1(D/K)^2 + \rho\beta_0 = 0. \qquad (10b)$$

A comparison of these equations with the uncoordinated decisions characterized by conditions 7a and 7b reveals that, for a given level of borrowing, the individual farmer does not invest enough in productive capital, the positive externality of physical capital on the moshav's credit rating is ignored, and this tendency is reinforced by the element of risk aversion.[6] The comparison of borrowing behaviour under the two regimes is ambiguous, however. Uncoordinated borrowing is encouraged by neglect of the negative externality of debt on the moshav's credit rating, but discouraged by the element of risk aversion. In addition, individual borrowing behaviour may vary from the joint optimum because the (naively) expected value of the moshav's leverage may diverge from its actual value.

We believe these are significant effects that may seriously undermine the efficient functioning of the moshav, but it may well be that the greatest danger to the moshav's long-term health stems from dynamic effects that arise when moshav members are heterogeneous. In the present model, different attitudes to debt accumulation (stemming, for example, from different levels of risk aversion) may lead to a situation in which the debt positions of 'low-debt' members (possibly more thrifty and more efficient in production) and 'high-debt' members diverge to opposite extremes: 'high-debt' members acting as 'free riders' exploit the availability of better credit terms that their debt position merits, and steadily increase their leverage ratio, while 'low-debt' members, faced with worse credit terms than they deserve, constrict their borrowing behaviour and their productive activity.

We have not been able to carry out a formal analysis of this aspect of moshav financial cooperation but simulation runs reported in section 6 demonstrate that a divergent solution is possible. Clearly, when such is the case, 'low-debt' moshav members have a strong interest in disbanding the moshav's financial cooperative, or at least removing their support from those members who have exhibited what they view as irresponsible debt accumulation. Such attitudes have been much in evidence.

5.5 Empirical evidence

This section estimates the unknown reduced form parameters of the simultaneous equation system A.4 in the appendix. Our empirical analysis is based on data on five moshavim in the north-western part of the Negev district which were founded in the early 1950s and experienced a major financial crisis during the 1980s. The data were obtained from the Jewish Agency's Annual Agricultural and Demographic Census, and include observations on capital stock, debt (measured in shekels, in September 1983 prices) and other characteristics of 322 family farms, for the years 1982 and 1983.

Our estimation takes into account possible variation among the sample family farms as regards risk aversion, time preferences and managerial ability, through the inclusion of relevant characteristics such as the farmer's nativity (Z1: 1 = Israeli born, 0 = immigrant), and his farming experience, proxied by the number of years of managing a farm (Z2). The significance of these demographic characteristics in the explanation of labour supply, efficiency of production, and income distribution in the Israeli family farm sector has already been established by Sadan and Weintraub (1980), Berck and Levy (1986) and Levy (1987) who utilized survey data from the mid-1970s. These characteristics define the typical three generations of farmers in moshavim established in the early 1950s. The first-generation farmers are the moshav founders who immigrated to the newly established State of Israel from the Middle East and North Africa. The second-generation of farmers consists of the younger brothers and the elder sons of the first-generation farmers. The third-generation farmers are the Israeli-born sons of the first generation. (We shall use this three-way division to simulate the development path of the moshav over time in the next section.)

Following Haruvi and Kislev (1984), our estimation also takes into account moshav effects that complement the farmstead orientation underlying our theoretical approach. Such effects reflect structural characteristics of the moshav, such as age, land and water allotments, production quotas, regional affiliation, access to alternative marketing channels, quality of accounting information, etc. They are reflected in the inclusion of four dummy variables, M1 to M4.

Unbiased estimates of the full (direct plus indirect) effects of the system's predetermined variables can be found simply by ordinary least squares estimation of the reduced form A.4 parameters. These estimated effects are presented in Table 5.2, for two alternative specifications: with and without the dummy variables. The estimation results confirm that the full effects of the perceived mean of the cooperative's leverage on the individual member's investment is negative, as expected, and statistically significant; and so also are the estimated full effects of the individual member's initial debt and capital stock. This holds regardless of whether the dummy variables are included or not. The effects of these factors on individual members' borrowing were found to be statistically in significant when the dummy variables were included, but when the dummy variables are omitted the effects of $(MD/MK)_{-1}$ and D_{-1} on the individual member's borrowing are also negative and statistically significant. It is possible that the high degrees of correlation between $(MD/MK)_{-1}$ and M1 and M3 (0.667 and 0.565, respectively) militate against identification of their separate effects.

Table 5.2
Ordinary least squares estimates of the reduced form parameters[a]

Explanatory variables	Dependent variables: Demand for credit (d_i) With dummies	Without	Investment (I_i) With dummies	Without
(MD/MK)-1	120685.69	-2364900	-3131645.60	-1129461
	(0.261)	(7.867)	(2.303)	(1.471)
D-1	-0.018067	-0.080755	-0.315270	-0.400236
	(0.503)	(1.898)	(2.990)	(3.682)
K-1	-0.001336	-0.004727	-0.130267	-0.131789
	(0.323)	(0.946)	(10.735)	(10.331)
Nativity (Z1)	159159.82	226249	-205970.56	-286124
	(2.286)	(2.721)	(1.008)	(1.347)
Farming Experience (Z2)	4850.94	17004.83	-21239.16	-24243.04
	(1.817)	(6.191)	(2.710)	(3.456)
M1	896322.68	—	7718.24	—
	(9.582)		(0.028)	
M3[b]	271653.78	—	400820.71	—
	(4.674)		(2.349)	
M4	141865.67	—	-792089.08	—
	(1.953)		(3.714)	
Constant	-315823.52	3352956	1147354.90	788732
	(2.595)	(3.489)	(3.211)	(3.052)
R^2	0.497	0.255	0.390	0.317
F-test statistic	38.680	21.403	24.987	28.990

a Absolute value of t-ratios reported in parentheses below the estimates.

b One of the moshav dummy variables, M2, did not enter the regression equation due to insufficient tolerance.

Interpreted through the comparative statics analysis in section 5.3, and specifically properties 8b, 8c, 8e and 8f, these estimates indicate that the members perceived the cooperative's leverage as a random variable and had an aversion to risk, that is, $R_i\sigma_i^2>0$. The positive costs of risk bearing for the individual member, which are due to lack of information about the current borrowing and investment of the rest of the moshav's members, imply that the moshav's operation was not jointly coordinated, and indicate the existence of a 'free-rider' problem.

The estimates associated with the dummy variables are in general statistically significant and indicate the existence of structural differences among the sample moshavim which affect their members' borrowing and investment. One of these dummy variables (M2) did not enter the regression equation due to insufficient tolerance, indicating that the associated moshav's structure is very similar to that of the moshav taken as a reference. The members of these two moshavim (2 and 5) were found to behave more cautiously, borrowing less than the members of the other three moshavim.

The reduced form estimation results indicate further that Israeli-born farmers borrow more than immigrant farmers but invest less; and that veteran farmers borrow more and invest less than younger farmers. These differences in borrowing and investment behaviour among the cooperative's members are better illustrated by the following simulation which takes into account the moshav's three-generation population structure.

5.6 Simulation of the trajectories of the individual farm's debt and capital stock and the moshav's leverage

The estimated reduced forms of the i-th member farm's demand for credit and investment based on the specification that includes the dummy variables are[7]:

$$\begin{aligned} d_i = & -315823.52 + 896322.68\ M1 + 271653\ M3 + 141865.67\ M4 \\ & + 120685.69\ 9\ (MD/MK)_{-1} - 0.018067\ D_{-1i} - 0.001336\ K_{-1i} \\ & + 159159.82\ Z1_i + 4850.94\ Z2_i + e_{1i}, \qquad (11a) \end{aligned}$$

$$I_i = 1147354.90 + 7718.24\ M1 + 400820.71\ M3 - 792089.08\ M4 - 3131645.60\ (MD/MK)_{-1} - 0.315270\ D_{-1i} - 0.130267\ K_{-1i} - 205970.56\ Z1_i - 21239.16\ Z2_i + e_{2i}, \tag{11b}$$

where e_1 and e_2 are error terms. Recalling that $d_i = D_i - D_{-1i}$ and $I_i = K_i - K_{-1i}$, and taking the observed data for 1983 as a starting point, we can simulate the expected trajectories of the individual farm's debt and capital stock and the moshav's aggregate leverage. Note that the characteristic roots of the state-transition matrix of the difference equation system 11 are within the unit circle (0.9855692 and 0.8660968), and hence the trajectories of D_i and K_i converge to their trend curves.[8]

Our simulation considers the more cautious moshavim M2 and M5, and focuses on the division of the moshav's farmer population into three groups distinguished by nativity and number of years managing a farm:

$$G1 = \{i \mid Z1_i = 0 \cap Z2_i(t = 1983) = 28\}, \tag{12a}$$

$$G2 = \{i \mid Z1_i = 0 \cap Z2_i(t = 1983) = 18\}, \tag{12b}$$

$$G3 = \{i \mid Z1_i = 1 \cap Z2_i(t = 1983) = 5\}, \tag{12c}$$

The shares of these groups in the simulation population conform to their weights in the estimation sample: P(G1) = 2/6, P(G2) = 3/6 and P(G3) = 1/6. This is a characteristic inter-generation structure of Israeli moshavim established in the 1950s.

Table 5.3 presents the simulation results which arise from a hypothetically equal distribution of capital stock and debt among the participants in 1983 taken as the base sample's averages for this year. These simulation results show that, starting from equal levels of debt and capital, all members reduce their levels of indebtedness and their capital stock but at different speeds. Farmers of type G1 reduce their level of debt at a lower rate than the rest of the moshav's members. They also reduce their capital stock at a higher rate.[9] In contrast, farmers of the second generation reduce their level of debt at the highest rate and leverage their farmstead most moderately. The youngest farmers (G3) borrow more than their counterpart G2 members, but invest more in capital stock. A graphic representation of these trajectories is displayed in Figure 5.1. It highlights the divergence in leverage ratios between

Table 5.3
Simulated time trajectories of debt, capital stock and leverage 1983-1986[a]

	Member Type G1			*Member Type G2*		
Year	Debt	Capital	Leverage	Debt	Capital	Leverage
1983	755,599	2,638,012	0.2864	755,599	2,638,012	0.2864
1984	597,841	1,690,664	0.3536	549,332	1,903,056	0.2887
1985	452,550	804,404	0.5630	356,124	1,216,813	0.2927
1986	324,060	0	∞	180,345	447,626	0.4029

	Member Type G3			*Moshav average[b]*		
Year	Debt	Capital	Leverage	Debt	Capital	Leverage
1983	755,599	2,638,012	0.2864	755,599	2,638,012	0.2864
1984	645,430	1,973,195	0.3271	581,518	1,843,949	0.3154
1985	546,490	1,317,657	0.4147	419,994	1,096,419	0.3831
1986	463,234	942,418	0.4915	275,398	380,883	0.7231

a All money values are in September 30, 1983 Israeli Shekels (63.6872 Israeli Shekels=1 US dollar)

b Moshav average debt=$(2/6)D(G1)+(3/6)D(G2)+(1/6)D(G3)$;
Moshav average capital=$(2/6)K(G1)+(3/6)K(G2)+(1/6)K(G3)$;
Moshav leverage=moshav average debt/moshav average capital.

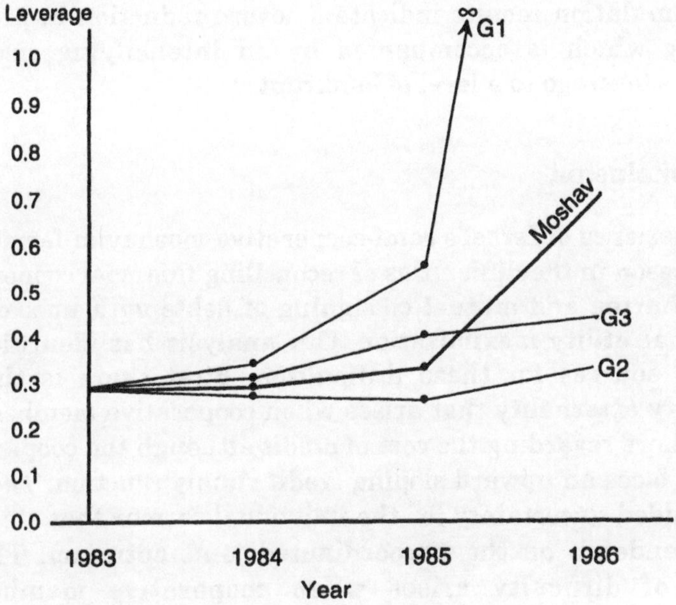

Figure 5.1 Time trajectories of farmers' leverage by generation and of the moshav's leverage

young-generation and immigrant farmers of the same moshav, which must undermine its cooperative structure.

In terms of the theoretical analysis, the disparate behaviour of the identified generations may evolve from differences in the rate of time preference, in information about other members' behaviour, in attitudes toward risk and in production efficiency. It is possible that the younger generation of farmers who have benefited from better schooling and better preparation for a moshav lifestyle have better information about other members' borrowing and investment and a lower degree of absolute risk aversion, and thus face lower marginal costs of risk bearing from an uncertain liquidation price. It is also possible that the younger-generation members are better farmers, and thus generate greater marginal added value from investment. This argument is supported by Berck and Levy's (1986) findings that immigrant and veteran (first generation) farmers tend to work less and also farm less efficiently than the younger generation of farmers.

The simulation results indicate a severe reduction in production capacity which is accompanied by an intensifying rise of the moshav's leverage to a level of bankruptcy.

5.7 Conclusion

The experience of Israel's semi-cooperative moshavim farmers is an object lesson in the difficulties of reconciling financial cooperation in credit-sharing and mutual co-signing of debts with uncoordinated individual utility maximization. Our analysis has identified three distinct sources for these difficulties. First there is the usual pecuniary externality that arises when cooperative members act as price takers regarding the cost of credit although the cooperative as a whole faces an upward sloping credit supply function. The second is the added uncertainty for the individual farmer that stems from his dependence on the uncoordinated joint optimum. The third source of difficulty arises when cooperative members are heterogeneous in their production efficiency and attitudes to debt-bearing. Dynamic simulation suggests that 'debt-prone' members of the cooperative will increase their debt position at the expense of 'debt-averse' members. This undermines the stability of the cooperative. Both theoretical considerations and empirical observation indicate that each of these factors is exacerbated during periods of general financial difficulty for farmers.

Financial cooperation has played an important role in developing the agricultural sector in Israel as in other countries, and also has a useful role to play in developing small manufacturing and service enterprises. In many cases it is a necessary tool for channelling credit to small landlords or craftsmen, and in any event offers important economies of scale in risk sharing, information and administration. The early success of the moshavim attest to the advantages of cooperation in developing an agricultural sector comprised of small landholdings. This specific form of cooperation provides the small farmstead with an infrastructure of mutual responsibility, while leaving wide scope for individual initiative. But the recent adverse experience of many moshavim highlights the need for a social and institutional framework that can reconcile the inherent difficulties of the moshav type of semi-cooperative. In Israel these social underpinnings have eroded over time. New institutional arrangements must be developed if the type of cooperation practised by the moshav is to remain viable.

Appendix: Mathematical appendix for section 5.3

Taking the second-order Taylor polynomial of $y(K_i, d_i)$ at $(K_{-1i},0)$,

$$y(K_i,d_i) \cong y(K_{-1i},0) + \frac{\partial y(K_{-1i},0)}{\partial K} I_i + 0.5 \frac{\partial^2 y(K_{-1i},0)}{\partial K^2} I_i^2$$

$$+ \frac{\partial y(K_{-1i},0)}{\partial d} d_i + 0.5 \frac{\partial^2 y(K_{-1i},0)}{\partial d^2} d_i^2 + \frac{\partial^2 y(K_{-1i},0)}{\partial y \partial d} I_i d_i, \tag{A.1}$$

in which case,

$$\frac{\partial y}{\partial d_i} \cong \frac{\partial y(\cdot)}{\partial d} + \frac{\partial^2 y(\cdot)}{\partial d^2} d_i + \frac{\partial^2 y(\cdot)}{\partial K \partial d} I_i \tag{A.2}$$

and

$$\frac{\partial y}{\partial I_i} \cong \frac{\partial y(\cdot)}{\partial K} + \frac{\partial^2 y(\cdot)}{\partial K^2} I_i + \frac{\partial^2 y(\cdot)}{\partial K \partial d} d_i. \tag{A.3}$$

By substituting A.2 and A.3 in 7a and 7b, respectively, the following reduced form is obtained:

$$\begin{bmatrix} d_i^* \\ \\ I_i^* \end{bmatrix} \cong \underbrace{\begin{bmatrix} -\left[\frac{\partial^2 y(\bullet)}{\partial d^2} - \alpha_1^2 R_i \sigma_i^2\right] & -\frac{\partial^2 y(\bullet)}{\partial K\, \partial d} \\ -\frac{\partial^2 y(\bullet)}{\partial K\, \partial d} & -\left[\frac{\partial^2 y}{\partial K^2} - \rho_i^2 \beta_1^2 R_i \sigma_i^2\right] \end{bmatrix}^{-1}}_{H}$$

$$\times \begin{bmatrix} \left(\frac{\partial y(\bullet)}{\partial d} - \alpha_o - \rho_i\right) & (-\alpha_1) & (-\alpha_1^2 R_i \sigma_i^2) & 0 \\ \left(\frac{\partial y(\bullet)}{\partial K} + \beta_o \rho_i - 1\right) & (-\beta_1 \rho_i) & 0 & (-\rho_i^2 \beta_1^2 R_i \sigma_i^2) \end{bmatrix} \begin{bmatrix} 1 \\ (MD/MK)_{-1} \\ D_{-1i} \\ K_{-1i} \end{bmatrix}. \tag{A.4}$$

The square matrix H is the Hessian of $V_i(d_i,I_i)$; and V_i has a (local) maximum at the critical point (d_i^*,l_i^*) if

$$H_{11} = \alpha_1^2 R_i \sigma_1^2 - \frac{\partial^2 y(K_{-1i},0)}{\partial d^2} > 0, \quad (A.5)$$

$$H_{22} = \rho_i^2 \beta_1^2 R_i \sigma_i^2 - \frac{\partial^2 y(K_{-1i},0)}{\partial K^2} > 0, \quad (A.6)$$

and

$$det\, H > 0 \quad (A.7)$$

As $\partial^2 y/\partial d^2$ and $\partial^2 y/\partial K^2$ are both negative by assumption, conditions A.5 and A.6 are satisfied. Moreover, as F, the farm's value added function, is concave *det* H must be positive. To see this, denote by $\tilde{H}$ the Hessian of F; then $\tilde{H}$ is also the Hessian of y (which differs from F only by a linear term); and as F is concave $det\, \tilde{H} > 0$. By straightforward calculation $det\, H = det\, \tilde{H} + \alpha_1^2 R_i^2 \rho_i^2 \beta_1^2 \sigma_i^4 - (\partial^2 y/\partial d^2)\rho_i^2 \beta_1^2 R_i \sigma_i^2 - (\partial^2 y/\partial K^2)\alpha_1^2 R_i \sigma_i^2 > det\, \tilde{H} > 0$. Thus, second-order conditions for maximum are also met.

Notes

1 As Zusman (1983) has pointed out, the institutional mechanism which a cooperative adopts to resolve issues of social choice is a key determinant of the way it functions.

2 See also Hochman, Levy, Bar-Niv and Bar-Nis (1986) for a comprehensive case study of the financial crisis in five moshavim.

3 Zusman (1983) is an important step in this direction.

4 Financial cooperation, as practised in the moshav, implies floating interest terms for the individual farmer: interest charges are determined *ex post* and equal the moshav's current average cost of capital. As Table 5.1 shows, an overwhelming proportion of moshav debt is short-term and must be rolled over at current interest rates at short intervals, hence current average interest charges are strongly influenced by the current leverage. In practice, inadequate accounting systems cause

added delay before the moshav's current capital costs are known to the farmer.

5 See discussion in Freund (1956) and recent applications by Yassour, Zilberman and Rausser (1981) and Collender and Zilberman (1985). As regards the generality of this framework Hammond (1974) has argued that the easy-to-analyze utility curve of constant absolute risk aversion can be used in place of non-constant absolute risk aversion when the rival choices in any pair-wise comparison yield uncertain payoffs that are either simply-intertwined or one stochastically dominates the other. In our particular case the former condition holds: our assumptions about ε_i implies that for any pair of chosen values of the decision variables, d_i and I_i, the cumulative distribution functions of the random payoffs $(c_i + \rho_i S_i)$ cross only once.

6 The model indicates under-investment given a level of borrowing, but as there may well be over-borrowing (see below in the text) investment levels may also exceed the joint-optimum level of investment. Of course this is only a partial analysis of optimal investment in agricultural capacity. Naive price expectations are a common reason for suboptimal investment levels.

7 We also simulate debt, capital and leverage trajectories using the estimated reduced form in which the moshav dummies are omitted. The simulations obtained also exhibit a large decline in capital and debt, and strongly indicate the more cautious behaviour of moshav members of type G2 and G3.

8 The state-transition matrix is

$$A = \begin{pmatrix} 1 - 0.018067 & -0.001336 \\ -0.315270 & 1 - 0.130267 \end{pmatrix}$$

and its characteristic roots are found by $\lambda_{1,2} = 0.5[tr\,A \pm (tr\,A - 4det\,A)^{0.5}]$. They are within the unit circle, and so the solution to the homogeneous part of the difference equation system 11, $c_1\lambda_1^t + c_2\lambda_2^1$, converges to zero as t goes to infinity; and the trajectories of D and K approach their trend curves.

9 We place now lower bound on negative values of I_i, allowing a high rate of disinvestment consistent with negative rates of gross investment. Alternative assumption, for example, non-negative gross investment and a fixed depreciation rate, could also be incorporated in our framework.

References

Berck, P. and Levy, A. (1986), 'The costs of equal land distribution: The case of Israeli moshavim', *American Journal of Agricultural Economics*, vol. 68, pp. 605–14.

Collender, R.N. and Zilberman, D. (1985), 'Land allocation under uncertainty for alternative specifications of return distributions', *American Journal of Agricultural Economics*, vol. 67, pp. 779–86.

Freund, R.J. (1956), 'An introduction of risk into a risk-programming model', *Econometrica*, vol. 24, pp. 253–63.

Hammond, S. (1974), 'Simplification of choice under uncertainty', *Management Science*, vol. 20, pp. 1047–72.

Haruvi, N. and Kislev, Y. (1984), 'Cooperation in the moshav', *Journal of Comparative Economics*, vol. 8, pp. 54–77.

Hochman, E., Levy, A., Bar-Niv, R. and Bar-Nis, Z. (1986), *Evaluation feedback and control systems of the aid program to distressed moshavim in the Negev*, Settlement Department of the Jewish Agency, Beer Sheva, Israel (in Hebrew).

Levy, A. (1987), 'Income inequality and the distribution of ownership of productive resources: Theory and application with lognormal distribution', *Journal of Policy Modeling*, vol. 9, pp. 321–36.

Sadan, E. and Weintraub, D. (1980), 'Ethnicity, nativity, and economic performance of cooperative smallholding farms in Israel', *Economic Development and Cultural Change*, vol. 28, pp. 487–507.

Stiglitz, J.E. (1972), 'Some aspects of pure theory and corporate finance: Bankruptcy and turnovers', *The Bell Journal of Economics*, vol. 3, pp. 458–83.

—— (1975), 'Some aspects of pure theory and corporate finance: Bankruptcy and takeovers', *The Bell Journal of Economics*, vol. 6, pp. 711–4.

Yassour, J.D., Zilberman, D. and Rausser, G.C. (1981), 'Optimal choices among alternative technologies with stochastic yield', *American Journal of Agricultural Economics*, vol. 63, pp. 718–24.

Zusman, P. (1983), 'Collective choice, Pareto optimality and the organization of cooperatives — the case of agricultural credit association', *Journal of Economic Behavior and Organization*, vol. 4, pp. 183–204.

6 The consequences of mutually secured debts: The case of Israeli moshavim

The effects of the moshav's organizational principle of mutual responsibility for members' debts on investment, consumption and borrowing are studied within the framework of an optimal control model and summarized by a number of optimality conditions. The effects of the individual member's position and the moshav's financial position on the individual member's investment and borrowing are estimated and tested further in two cross-sectional regression analyses, which also take into account observed variations in characteristics among the family farms.

6.1 Introduction

As has been shown in the previous chapter, financial externalities might arise from the moshav's organizational principles of mutual responsibility. These externalities can have considerable adverse effects on the capital investment and borrowing of the more efficient farms, relative to less efficient farms, especially in periods of recession when the financial position of the moshav is worsened. These effects are studied in the present chapter within the framework of an optimal control model and summarized by a

Reprinted with permission from the *Journal of Economics and Finance*, vol. 17, no. 2, Summer 1993, pp. 93–108, with modifications.

number of optimality conditions. The model's implications with regard to the individual farmer's borrowing, investment and consumption are then discussed. Subsequently, the effects of the individual's position, the moshav's position and socio-demographic factors on the individual member's investment and borrowing are estimated with two different types of data. The first data base provides micro information on 135 farms in two moshavim in 1983, while the second includes aggregate information on eighty-two moshavim for the same year. Finally, the chapter is concluded with a brief summary.

6.2 Intertemporal model of moshav members' borrowing, investment and consumption

This section presents a simple formulation of the economic behaviour of a family farm in a moshav. The framework is dynamic and takes into account the unique and essential relationships between the single unit and the moshav organization as regards the principles of mutual responsibility for members' debts, and sharing of collective marketing and financial services provided by a purchasing organization. A purchasing organization is common to a number of nearby moshavim typically affiliated to the same ideological movement. In addition to purchasing agricultural products, it provides banking services to the moshavim and plays an important role in Israel's so called 'gray credit market'. Single farms do not have direct access to the purchasing organization. They settle their business affairs with the moshav's secretary and accounting offices. These authorized offices deal with the purchasing organization. Hence, the farm's debt is to the moshav, and the moshav's debt is to the purchasing organization.

The economic environment of the family farm can be characterized by the motion equations of its stock of productive capital and amount of debt:

$$\dot{K} = I - \delta K \tag{1}$$

$$d \equiv \dot{D} = C + I + i(AD)D - V(K,N) - w(1 - N),\ 0 < N < 1 \tag{2}$$

where

K is the stock of productive capital in constant purchasing prices on the farm,

D is the farm household debt to the moshav ($D \gtreqless 0$),

I is the farm's current gross investment in productive capital,

d is the farm's current borrowing,

δ is the rate of depreciation of capital,

i is the interest rate set by the purchasing organization,

AD is the moshav's average debt (total moshav debt divided by the number of family farms),

N is the on-farm labour supplied by the family household,

w is the wage rate for off-farm employment,

V is the on-farm value added assumed to be an increasing and concave function in both K and N, and

C is the farm household's consumption.

In this framework, the implication of the moshav's financial structure — particularly that debts are mutually secured by all members of the moshav — is that the interest rate paid by the individual farm is that which is set by the purchasing organization for the moshav as a whole, and is thus a function of the moshav's average debt:

$$i = i(AD), \text{ and } i'(AD) > 0.\text{[1]} \tag{3}$$

Assuming the farmer's temporal utility can be represented as an increasing, convex function of current consumption, u(C), and that $\lim_{C \to \infty} u'(C) = 0$, the farmer's decision problem is postulated as choosing consumption, investment and on farm labour[2] over a known finite horizon (0, T) so as to maximize the value of the discounted utility stream and the 'salvage value' S(T) measured in utiles and associated with the assets of the farm at the terminal time T

$$\max \int_0^T e^{-rt}\, U(C(T))\, dt + S(T) \tag{4}$$

subject to the constraints (1) and (2), $C \geq 0$, $K(0) > 0$ and $K(T) \geq 0$.

The farm's salvage value should incorporate the effects of the members' own debt (D) and the moshav's average debt (AD). Both have a negative effect on the farm's resale value, the latter because of the mutual responsibility for debts and the effect of the moshav's average debt on its cooperative reputation. We therefore specify the farm's salvage value as

$$S_T = R(AD_T)K_T - M(AD_T, D_T) \tag{5}$$

where R is a function which translates K (measured as accumulated net investments in constant prices) to its resale value in utiles. It is assumed that R represents the moshav's reputation and hence decreases with AD_T. M denotes the loss of utility due to the member's liability for his own and the moshav's debt. Because of the mutual co-signing principle, M is assumed to increase with the farm's own debt and the moshav's average debt. Summing up, we assume that

$$\frac{dR}{dAD_T} < 0, \frac{\partial M}{\partial D_T}, \frac{\partial M}{AD_T} > 0 \text{ and } \frac{\partial^2 M}{\partial D_T \partial AD_T} \geq 0.$$

The Hamiltonian for the problem specified in 4 is

$$H = e^{-rt} U(V(K, N) + w(1 - N) + d - I - i(AD)D) + \lambda_1(I - \delta K) + \lambda_2 d. \tag{6}$$

The variables K, D, N, C, I, λ_1 and λ_2 must obey the constraints and the auxiliary equations

$$\dot{\lambda}_1 = -e^{-rt} U_C V_K + \lambda_1 \delta \tag{7a}$$

$$\dot{\lambda}_2 = e^{-rt} U_C i(AD) \tag{7b}$$

the optimality conditions for interior solution (i.e., assuming that control constraints are not binding)

$$\frac{\partial H}{\partial N} = e^{-rt} U_C(V_N - w) = 0 \tag{8a}$$

$$\frac{\partial H}{\partial I} = -e^{rt} U_C + \lambda_1 = 0 \qquad (8b)$$

$$\frac{\partial H}{\partial d} = e^{-rt} U_C + \lambda_2 = 0 \qquad (8c)$$

and the transversality conditions

$$K(T) \geq 0, \lambda_1(T) \geq R(AD_T)$$

$$K(T) [\lambda_1(T) - R(AD_T)] = 0 \qquad (9a)$$

$$\lambda_2(T) = - \frac{\partial M}{\partial D} (D_T, AD_T). \qquad (9b)$$

It is important to note that in the derivation of the auxiliary equation 7b we assume that the single farm considers its effect on the moshav's average debt to be negligible, that is, $\partial AD/\partial D = 0$. This assumption reflects the 'free-rider' problem characteristic of price pooling, and is justified by the fact that a typical moshav comprises about seventy small farms endowed with equal amount of land and water allotment.

It is also important to note that the path of AD is only known *ex post*. Thus, the above analysis should be viewed as adopting the common practice of relying on what is called certainty equivalence. This procedure takes the solution to the certainty model and replaces the unknown AD with their conditional expected value given the information available. Our impression from working with several of the financially distressed moshavim is that, due to an inefficient and slow accounting system, the information available to a moshav's member is on the values of AD and D a year ago (AD_{-1} and D_{-1}); and that due to a severe lack of co-ordination of and information about the allocation of credit, there is a common belief among the moshav's members that the discrepancy between AD and AD_{-1} is nothing but a white noise. Consequently, the econometric analyses will consider the one-year lages of the state variables as explanatory variables.

6.3 Model's implications

In this section we present the model's implications as regards members' debts, capital stocks and consumption.

6.3.1 Effect of the moshav average debt on member's debt

From the optimality conditions 8b and 8c

$$\lambda_1(t) = -\lambda_2(t). \tag{10}$$

This result and the transversality conditions imply that for K(T) > 0

$$R(AD_T) = \frac{\partial M}{\partial D}(D_T, AD_T). \tag{11}$$

Given the expected AD_T, the member's terminal own debt can be found from equation 11.

The moshav's rule of debt repayment (M) plays an important role in the determination of the members' terminal debts.[3] The total differential of equation 11 implies

$$\frac{dD_T}{dAD_T} = \frac{\frac{dR}{dAD_T} - \frac{\partial^2 M}{\partial D_T \partial AD_T}}{\frac{\partial^2 M}{\partial D_T^2}} \tag{12}$$

and in recalling the assumptions that $\frac{dR}{dAD_T} < 0$ and $\frac{\partial^2 M}{\partial D_T \partial AD_T} \geq 0$ we conclude that

$$\frac{dD_T}{dAD_T} \gtrless 0 \text{ as } \frac{\partial^2 M}{\partial D^2} \lessgtr 0 .$$

That is, given a lenient rule of debt repayment $\left(\frac{\partial^2 M}{\partial D^2} < 0\right)$, a larger expected terminal moshav's average debt encourages the accumulation of debts by individual members. Conversely, given a punitive rule $\left(\frac{\partial^2 M}{\partial D^2} > 0\right)$, a larger expected terminal moshav's average debt discourages the accumulation of debts by the moshav's members.

6.3.2 Effect of the moshav's average debt on capital stock

The transversality condition (9a) implies that for $K(T) > 0$

$$\lambda_1(T) = R(AD_T) \tag{13}$$

and since $dR/dAD < 0$, the larger the expected AD_T the lower the shadow price of the farm's capital ($\lambda_1(T)$), and thus, the smaller the terminal stock of capital a member would like to hold. This indicates another possibility which may arise if, as is likely, there are exogenous limits on the amount which may be borrowed, or if the marginal utility of consumption does not vanish asymptotically. Under such circumstances, if AD_T is expected to be very large, there might be no feasible level of consumption, C_T, that satisfies the equation $e^{-rT}U_C(C_T) = R(AD_T)$, and hence $K(T) = 0$. In other words, if the rest of the moshav members are accumulating large debts, the best course of action for an individual member might be to liquidate the farm's productive assets. We therefore expect to find a positive association between the average debt of the moshav and the proportion of its units not in active operation in the long run.

From equation (10) we can further obtain that

$$\frac{\dot{\lambda}_1}{\lambda_1} = \frac{\dot{\lambda}_2}{\lambda_2} \tag{14}$$

and reconsidering 7a, 7b and 8b we can show that along the optimal path the marginal product of capital should be equal to the rental cost

$$V_K(K, N) = i(AD) + \delta. \tag{15}$$

By totally differentiating equation 15 and the optimality condition 8a ($V_N(K,N) = w$) and assuming that w remains the same we obtain that

$$dk = \frac{i'(AD)}{V_{KK} - \frac{V_{KN}^2}{V_{NN}}} dAD. \tag{16}$$

In recalling the assumptions that $i' > 0$ and V is concave (i.e., $V_{KK} < 0$, $V_{NN} < 0$ and $V_{NN} V_{KK} - V_{KN}^2 > 0$), an increase in the moshav's current average debt reduces the capital stock an individual farm is willing to hold. Note, however, that if the credit-sharing system is abolished, farmers whose debt is equal to, or greater than, the average debt would seek to hold less capital than under credit sharing. This is due to the fact that under private credit arrangements the marginal cost of debt includes the effect of the incremental debt on the interest rate (that is, $i + i'(D)D$ and not just i).

To fix ideas and motivate the subsequent empirical analysis, let us consider the special case in which V is Cobb-Douglas:

$$V = AD^{\alpha_1} N^{\alpha_2}, 0 < \alpha_1, \alpha_2 < 1. \tag{17}$$

In this case, equation (16) becomes

$$dK = \left[\frac{i'(AD)}{\alpha_1 (\alpha_1 - 1) - \alpha_1^2 \alpha_2/(\alpha_2 - 1)}\right] \frac{K^2}{V} dAD \tag{18}$$

or equivalently,

$$\frac{dK}{K} = \left[\frac{i'(AD)}{\alpha_1 (\alpha_1 - 1) - \alpha_1^2 \alpha_2/(\alpha_2 - 1)}\right] (V/K)^{-1} dAD. \tag{19}$$

In this context, the ratio of value added to capital (V/K) can be viewed as a measure of farm efficiency. Thus, whatever the direction of the debt, less efficient farms may be expected to respond to changes in the current average debt of the moshav by changing their current productive capital stock at a faster rate than more efficient farms.

6.3.3 Effect of the moshav's average debt on consumption

By differentiating both sides of the optimality condition 8b with respect to t we obtain

$$re^{-rt}\, U_C - e^{-rt}\, U_{CC}\dot{C} + \dot{\lambda}_1 = 0 \tag{20}$$

and by substituting (7a) and (8b) for $\dot{\lambda}_1$ and λ_1

$$[r + \delta - V_K\,(K, N)]\, U_C - U_{CC}\dot{C} = 0. \tag{21}$$

In recalling equation (15) and Pratt's (1964) measure of absolute risk aversion $RA = -U_{CC}/U_C$, equation 21 can be rendered as follows:

$$\dot{C} = [i(AD) - r]\,\frac{1}{RA}. \tag{22}$$

This result implies that

$$\dot{C} \gtreqless 0 \text{ as } i(AD) \gtreqless r.$$

The underlying rationale is that the more myopic the member (i.e., the larger *r*) and the lower the costs of credit, the greater his or her consumption today and the smaller in future periods. Since the cost of credit rises with AD, the cooperative organization of the moshav, in comparison to private farming, encourages consumption in earlier periods by those members whose debts are greater than the average.

6.4 Empirical findings

The empirical analysis presented in this section comprises two parts. The first part tests whether a rise in the moshav's average debt reduces the stock of productive capital, and whether less efficient farms change their capital stock at a faster rate than more efficient farms. The test is based on equation 19, and is carried out with 135 observations on individual farms in two moshavim. The second part of the empirical analysis estimates the investment-borrowing simultaneous equation system which is defined in accordance with the solution to the optimization problem presented in the second section. In order to avoid a confusion between the effect of the moshav's financial position and the general moshav's effect, which is inherent in utilizing individual farm observations from a small number of moshavim, the estimation of the investment-borrowing system is performed with aggregate data on eighty-two moshavim.

6.4.1 *Empirical evidence on the effect of the average debt on the individual farm capital stock*

Our empirical test of the effect of the moshav's average debt on the individual farm's capital accumulation is based on data of two selected moshavim in which the phenomenon of debt accumulation is extremely noticeable. The data were obtained from the moshavim's ledgers and from the Jewish Agency Agricultural-Demographical Annual Censuses, and include observations on capital stock, debt, value added (measured in 10,000 shekels in September 1983 prices) and characteristics of 135 family farms for the years 1982 and 1983. In each moshav the distribution of debts among the members conforms roughly to a lognormal curve, and exhibit a substantial degree of inequality. The mean, median and mode of these distributions increase significantly as time progresses.

With these pooled cross-sectional observations we continue the analysis from part two of the third section by testing whether a rise in the moshav's average debt reduces or increases the individual farm's productive capital stock, and whether the rate of change varies with the farm's level of efficiency. We conduct this test within the framework of equation 19 and subject to the simplifying assumption that $i''(AD) = 0$. We also take into account possible variation among the family farms through the inclusion of observed characteristics such as farm age (FAGE), family size (SIZE) and off-farm occupation of the head of the family (OFOC). The last variable is defined as follows:

$$OFOC = \begin{cases} 1 & \text{if high skill and professional employment} \\ 0 & \text{otherwise.} \end{cases}$$

The following equation presents the ordinary least squares' estimates of the regression coefficients, where the t-ratios of these estimates are indicated in the parentheses:

$$\frac{K_t - K_{t-1}}{K_{t-1}} = \underset{(0.450)}{-\,0.04435} - \underset{(3.256)}{0.925E10^8}(V/K)^{-1}_{t-1}(AD_t - AD_{t-1})$$

$$- \underset{(2.230)}{0.00605}\ FAGE + \underset{(0.403)}{0.00345}\ SIZE$$

$$- \underset{(0.831)}{0.07857}\ OFOC + \text{residual.} \qquad (23)$$

Here, $R^2 = 0.127$, $\hat{F} = 4.087$ and the number of degrees of freedom is 130. Although the model explains only a small proportion of the variance of the rate of capital accumulation, the F test shows that the estimates are simultaneously significant.[4]

The significantly negative coefficient associated with $(V/K)^{-1}_{t-1}$ $(AD_t - AD_{t-1})$ indicates that a rise in the moshav's average debt reduces the stock of productive capital, and that the less efficient farms change their capital stock at a faster rate than the more efficient farms.

The negative and significant estimate associated with FAGE indicates that, *ceteris paribus*, the newly established farms invest more than the veteran ones. Since in the Israeli moshavim farm age and farmer age are positively and highly correlated, this result can be further attributed to life-cycle aspects. The effect of family size on farm investment may be viewed as the discrepancy between two opposing effects. On the one hand, a large family, *ceteris paribus*, may have a large labour force and hence a relatively high income. On the other hand, a large family spends much on consumption. Since the estimate associated with SIZE is not significantly different from zero, it is possible that these effects offset one another.

Many of the moshavim's members also work off the farm. High skill off-farm employment can successfully compete with income from farming and hence might reduce investment. The estimation result, however, indicates that, *ceteris paribus*, the rate of capital accumulation is insignificantly affected by off-farm employment.

6.4.2 Estimation of the investment-borrowing behaviour with aggregate data on eighty-two moshavim

The set of the first-order conditions for maximum utility presented in the previous section constitutes a simultaneous equation system in which the control variable I (investment), d (borrowing) and N (labour) are the dependent variables; and the one-period laged state variables D_{-1}, K_{-1} and AD_{-1} are the independent variables. The following estimation of this system is carried out with data provided by *The Jewish Agency Agricultural-Demographical Census* for 1983 which encompasses eighty-two moshavim in Israel's Negev (southern) region. This data source does not include information on labour. Under the assumption of equal amount of on-farm work days in all the sampled moshavim, the empirical analysis is restricted to the estimation of the investment-borrowing structural and reduced-form parameters. In recalling that each observation represents a moshav and that there is a variation in the moshav's number of family farms, the variables D_{-1}, K_{-1}, I and d are taken as average values (in 1983 million shekels), and thus indicate the position and behaviour of a representative member farm.

The analysis also takes into account the effects of the moshav's population structure on investment and borrowing through the inclusion of the rate of Israeli-born farmers (RIBF) and the average farmer age (AGE) in the moshav. The interaction of these socio-demographic variables captures the distinct three-generations structure, which is typical to the moshavim included in the sample. The first generation comprises Jewish refugees from Middle Eastern and North African countries who came to Israel in the early 1950s and settled in the newly established moshavim. They had in 1983 an average of twenty-eight years of farming experience, but suffered from lack of country-specific skill and a low level of education. The second generation of farmers comprises the younger brothers and the elder sons of the first-generation farmers. They had been also born abroad, but because of their younger age enjoyed

Israeli schooling and other benefits associated with growing up in Israel, which equipped them with the new country-specific skill. Members of this generation of farmers had in 1983 an average of eighteen years of farming experience. The third generation of farmers are the younger Israeli-born sons of the first-generation farmers, and had a relatively short farming experience of about five years in 1983.

It is important to note that with these cross-sectional data the average debt in a moshav (AD) is now interpreted as the representative farm's debt and hence can no longer be viewed as a source of external effects as indicated in the conceptual analysis. In order to incorporate possible external effects of the cooperative's financial position on the representative member, the regression equations include the moshav debt-capital ratio (leverage) at the end of the last period ($MDCR_{-1}$).

Consequently, the following analysis tests: (1) the effects of the representative member's position, as indicated by D_{-1} and K_{-1}, on his/her investment and borrowing; (2) the effects of the demographic structure of the moshav (RIBF and AGE) on investment and borrowing; and (3) the effects of the moshav's financial position, as reflected by $MDCR_{-1}$, on the representative member's investment and borrowing. The estimates of these effects and their t-ratios (in parentheses) are presented in Table 6.1 and Table 6.2. While Table 6.1 indicates only the direct effects of the exogenous variables, D_{-1}, K_{-1}, RIBF, AGE and $MDCR_{-1}$ on the representative member's current investment and borrowing, the estimated parameters in Table 6.2 also include the indirect effects and hence exhibit the full effects of the independent variables on the representative member's investment and borrowing. The age variable is excluded from the borrowing equation by the estimation procedure due to low levels of tolerance. Therefore, and in order to obtain identification, this variable is also excluded from the borrowing equation in the three-stage least squares estimation. Furthermore, best estimation results of the structural parameters are obtained when RIBF is omitted from the investment equation.

Table 6.1
Three-stage least squares estimates of the investment-borrowing simultaneous equations' structural parameters

	Dependent variables	
Explanatory variables	**I**	**d**
I	—	1.096 (1.804)
d	2.234 (1.002)	—
D_{-1}	0.948 (1.094)	-0.657 (1.954)
K_{-1}	-0.419 (1.989)	0.337 (2.245)
RIBF	—	0.205 (1.480)
AGE	0.032 (0.786)	—
$MIDCR_{-1}$	-0.797 (0.510)	0.440 (0.542)
Constant	-1.081 (0.626)	-0.388 (1.576)

Table 6.2
Ordinary least squares estimates of the investment-borrowing reduced-form's parameters

Explanatory variables	*Dependent variables* I	d
D_{-1}	0.358 (1.399)	-0.436 (2.375)
K_{-1}	-0.230 (5.271)	0.086 (2.612)
RIBF	-0.317 (1.838)	0.169 (2.095)
AGE	-0.022 (2.104)	—
$MDCR_{-1}$	-0.129 (0.197)	0.772 (1.663)
Constant	1.344 (2.468)	-0.120 (1.039)
R^2	0.496	0.130
R^2 adjusted	0.463	0.085
F-test statistic	14.972	2.887
Degrees of freedom	76	77

The estimation results lead to the following conclusions.

1. Investment and borrowing are mutually dependent — the availability of credit increases investment, which in turn increases borrowing. The former effect is statistically insignificant, whereas the latter is significant.

2. The direct and full effects of the representative member's debt on his/her levels of investment are positive but statistically insignificant, whereas the direct and full effects of the representative member's debt on his/her borrowing are both negative and statistically significant. The full effect of the representative member's debt on borrowing is moderated by the positive direct effect of debt on investment, which is transmitted through the positive direct effect of investment on borrowing. These results indicate that in view of their relatively large debts and the high interest rates, farmers reduce their current borrowing, but not necessarily at the expense of investment in production capital.

3. As can be reasoned by a diminishing marginal product's argument, the direct and full effects of the representative farmer's capital stock on net investment are negative and statistically significant. In contrast, the direct and indirect effects of the representative farm's capital stock on borrowing are positive and statistically significant. A possible explanation is that a large stock of capital may be associated with a large production activity which necessitates a large credit for buying perishable inputs. Note that the full effect of the capital stock on borrowing is moderated by a negative indirect effect stemming from the negative effect of capital stock on investment and the positive effect of investment on borrowing.

4. The estimates associated with RIBF are statistically significant and indicate that, all other things being equal, Israeli-born farmers invest less and borrow more than their immigrant counterparts. The OLS estimation of the reduced form also reveals a significant negative effect of age on investment. Since the interaction of RIBF and AGE captures the three-generation structure of the moshav's farmer population, these results can be

interpreted as indicating that the plausibly less efficient farmers of the first and third generations 'free rode' the more efficient farmers of the second generation whose performances improved the moshav's financial position as reflected by the debt-capital ratio.

5. The estimates associated with $MDCR_{-1}$ indicate that the moshav's leverage deters individual's investment and encourages further individual's borrowing. It is important to note that only the latter effect is statistically significant. In view of the previous result, the estimates of the effects of $MDCR_{-1}$ confirm the *a priori* expectations of a 'free-rider' problem in Israel's semi-cooperative villages.

6.5 Conclusion

In this chapter, the economic implications of mutually secured debts in Israel's semi-cooperative villages were conceptually and empirically analysed. The conceptual model suggested that there should be a negative relationship between the stock of capital the individual farm is willing to hold and the moshav's average debt, and that less efficient farms tend to respond to changes in the moshav's average debt by changing their productive capital stock at a faster rate than more efficient farms. This hypothesis was supported by the estimation results which referred to 135 family farms in two financially distressed moshavim.

The conceptual model also suggested that the individual's decision on investment and borrowing are made simultaneously and are affected by the individual member's position as regards debt and capital stock and by the moshav's financial position. The estimation of the investment-borrowing simultaneous equation system with aggregate data on eighty-two moshavim yielded statistically significant and meaningful results. The estimates associated with the socio-demographical variables, included in the analysis to capture the typical three-generation structure of the moshav's farmer population, indicated that the less efficient farmers of the first and third generations 'free rode' the more efficient farmers of the second generation and increased the moshav's debt-capital ratio. It was found, in turn, that a rise in the moshav's leverage deterred investment and encouraged further borrowing and thus perpetuated and intensified the moshav's financial problem.

Other conclusions stemming from the conceptual model that were not tested in the empirical analysis are that the level of consumption varies directly with the average debt of the moshav. In comparison to private farming, the cooperative organization of the moshav encourages consumption in earlier periods by those members whose debts are greater than the average. Finally, the moshav's rule for setting members' debts affects the impact of the moshav's average debt on the individual member's current debt. If the rule is lenient, a large expected moshav's debt will encourage the accumulation of debt by members; whereas if the rule is punitive, it will discourage debt accumulation.

Notes

1 A similar relationship between the interest rate and debt was also assumed by Hochman, Hochman and Razin (1973). For further discussion of the financial aspects in moshavim see Haruvi and Kislev (1984) who specified the interest rate as a function of both borrowing and the moshav's cooperative revenue. For simplicity, and since our empirical analysis focuses on moshavim that borrow much more than they earn, we chose to disregard the latter factor.

2 The allocation of time between leisure and labour is disregarded. It is assumed, for simplicity, that a fixed proportion of the time is devoted to work.

3 For further analysis of the selection of repayment rules of members' debt in agricultural cooperatives and their efficiency and welfare consequences see Zusman (1983 and 1988).

4 A higher R^2 is obtained when equation (18) is fitted to the data. The effect of the moshav's average debt on the desired level of capital stock remains negative and highly significant. The following equation presents the OLS estimates of the regression coefficients, and their t-ratios are given in the parentheses:

$$K_t - K_{t-1} = \underset{(0.734)}{11306.578} - \underset{(10.231)}{0.285E10^{-7}} (V/K^2)^{-1}_{t-1} (AD_t - AD_{t-1})$$

$$- \underset{(0.923)}{790.1680} \text{ FAGE} - \underset{(1.203)}{3250.362} \text{ SIZE}$$

$$- \underset{(1.658)}{55389.627} \text{ OFOC} + \text{residual}$$

$$R^2 = 0.463 \text{ and } \hat{F} = 26.481.$$

References

Haruvi, N. and Kislev, Y. (1984), 'Cooperation in the Moshav', *Journal of Comparative Economics*, vol. 8, pp. 54–77.

Pratt, J.W. (1964), 'Risk Aversion in the Small and the Large', *Econometrica*, vol. 32, pp. 122–36.

Hochman, E., Hochman, O. and Razin, A. (1973), 'Demand for Investment in Productive and Financial Capital', *European Economic Review*, vol. 4, pp. 67–83.

Zusman, P. (1983), 'Collective Choice, Pareto Optimality and the Organization of Cooperatives — The Case of Agricultural Credit Associations', *Journal of Economic Behavior and Organization*, vol. 4, pp. 183–204.

—— (1988), *Individual Behaviour and Social Choice in a Cooperative Settlement: the Theory and Practice of the Israeli Moshav*, The Magnes Press, The Hebrew University at Jerusalem.

7 Risk spreading in farmers' production choice: Evidence from India

Co-authored by Khorshed Chowdhury

This chapter analyzes risk-spreading behaviour in India's most agriculturally advanced state — Punjab. A mean-variance model of optimal land allocation — in which farmers are postulated to be risk averse, maximizing expected utility from value added from growing cereals, perceiving the deviation of the farm-gate prices from the government guaranteed prices in accordance with an autoregressive process, and expecting yields' means and variances to be proportional to the area under cultivation — is developed and estimated with panel data. Estimates of farm-land allocations determinants are obtained under a wide range of alternative assumptions about the expectation formation mechanism and the issue of 'money illusion'.

7.1 Introduction

In many developing countries, and in India in particular, the green revolution which started in the 1960s has advanced agricultural technology through the introduction of new irrigation methods, machinery, improved hybrids, fertilizers, herbicides, pesticides, and the like. The green revolution has also been expressed through improved methods of managing the individual agrobusiness.[1] Farming, perhaps more than any other industry, is vulnerable to uncertainty about yields and input and output prices resulting in extensive policy interventions. Since the early 1950s there have been important developments in financial economic theory with regard to the implication of uncertainty on the choice of portfolio and activity set. One of the most appealing methods of determining the optimal choice of activities is derived from Markowitz' (1952) mean-variance portfolio selection model which stresses the desirability of diversification of the individual's asset holdings in order to moderate the costs of risk bearing and to achieve maximum expected utility from the proceeds of these assets. The application of the mean-variance approach in agricultural economics is discussed by Berck (1981), Yassour, Zilberman and Rausser (1981), Levy (1982), Collender and Zilberman (1985), and Levy, Justman and Hochman (1989) and others.

This chapter investigates whether these conceptual developments in decision-making under uncertainty have been incorporated by the participants of the green revolution as experienced in one of the most agriculturally advanced state of India — Punjab. In particular, the effects of Punjabi farmers' decisions regarding the allocation of land between major cereals — wheat and gram in winter and rice and maize in summer — on input and output price expectations and to variations in yields during the period 1966 to 1987 are compared to those advocated by the mean-variance portfolio selection model. Estimates of the determinants of the land allocated for growing these cereals are essential for evaluating food supply stabilization programs.

Punjab has been the epicenter of the green revolution in Asia. Consequently, the experience of this state in the context of the green revolution has wider interest. Punjab has developed from a food-deficit state with a stagnant agricultural sector during the first half of the century (1906–1946) into the granary of India within a span of four decades. Since the advent of the green revolution during the mid-1960s the rate of growth of foodgrains output in Punjab has been running at almost two and a half times that of the rest of India. Per capita output of food is four times higher in Punjab than the national average. Eighty-four per cent of the geographical area of the state is under crop production. Almost all of it is high yielding hybrid varieties. Over 91 per cent of the gross cropped area is irrigated. Rice and wheat are produced on entirely irrigated lands. Fertilizer use per hectare is around 157 kilograms which is four and a half times the national average.

Punjab has three distinct agroclimatic sub-zones. The foothills of the Shiwaliks in the Himalayas in the north, and the areas bordering the Thai desert in the south of the state consist of two sub-zones which do not have ideal conditions for the production of hybrid wheat and rice varieties. The middle sub-zone covering seven districts consists of plains with fresh and potable underground water with high tube-well irrigation potential. The entire middle sub-zone has similar annual rainfall levels (averaging 650 millimeters), soil texture, micro-nutrients, climate and crop husbandary practices. These factors induced us to restrict our analysis to the seven districts of the homogeneous agro-climatic middle zone. These districts also have a well-developed rural infrastructure: all villages have access to electricity, all weather roads, regulated grain markets and efficient input supply.[2]

Table 7.1 reveals that between 1953 and 1986 the per hectare yield of wheat and rice has been rising at unprecedented rates. In contrast, the rate of growth of the per-hectare yield of maize has been substantially smaller, and the per-hectare yield of gram has been stagnant, with high variability, during the 1950s, 1960s and 1970s, and has significantly fallen during the 1980s. Table 1 reveals further that these trends in the per-hectare yield of cereals have been accompanied by a dramatic shift in land allocation in Punjab in favour of wheat as the major winter crop, followed by rice as the major summer crop. This development in per-hectare yield and croping patterns might indicate the important role of trends and variations in yield per hectare in determining the farm-land allocation in Punjab.

Since 1966, the government of India has followed a floor price system, particularly for wheat and rice. In view of policymakers' interest, a number of empirical studies on Punjab agriculture attempting to estimate acreage and output price elasticities have been reported in the economic literature within India and

Table 7.1
Yield per hectare and cropping pattern in Punjab

Years	Summer Cereals		Winter Cereals	
	Rice	Maize	Wheat	Gram
Yield per Hectare (Kilograms)				
1953–56	892	1300	901	800
1963–66	1223	1265	1510	760
1973–76	2823	1550	2797	820
1983–86	3094	1910	3289	580
Area (thousands of hectares)				
1953–56	210.3	390 .0	1624.3	1262.7
1963–66	306.3	548.0	2059.3	493.0
1973–76	1255.3	836.0	5418.3	302.3
1983–86	5024.3	509.3	10195.3	69.7

Source: Chaudhri, Singh, Deb and Piraziziy (1991)

internationally. Most of these studies deal with wheat and have varied coverage of districts, periods, model specifications, estimation procedures with widely divergent results. Krishna (1963), using a partial adjustment model with naive price expectation, reported wheat acreage elasticity of 0.14 for greater Punjab during the period 1914–43. Krishna and Raychaudhuri (1980) found wheat acreage elasticity of 0.276 for the period 1957–69. Cummings (1975) obtained an estimate for Punjab wheat acreage elasticity of 0.13 with 1950–67 data. Kaul (1967) reported an elasticity of 0.12 for five districts in Punjab, and Kaul and Sidhu (1971) found an elasticity of 0.15 for Punjab as a whole. These results are representative of over forty-five studies with wheat acreage elasticity estimates ranging between 0.004 and 0.37 depending on the period, coverage and estimation procedure.[3]

The historical addivity of acreage and yield elasticities to output elasticity does not hold for recent years. The summation of acreage and yield elasticities has diverged from the directly estimated output elasticity for recent data as reported by Krishna and Chibbar

(1983), Ray (1983) and Ray and Subramanian (1983). One major reason for these divergences is the exclusion of the uncertainty about yields and the associated costs of risk bearing with respect to prices, outputs and interactions. These issues have not been explored in the context of agriculture in Asia or India. Implications of unstable and risky markets in agriculture have been examined by Wright (1979), Newberry and Stiglitz (1981) and Scandizzo, Hazell and Anderson (1984).

This chapter analyzes the land allocation between the major cereals in Punjab within a mean-variance model of optimal land allocation in which farmers are postulated to be risk averse, maximizing expected utility from value added from growing cereals, perceiving the deviation of the farm-gate prices from the government guaranteed prices in accordance with an autoregressive process, and expecting yields' means and variances to be proportional to the land under the various cereals. The mean-variance model and the properties of the derived optimal land allocation are presented in section 7.2. The procedure and data for estimating the determinants of the optimal land allocation are described in section 7.3. The estimation results, under alternative assumptions about the expectation formation mechanism and the issue of 'money illusion', are displayed and interpreted in section 7.4. Concluding remarks and policy implications are given in section 7.5.

7.2 Mean-variance model of optimal land allocation

The mean-variance portfolio approach to land allocation is based on the assumption that there is uncertainty about prices and yields and that farmers are risk averse and allocate land to the various crops so as to maximize the expected utility from the proceeds from these activities. In view of the price stabilization policy practiced by the Indian government, our analysis incorporates the assumption that farmers' perception of the current market price deviation from the guaranteed price follows a deterministic autoregressive process, such as the naive or adaptive expectations' mechanisms. Thus, it is the probability distribution of yields that underlies the mean-variance portfolio model of farm land allocation constructed below.

Let L_k be the number of hectares allocated to growing crop k and $\tilde{f}_k(L_k)$ the corresponding production function of crop k. The determination of the farm land allocated to growing crop k takes into account random disturbances in production. These disturbances are assumed to be proportional to the scale of operation — the land allocated to the k-th activity. Hence,

$$\tilde{f}_k((L_k) = f_k(L_k) + L_k \varepsilon_k \tag{1}$$

for every k = 1, 2, ..., K. Here, f_k is a non-decreasing function of L_k, and ε_k is a random variable indicating the fluctuations in the per-hectare yield of crop k comprising the marginal effect of the uncontrolled physical conditions on the yield of crop k. It is assumed that ε_k is normally distributed with mean zero and variance σ_k^2. Moreover, since any pair of crops k and ℓ grown simultaneously is exposed to common uncontrolled growing conditions, the covariance of ε_k and ε_ℓ ($\sigma_{k\ell}$) is not necessarily equal to zero. It is positive (negative) when these crops have similar (opposite) responses to uncontrolled growing conditions.

The determination of land allocation on the farm is also based on the following assumptions:

(i) The production costs of crop k are proportional to the land allocated to growing this crop. That is

$$C_k = c_k(w^e)L_k \tag{2}$$

where w^e is a vector of the expected prices of all the other inputs involved in the production of crop k, and c_k is the associated cost function per hectare.

(ii) The farmers are identical and endowed with equally small amount of land. They are price takers in both the markets of outputs and inputs. They face governmentally guaranteed prices for their produce (P_k^g) and form their expectations about the deviation of the realized farm-gate price (P_k) from the guaranteed price in accordance with Cagan's (1956) adaptive expectation model. Thus, the k-th crop market price perceived by the farmers (P_k^e) is found from:

$$P_{kt}^e = P_{kt}^g + \beta \sum_{j=0}^{\infty} (1 - \beta)^j (P_{k\,t-1-j} - P_{k\,t-1-j}^g)$$

$$= P_{kt}^g + \frac{\beta(P_{k\,t-1} - P_{k\,t-1}^g)}{1 - (1 - \beta)\mathcal{L}} \tag{3}$$

where $\mathcal{L}$ denotes the lag operator, and $0 < \beta < 1$ the expectation-correction coefficient. Similarly, the price of the i-th production input perceived by the farmers (w_i^e) is based on the adaptive expectation hypothesis and hence can be expressed as:

$$w_{it}^e = \frac{\beta\, w_{i\,t-1}}{1 - (1 - \beta)\mathcal{L}} \tag{4}$$

where $w_{i,\,t-1}$ is the last season's price of the i-th input.

(iii) The farmers level of satisfaction from the value added generated on the farm (Y) can be found by using the negative exponential utility function, which reflects a constant degree of absolute risk aversion (R):

$$u(Y) = 1 - e^{-RY}\,. \tag{5}$$

Assuming that farmers are expected utility maximizers and recalling the abovementioned assumptions, the farmers' decision problem can be expressed as

$$\max_{\{L_1,\, \ldots,\, L_k\}} E\,[u(Y)]$$

subject to the value-added constraint

$$Y = \sum_{k=1}^{K} \left\{ P_k^e\, [f_k(L_k) + L_k\, \varepsilon_k] - L_k\, c_k(w^e) \right\} \tag{6}$$

and the land constraint

$$\sum_{k=1}^{K} L_k = 1. \tag{7}$$

Since the farm's total value added (Y) is a linear combination of the normally distributed disturbances $\varepsilon_1, ..., \varepsilon_k$, Y is also normally distributed with mean and variance as given below:

$$E(Y) = \sum_{k=1}^{K} [P_k^e f_k(L_k) - L_k c_k(w^e)] \tag{8}$$

$$VAR(Y) = \sum_{k=1}^{K} P_k^{e^2} \sigma_k^2 + \sum_{k=1}^{K} \sum_{\ell \neq k}^{K} P_k^e P_\ell L_k L_\ell \sigma_{k\ell}. \tag{9}$$

Following Freund (1956), it can be shown that since u is negative exponential and Y is normally distributed, E[u(Y)] is equal to one minus the moment-generating function of the normal distribution. Hence, maximizing E[u(Y)] is equivalent to maximizing [E(Y) - 0.5Rvar(Y)].[4] Considering this equivalence and the land constraint, the corresponding Lagrangian is given by:

$$J = \sum_{k=1}^{K} [P_k^e f_k(L_k) - L_k c_k(w^e)] - \frac{1}{2} R \left[\sum_{k=1}^{K} P_k^2 L_k^2 \sigma_k^2 + \sum_{k=1}^{K} \sum_{\ell \neq k}^{K} P_k^e P_\ell^e L_k L_\ell \sigma_{k\ell} \right]$$

$$+ \lambda \left(1 - \sum_{k=1}^{K} L_k \right). \tag{10}$$

While the first term on the right-hand side indicates the expected value added, the second term indicates the costs of risk bearing for the farmer stemming from uncertainty about the yields, and the third term displays the value of unused land on the farm where λ is the shadow price of land.

The necessary conditions for maximum constrained expected utility are:

$$\frac{\partial J}{\partial L_k} = P_k^e f_k' (L_k^*) - c_k(w^e) - R\left[P_k^2 \sigma_k^2 L_k^* + \sum_{\ell \neq k}^{K} P_k^e P_\ell^e L_\ell \sigma_{k\ell}\right] - \lambda^* = 0 \qquad (11)$$

for every $k = 1,\ldots,K$.

These conditions imply that the farmer's expected utility is maximized when the allocation of land between the K cereals under consideration is such that the increment in the expected revenue from an infinitesimal increase in the land allocated to any of them is offset by the additional costs of production and risk bearing and the forgone rent on land.

Our empirical analysis is focused on the two major cereals grown in the Punjab in each season — wheat and gram in winter and rice and maize in summer. Therefore, K is set to be equal to two hereafter. In order to obtain a closed-form solution to the optimal land allocation between these cereals it is assumed further that the expected yield of each crop is proportional to the land allocated to that crop. That is,

$$f_k(L_k) = \bar{y}_k L_k \qquad (12)$$

for every $k = 1, 2$ where $\bar{y}_k$ denotes the expected per hectare yield of crop k.

The set of necessary conditions 11 implies that an interior solution to the land allocation problem requires an equality between the marginal contributions of land allocated for growing each of the abovementioned cereals to the farmer's expected utility:

$$P_1^e \bar{y}_1 - c_1(w^e) - R P_1^{e^2} L_1^* \sigma_1^2 - R P_1^e P_2^e L_2^* \sigma_{12} = P_2^e \bar{y}_2 - c_2(w^e)$$
$$- R P_1^e P_2^e L_1^* \sigma_{12} - R P_1^{e^2} L_2^* \sigma_2^2. \qquad (13)$$

When the above condition is satisfied, both L_1^* and L_2^* are positive. Furthermore, if the land constraint is binding, then

$$L_2^* = 1 - L_1^* \tag{14}$$

and the amount of land allocated for growing crop 1 is given by

$$L_1^* = \frac{[P_1^e \bar{y}_1 - c_1(w^e)] - [P_2^e \bar{y}_2 - c_2(w^e)] + R(P_2^{e^2} \sigma_2^2 - P_1^e P_2^e \sigma_{12})}{R(P_1^{e^2} \sigma_1^2 - 2P_1^e P_2^e \sigma_{12} + P_2^{e^2} \sigma_2^2)} . \tag{15}$$

It is important to note that the second-order condition for maximum expected utility requires that

$$R (P_1^{e^2} \sigma_1^2 - 2 P_1^e P_2^e \sigma_{12} + P_2^{e^2} \sigma_2^2) > 0 \tag{16}$$

as long as farmers are risk averse ($R > 0$).

As can be expected, equations 15 and 16 reveal that the amount of land allocated to cereal 1 increases with the expected per hectare profit differential between cereal 1 and cereal 2 and decreases with the per hectare yield variance of cereal 1. However, the effects of the perceived own price, cross price, cross yield variance and yields covariance on the amount of land allocated for growing cereal 1 are not obvious. These effects are summarized in the following propositions. The proofs of these propositions and a detailed derivation of the interior solution are provided in the mathematical appendix.

Proposition 1: (The perceived own price effect)

$$\frac{\partial L_1^*}{\partial P_1^e} \gtreqless 0 \text{ as } \bar{y}_1 \gtreqless R[P_1^e \sigma_1^2 - (2L_1^* - 1)P_2^e \sigma_{12}].$$

In accordance with the price expectation mechanism specified in equation 3, an increase in the perceived price of any of the cereals can result from a relatively high realized price in the previous period and/or an increase in the price guaranteed by the government. Proposition 1 indicates that farmers do not necessarily increase, and might even reduce, the amount of land allocated for growing cereal 1 when they expect a rise in this cereal's market price. The underlying rationale is that the rise in the costs of risk bearing from increasing the amount of land under cereal 1 might offset, or even exceed, the expected returns from doing so. The greater the per hectare yield variation of cereal 1 (σ_1^2) and the smaller the expected per hectare yield of cereal 1 ($\bar{y}_1$), the smaller the effect of P_1^e on L_1^*. Moreover, if cereals 1 and 2 have different responses and levels of resistance to harsh climatic conditions and diseases so that σ_{12} is small or even negative, and if initially $L_1^* > 0.5$, farmers will be even more reluctant to increase the amount of land under cereal 1 despite the expected increase in this cereal market price.

Proposition 2: (The perceived cross price effect)

$$\frac{\partial L_1^*}{\partial P_2^e} \gtreqless 0 \text{ as } 2R(P_2^e \sigma_2^2 - P_1^e \sigma_{12})(1 - L_1^*) - \bar{y}_2 \gtreqless 0.$$

A rise in the expected price of cereal 2 increases the expected returns on that crop, but also raises the variance of those returns and hence the costs of risk bearing. Thus, a rise in the expected price of cereal 2 increases (decreases) the area under cereal 1 if the increase in the costs of risk bearing are greater (smaller) than the increase in the expected returns.

Proposition 3: (The cross yield variance effect)

$$\frac{\partial L_1^*}{\partial \sigma_2^2} \gtreqless 0 \text{ as } [P_2^e \bar{y}_2 - c_2(w^e)] + R(P_1^{e^2} \sigma_1^2 - P_1^e P_2^e \sigma_{12}) \gtreqless [P_1^e \bar{y}_1 - c_1(w^e)].$$

This proposition indicates that as long as the land constraint is binding, the area under cereal 1 does not necessarily increase with the level of uncertainty about the per-hectare yield of cereal 2. It is suggested that an increase in σ_2^2 would most likely increase L_1 when the growing and market conditions are less favourable for cereal 1.

Proposition 4: (The yields covariance effect)

$$\frac{\partial L_1^*}{\partial \sigma_{12}} \gtreqless 0 \text{ as } [P_1^e \bar{y}_1 - c_1(w^e)] - [P_2^e \bar{y}_2 - c_2(w^e)] \gtreqless R(P_1^{e^2} \sigma_1^2 - P_2^{e^2} \sigma_2^2) .$$

This proposition indicates that if the risk-adjusted marginal expected return on cereal 1 is greater (smaller) than that on cereal 2, the larger (smaller) the per-hectare yield covariance the larger (smaller) the area under cereal 1.

By symmetry, propositions 1 to 4 also describe the properties of the optimal allocation of land to cereal 2. However, it might be that under certain circumstances farm land is fully allocated for growing only one of the cereals. In terms of the model, such a corner solution evolved when the combination of growing conditions (e.g., land fertility and yield variation) and market conditions (e.g., perceived output and input prices) is more favourable for one of the crops, irrespective of the scale of operation.

7.3 Estimation procedure and data

For estimating the effects of the determinants of land allocation between the major cereals, a first-order Taylor's approximation of equation 15 is considered:

$$L_{1t} = a_0 + a_1 P_{1t}^e + a_2 P_{2t}^e + a_3 \bar{y}_{1t} + a_4 \bar{y}_{2t} + a_5 \sigma_{1t}^2 + a_6 \sigma_{2t}^2 + a_7 \sigma_{12t} + a_8 w_{1t}^e + a_9 w_{2t}^e + \eta_{1t} \quad (17)$$

and by symmetry

$$L_{2t} = b_0 + b_1 P_{1t}^e + b_2 P_{2t}^e + b_3 \bar{y}_{1t} + b_4 \bar{y}_{2t} + b_5 \sigma_{1t}^2 + b_6 \sigma_{2t}^2 + b_7 \sigma_{12t} + b_8 w_{1t}^e + b_9 w_{2t}^e + \eta_{2t} \quad (18)$$

where w_1^e is the perceived price index of fertilizers, w_2^e is the perceived price of herbicides and pesticides, t is a time index, $a_0,\ldots,a_9$ and $b_0,\ldots,b_9$ are scalars and η_1 and η_2 are the approximation errors.

It is assumed that the farmers infer the values of $\bar{y}_1$, $\bar{y}_2$, σ_1^2, σ_2^2 and σ_{12} by calculating moving averages, variances and covariances with past observed values of the per hectare yields y_1 and y_2 over a predetermined period of M growing seasons:

$$\bar{y}_1 = \frac{1}{M}\sum_{m=1}^{M} y_{1,\,t-m} \tag{19}$$

$$\bar{y}_2 = \frac{1}{M}\sum_{m=1}^{M} y_{2,\,t-m} \tag{20}$$

$$\sigma_{1t}^2 = \frac{1}{M}\sum_{m=1}^{M} (y_{1,\,t-m} - \bar{y}_{1t})^2 \tag{21}$$

$$\sigma_{2t}^2 = \frac{1}{M}\sum_{m=1}^{M} (y_{2,\,t-m} - \bar{y}_{2t})^2 \tag{22}$$

$$\sigma_{12t} = \frac{1}{M}\sum_{m=1}^{M} (y_{1,\,t-m} - \bar{y}_{1t})(y_{2,\,t-m} - \bar{y}_{2t})). \tag{23}$$

The effects of these per hectare yield distribution moments and the perceived output and input prices on land allocation between cereal 1 and cereal 2 are indicated by the unknown parameter vectors a and b.

Equations 17 and 18 include the perceived prices of the two cereals under consideration and the perceived prices of two aggregate agricultural inputs — fertilizers and pesticides and herbicides. These perceived output and input prices are assumed to be constructed in accordance with the adaptive expectations mechanism portrayed by equations 3 and 4, respectively. Obviously, the perceived prices cannot be accurately calculated for the sample's early years due to a too short historical time series and hence equations 17 and 18 cannot be used straightforwardly for estimating the unknown parameters $a_0,...,a_9$ and $b_0,...,b_9$. However, the substitution of these expectation formation mechanisms into equations 17 and 18, and the multiplication of both sides of the resultant equations by $[1 - (1 - \beta)\mathcal{L}]$ lead to the following estimable regression equations system:

$$
\begin{aligned}
L_{1t} - (1 - \beta)L_{1\,t-1} &= \beta a_0 + a_1 [\beta P_{1\,t-1} + (P^g_{1t} - P^g_{1\,t-1})] \\
&+ a_2 [\beta P_{2\,t-1} + (P^g_{2t} - P^g_{2\,t-1})] + a_3 [\bar{y}_{1t} - (1 - \beta)\,\bar{y}_{1\,t-1}] \\
&+ a_4 [\bar{y}_{2t} - (1 - \beta)\,\bar{y}_{2\,t-1}] + a_5 [\sigma^2_{1t} - (1 - \beta)\,\sigma^2_{1t-1}] \\
&+ a_6 [\sigma^2_{2t} - (1 - \beta)\,\sigma^2_{2t-1}] + a_7 [\sigma_{12t} - (1 - \beta)\,\sigma_{12\,t-1}] \\
&+ a_8 [\beta\, w_{1\,t-1}] + a_9 [\beta\, w_{2\,t-1}] + [\eta_{1t} - (1 - \beta)\,\eta_{1\,t-1}] \qquad (24)
\end{aligned}
$$

$$
\begin{aligned}
L_{2t} - (1 - \beta)L_{2\,t-1} &= \beta b_0 + b_1 [\beta P_{1\,t-1} + (P^g_{1t} - P^g_{1\,t-1})] \\
&+ b_2 [\beta P_{2\,t-1} + (P^g_{2t} - P^g_{2\,t-1})] + b_3 [\bar{y}_{1t} - (1 - \beta)\,\bar{y}_{1\,t-1}] \\
&+ b_4 [\bar{y}_{2t} - (1 - \beta)\,\bar{y}_{2\,t-1}] + b_5 [\sigma^2_{1t} - (1 - \beta)\,\sigma^2_{1t-1}] \\
&+ b_6 [\sigma^2_{2t} - (1 - \beta)\,\sigma^2_{2t-1}] + b_7 [\sigma_{12t} - (1 - \beta)\sigma_{12\,t-1}] \\
&+ b_8 [\beta\, w_{1\,t-1}] + b_9 [\beta\, w_{2\,t-1}] + [\eta_{2t} - (1 - \beta)\,\eta_{2\,t-1}]. \qquad (25)
\end{aligned}
$$

The estimation procedure iterates on the expectation correction coefficient by assigning a different value of β in each iteration. In this case, the terms in brackets on the right-hand side of equations 24 and 25 become the regressors explaining the partial adjustment of the land allocated for growing the cereals under consideration. The associated parameters $a_0,...,a_9$ and $b_0,...,b_9$ are estimated for ten alternative values of β ranging between 0.1 to 1 in intervals of 0.1. In doing so, a wide range of expectation formation mechanism is explored: when β is set to be 1 the parameter vectors **a** and **b** are estimated under the naive expectation's assumption that only the last observed price matters; but as β decreases, the weights given to recent observations in forming the farmers' price expectations decline, and when β receives its lower value these parameter vectors are estimated under the assumption that a relatively small adjustment of the price expectations is required since farmers are endowed with almost perfect foresight. It is assumed that $[\eta_{1t} - (1 - \beta)\eta_{1t-1}]$ and $[\eta_{2t} - (1 - \beta)\eta_{2t-1}]$ can be regarded as error terms having zero means.

The estimation of the land allocation equations are also conducted under two alternative assumptions concerning the issue of 'money illusion'. The first assumption regards the Punjabi farmers as immune to 'money illusion', and, consequently, estimates of the land allocation equations are derived with the current prices of the various outputs and inputs deflated by the Indian wholesale price index with 1970/71 as a base year. In contrast, the second assumption regards the Punjabi farmers as suffering from 'money illusion' and hence the current prices of outputs and inputs are considered in the estimation process.

As explained in section 7.2, the econometric analysis is restricted to the seven districts of the homogeneous agroclimatic middle zone of Punjab. Annual observations on area sown (in hectares), yields (in kilograms per hectare) 'farm-gate price' of outputs, and governmentally guaranteed prices (in Indian rupees per ton) for the winter cereals, wheat and gram, and the summer cereals, rice and maize, as well as fertilizers price index, pesticides and insecticides index price , are collated for these districts for the period of years following the inception of the green revolution: 1961/2–1985/6. These data are extracted from various issues of: *Area, Production and Yield of Principle Crops in India, Vol. 2, Statistical Abstract of Punjab,* and *Farm Harvest Prices.*

In recalling the time-series cross-section's composition of the data base, Kmenta's (1986) cross-sectionally hetroscedastic and timewise autoregressive estimation method is applied. Similar results are obtained with Zellner's (1962) estimation method of seemingly unrelated regression equations which assumes that there is a contemporaneous correlation between the above-mentioned error terms.

7.4 Estimation results

The estimation results of the land allocation equations 24 and 25 obtained with Kmenta's (1986) pooled time-series cross-section estimation method are summarized in Tables A7.1–A7.4 which appear in the Appendix at the end of the book. Tables A7.1 and A7.2 present the estimation results of the land allocation equations for the major summer crops (rice and maize) without and with the assumption that the Punjabi farmers suffer from 'money illusion', respectively; and, similarly, Tables A7.3 and A7.4 display the estimation results of the land allocation equations for the major winter cereals (wheat and gram). The Buse's R-square indicate that in the case of the summer cereals a better fit is obtained under the assumption that the Punjabi farmers suffer from 'money illusion', but in the case of the winter cereals the Buse's R-squares do not change substantially by the elimination of the 'money illusion' assumption. Overall, best estimation results are obtained when the total number of lags, M, in the moving averages, variances and covariances of yields is set equal to 5; and, subsequently, the estimation period is 1966/7–1985/6. Each cell in Tables A7.1–A7.4 indicates the estimated coefficient, t-ratio and elasticity around the mean. It is important to note that the elasticities are computed as the product of the estimated values of $a_0,...,a_9$ and $b_0,...,b_9$ and the corresponding ratios of the average value of the independent variables to the average value of the dependent variables where the dependent and independent variables are those presented in equations 17 and 18. Therefore, the computed elasticities indicate the percentages of change in land under each of the pair of cereals under consideration stemming from a 1-per-cent increase in the perceived prices, per hectare-yield averages, variances and covariance, and input prices. It should be mentioned that although there is a certain degree of inaccuracy in the computation of the perceived prices for the sample's early years, this inaccuracy is subsequently moderated by averaging over a sufficiently long period of years. The estimation results are presented, discussed and interpreted hereafter.

The effect of the perceived price of rice

Under the assumption that there is no 'money illusion', the effects of the perceived price of rice on land allocation between rice and maize is statistically insignificant. When it is assumed that the Punjabi farmers suffer from 'money illusion', the perceived price of rice has a statistically positive effect on the land allocated to rice, but statistically insignificant effect on land allocated to maize.

Nevertheless, the rice land elasticity is small and ranges between 0.0161 to 0.0480.

The effect of the perceived price of maize

Under the assumption that there is no 'money illusion', the effect of the perceived price of maize on the land allocated to rice is not significantly different from zero. This factor has a significantly positive effect on the land allocated to maize only for high values of β and the maize land elasticity in these cases ranges between 0.758 and 1.0484. Similar results are obtained under the alternative assumption that there is 'money illusion', but the maize land elasticity is substantially smaller than that obtained under the 'no-money illusion' assumption and ranges between 0.0102 to 0.0147.

The effect of the perceived price of wheat

Under the assumption that there is no 'money illusion', the effect of the perceived price of wheat on land under wheat is negative and statistically significant for $0.1<\beta<0.8$, and the wheat-land elasticity is substantial and ranges between -0.4676 and -1.2042. Correspondingly, the effect of the perceived price of wheat on land allocated to gram is significantly positive for $0.1<\beta<0.3$ with elasticity ranging between 1.2642 and 1.6804, but insignificantly different from zero for larger values of β. In view of the necessary condition for maximum expected utility (equation 13), propositions 1 and 2 and the data, these results indicate, perhaps, that the Punjabi farmers bear a considerable risk from the uncertainty about the yield of wheat, but which is moderated by the negative covariance between the per hectare yields of wheat and gram. Note, further, that under the assumption that there is 'money illusion', the perceived price of wheat affects the land allocation in a similar way, but the elasticities are substantially smaller: a rise in the perceived price of wheat reduces the area under wheat by only 0.0066 to 0.0086 per cent and increases the area under gram by only 0.0167 to 0.0184 per cent.

The effect of the perceived price of gram

Regardless of whether or not the Punjabi farmers suffer from 'money illusion', the effect of the perceived price of gram on the amount of land allocated to gram is negative and significant while on the area under wheat it is not significantly different from zero for the entire range of β. Note, however, that the elasticity of gram-land with respect to this factor is substantial only under the assumption that there is no 'money illusion' and, in general, declines as β goes to 1 (i.e., the naive expectations case) and ranges between -0.4971 and -3.0063. Under the assumption of 'money illusion' the gram land elasticity also declines with β but is substantially smaller, in absolute terms, and ranges between -0.0042 and -0.0339. Similar to the previous case, these results indicate that the Punjabi farmers are risk averse and exposed to considerable costs of risk bearing stemming from the uncertainty involved in growing gram, although these costs are moderated by the negative covariance between the per hectare yields of wheat and gram.

The effect of the perceived average yield of rice

As expected by the conceptual model, the estimated effect of the perceived average yield of rice on the land under rice, with and without 'money illusion', is found to be significantly positive for the entire range of β, but the corresponding elasticity is small and slightly increases with β from 0.0623 to 0.1427 if the Punjabi farmers do not suffer from 'money illusion' and from 0.0717 to 0.0847 if they do suffer from 'money illusion'. Correspondingly, in the case that the Punjabi farmers do not suffer from 'money illusion', the estimated effect of the perceived average yield of rice on land under maize is significantly negative for the entire range of β, and the elasticity is small and only increases slightly, in absolute terms, from -0.0323 to -0.0367 as β rises. Under the alternative assumption that the Punjabi farmers suffer from 'money illusion', the estimated effect of the perceived average yield of rice on the area under maize is negative and statistically significant only for $0.1 < \beta < 0.3$ and the associated elasticity is small and declines, in absolute terms, from -0.0422 to -0.0322 as β increases.

The effect of the perceived average yield of maize

As stipulated in the conceptual framework, the estimated effect of the perceived average yield of maize on the land under rice, with and without 'money illusion', is negative and statistically significant for the entire range of β. However, the corresponding elasticity is small. In the case where the Punjabi farmers do not suffer from 'money illusion', it initially increases, in absolute terms, with β and reaches a peak of -0.0686 when β is equal to 0.6 and then declines gradually, in absolute terms, to -0.0211 as β goes to 1. Where farmers suffer from 'money illusion', the rice-land elasticity increases generally, in absolute terms, with β from -0.0474 to -0.0662. Correspondingly, the estimated effect of the perceived average yield of maize on the land under maize, with and without 'money illusion', is positive and statistically significant, but the corresponding elasticity is small. If the Punjabi farmers do not suffer from 'money illusion' the maize-land elasticity with respect to this factor rises, in general, with β from 0.0253 to 0.0500; and if they suffer from 'money illusion' it rises slightly more with β from 0.0263 to 0.0847.

The effect of the perceived average yield of wheat

The estimated effect of the perceived average yield of wheat on land under wheat is, as expected, positive and statistically significant for the entire range of β, regardless of whether or not the Punjabi farmers suffer from 'money illusion'. However, the wheat-land elasticity is small and slightly increases with β: from 0.0269 to 0.0752 if the money illusion assumption prevails and from 0.0257 to 0.0796 if there is no 'money illusion'. Correspondingly, the estimation results indicate that although the number of hectares allocated to gram declines significantly with the perceived average yield of wheat, the gram-land elasticity with respect to this factor is small and rises with β, in absolute terms, from -0.0284 to -0.1430 if there was 'money illusion' and from -0.0382 to -0.1762 if there was no 'money illusion'.

The effect of the perceived average yield of gram

Under both the 'money illusion' assumption and the 'no-money illusion' assumption, the estimated effects of the perceived average yield of gram on land allocation between wheat and gram are very similar. As expected, the perceived average yield of gram reduces the area under wheat. This result is statistically significant for the entire range of β, but the associated elasticity is small and ranges, in both cases, between -0.0025 to -0.0034. The effect of this factor on land allocated to gram is positive but statistically insignificant.

The effect of the perceived yield variance of rice

As expected in the conceptual analysis, the estimated effect of the yield variance of rice on the land allocated to rice, with and without 'money illusion', is negative for almost the entire range of β, but statistically insignificant. The effect of this factor on land allocated to maize, with and without 'money illusion', is positive. If there were 'money illusion', it is statistically significant for the entire range of β, whereas if there were no 'money illusion', it is statistically significant only for high values of β (i.e., $\beta > 0.7$). In both cases, the maize-land elasticity with respect to the rice-yield variance is small and rises with β from 0.0001 to 0.0023.

The effect of the perceived yield variance of maize

Contrary to the conceptual analysis, the estimated effect of the maize-yield variance on the area under maize, with and without 'money illusion', is positive and statistically significant for the entire range of β. However, the maize-land elasticity with respect to the maize-yield variance is small in both cases and ranges between 0.0011 and 0.0018. The estimated effect of the maize-yield variance on the area under rice, with and without 'money illusion', is positive and statistically significant for the entire range of β and indicates, probably, the Punjabi farmers' desire to spread risk in order to reduce the total costs of risk bearing as suggested in proposition 3. However, the rice-land elasticity with respect to the maize yield variance is small and ranges in both cases between 0.0013 to 0.0017.

The effect of the perceived yield variance of wheat

The estimated effect of the wheat-yield variance on the area under wheat, with and without 'money illusion', is positive and statistically significant for almost the entire range of β. However, the wheat-land elasticity with respect to wheat-yield variance is small in both cases and ranges between 0.0007 and 0.0014. Note that, similarly to the aforementioned estimated effect of maize-yield variance on area under maize, this finding is contrary to the properties of the mean-variance conceptual analysis. Moreover, the estimated effect of the wheat-yield variance on the area under gram, with and without 'money illusion', is negative and statistically significant for almost the entire range of β. However, the gram-land elasticity with respect to the wheat-yield variance is small and ranges in both cases between -0.0013 to -0.0041.

The effect of the perceived yield variance of gram

As expected by the conceptual analysis, the effect of the gram-yield variance on the area under gram, with and without 'money illusion', is negative and statistically significant for almost the entire range of β excluding the limiting case of naive expectations. However, the gram-land elasticity with respect to the gram-yield variance is very small and ranges between -0.00001 to -0.000033. The effect of this factor on the area under wheat is positive but statistically significant only for β equal to 0.5 if there is 'no-money illusion' and for $0.1 < \beta < 0.4$ if the Punjabi farmers suffer from 'money illusion'. Moreover, the corresponding elasticity is very small and equal to 0.00001.

The effect of the perceived rice-maize yield covariance

The sample covariance of per-hectare yields of rice and maize is negative and therefore suggests that these crops have different responses to uncontrolled growing conditions, or, otherwise, that the Punjabi farmers have a significantly better ability and/or incentive to control the growing conditions of one of these crops than the other. While the per hectare yield covariance, with and without 'money illusion', has a positive and statistically significant effect on the area under rice for the entire range of β, it has a negative, though statistically insignificant, effect on the area under maize. In recalling that the elasticity of rice-land with respect to per-hectare yield covariance is very small (0.0005), farmers in the Punjab will slightly increase the area under rice once the responses of rice and maize to uncontrolled growing conditions become more similar (e.g., through the introduction of new hybrids and/or improved growing technology).

The effect of the perceived wheat-gram yield covariance

The sample covariance of per-hectare yields of wheat and gram is negative and therefore suggests that these crops have different responses to uncontrolled growing conditions. The per-hectare yield covariance, with and without 'money illusion', has a positive effect on the area under gram, which is statistically significant only for $0.3<\beta<0.5$. Note, however, that the corresponding elasticity is very small and equal to 0.0001. Moreover, the effect of per hectare yield covariance on the area under wheat is negative but statistically insignificant. That is, as the responses of wheat and gram to uncontrolled growing conditions become more similar, farmers in the Punjab will only slightly increase the area under gram.

The effect of the perceived price of fertilizers

The estimation results indicate that a rise in the perceived price of fertlizers increases the area under both wheat and gram, possibly at the expense of other winter crops excluded from the analysis and which utilize fertilizers more intensively. The wheat-land elasticity and the gram-land elasticity are substantial if the Punjabi farmers do not suffer from 'money illusion'. Moreover, as β declines, these land elasticities increase from 0.7885 to 8.7223, in the case of wheat, and from 0.8172 to 20.0721, in the case of gram. However, if the Punjabi farmers suffer from 'money illusion', the land elasticities of wheat and gram with respect to the perceived price of fertilizers are substantially smaller: between 0.0087 to 0.0856 and 0.0091 to 0.2074 in the cases of wheat and gram, respectively.

With regard to the summer crops, rice and maize, the estimation results indicate that a rise in the perceived fertilizers' price reduces the area under rice and increases the area under maize. This effect is more substantial as the Punjabi farmers give relatively moderate weights to recent observations in the formation of their expectations about input and output prices (i.e., smaller β) and do not suffer from 'money illusion'. In this case, the land-elasticity with respect to the perceived price of fertilizers can reach -10.811 and 4.5429 for rice and maize, respectively. However, these results are statistically insignificant at the 5-per-cent level.

The effect of the perceived prices of herbicides and pesticides

A rise in the perceived prices of herbicides and pesticides increases the area under rice and decreases the area under maize. This effect is more substantial if the Punjabi farmers do not suffer from 'money illusion' and give relatively moderate weights to recent observations in the formation of their price expectations. For example, in the extreme case where β is equal to 0.1, the land elasticities are 14.8688 per cent and -13.8393 per cent for rice and maize, respectively. With regard to the winter crops, a rise in the perceived price of herbicides and pesticides does not significantly affect the area under wheat but reduces significantly the area under gram, in particular, if the Punjabi farmers do not suffer from 'money illusion'. In this case the gram-land elasticity is substantial and increases in absolute terms from -2.4259 to -15.2895 as β declines.

7.5 Summary and policy implications

This chapter investigated the responses of farmers' decisions regarding land allocation between the major winter cereals (wheat and gram) and the summer cereals (rice and maize) in India's most agriculturally advanced state — Punjab. A mean-variance model of optimal land allocation was developed and estimated with panel data on seven districts of Punjab for the green revolution period 1966–1986. The estimation of the derived land allocation equations considered a wide range of assumptions about the input and output price expectation mechanism as well as the issue of 'money illusion'.

In general, the direction of the estimated effects are robust with respect to variation in the price-expectation's coefficient, β; but in many cases, the computed elasticity varies monotonically and significantly with this coefficient. The estimation results reveal that the costs of risk bearing play a significant, and in some cases dominant, role in determining the effects of the perceived prices of the various crops on the land allocation, leading in many cases to results which differ in both direction and magnitude from those obtained in previous studies on land allocation in India and which could not be explained if the Punjabi farmers have not been risk averse. It is also evident that the land allocation elasticties with respect to the perceived cereals' prices are very sensitive to the issue of 'money illusion'. The estimation results also indicate that the effects of the perceived per-hectare average yields on the land allocation in the Punjab are statistically significant and generally compatible with the hypotheses generated by the conceptual analysis. However, the land-allocation elasticities with respect to these factors are small. It is important to note that while the estimates of the effects of the yield-variances on land allocation are compatible with the conceptual analysis in the case of the summer crops (rice and maize), they are contrary to the properties of the conceptual framework in the case of the winter crops (wheat and gram). In each of these cases, the computed land elasticities with respect to yield-variances, with and without 'money illusion', are very small. The estimation results associated with the yield covariances indicated that the effect of a greater similarity in the responses of the winter and summer cereals to uncontrolled growing conditions will not substantially alter the land allocation in the Punjab. Finally, the estimation results highlight the substantial effect of the prices of fertilizers, herbicides and pesticides on the allocation of land in Punjab. The effects of these input prices were found to be very sensitive to the existence, or non-existence, of 'money illusion', and are intensified as the Punjabi farmers give more moderate weights to recent observations in the formation of their expectations about input and output prices.

Policymakers' reliance on food-grain output prices in recent decades as a major instrument, in our judgement, has been misplaced. The estimated price elasticities for earlier years with specific assumptions about expectations in current prices are vastly different from those reported in earlier studies. As such, it is desirable for the policymakers to be aware of the interactions involved and the range of estimated elasticities. Trends, growth and variations in yield per hectare seem to be more important in farm-households' land allocation decisions than price considerations only.

Research effort in some cereals only and neglect of others (e.g., wheat but not gram) might inappropriately affect area allocation and the farming system. Research and development efforts need to be focused on the farming system as a whole. Input prices, such as those of fertilizers, pesticides and herbicides, are important factors in farmers' decision. In many situations, they are even more important policy instruments than the output prices. Recent policy changes dealing with the removal of fertilizer subsidies should be attempted with a high degree of caution. There is need to re-estimate output supply responses at the national and regional levels before tinkering with input price policies.

Notes

1 See Schultz (1975), Chaudhri (1979) and Jamison and Lau (1982) for theory and evidence.
2 See Chaudhri and Dasgupta (1985), Chapter III.
3 For a review of studies on India and Punjab, see Gulati (1985).
4 See Hammond (1974) for a discussion of the generality of this framework.

References

Berck, P. (1981), 'Portfolio Theory and the Demand for Futures: The Case of California Cotton', *American Journal of Agricultural Economics*, vol. 63, pp. 466–74.

Cagan, P. (1956), *The Monetary Dynamics of Hyperinflation in Studies on the Quantity Theory of Money*, Friedman, Milton (ed.) Chicago, University of Chicago.

Chaudhri, D.P. (1979), *Education, Innovations and Agricultural Development*, Croom Holn Publishers, London.

Chaudhri, D.P. and Singh, H.S. (1989), *Strategy for Agricultural Development of Punjab, Haryana and Delhi (1990–2001 AD)*, Haryana Agricultural University and Agro-Econ. Research Centre, Delhi University.

Chaudhri, D.P. and Dasgupta, A.K. (1985), *Agriculture and the Development Process: A Study of Punjab*, Croom Helm Publishers, London.

Chaudhri, D.P., Singh, R.B., Deb, S. and Piraziziy, A. (1991), *Land Use, Sustainability and Agricultural Development in North West India (1951–88)*, Agricultural Economics Research Centre, Delhi University.

Collender, R.N. and Zilberman, D. (1985), 'Land Allocation Under Uncertainty for Alternative Specifications of Return Distributions', *American Journal of Agricultural Economics*, vol. 67, pp. 779–86.

Cummings, J.T. (1975), 'The Supply Response of Indian Farmers in the Post-Independence Period : Major Cereal and Cash Crops', *Indian Journal of Agricultural Economics*, vol. 30, no. 1 (January–March).

Freund, R.J. (1956), 'An Introduction of Risk into a Risk-Programming Model', *Econometrica*, vol. 24, pp. 253–63.

Government of India, *Area, Production and Yield of Principal Crops in India*, vol. II, various issues, Directorate of Economics and Statistics, Ministry of Agriculture, New Delhi.

——, *Farm Harvest Prices*, various issues, Directorate of Economics and Statistics, Ministry of Agriculture, New Delhi.

Government of Punjab, *Statistical Abstract of Punjab*, various issues, Statistical Advisors Office, Chandigarh.

Gulati, A. (1985), 'Supply Response of Wheat in India : Model Review and Estimation', Business Economics Working Paper No. 2, University of Delhi.

Hammond, S. (1974), 'Simplification of Choice Under Uncertainty', *Management Science*, vol. 20, pp. 1047–72.

Jamison, D.T. and Lau, L.J. (1982), *Farmer Education and Farm Efficiency*, John Hopkins University Press, Baltimore.

Kaul, J.L. (1967), 'A Study of Supply Response to Price of Punjab Crops', *Indian Journal of Economics*, vol. 58, no. 188 (July).

Kaul, J.L. and Sidhu, D.S. (1971), 'Acreage Response to Prices for Major Crops in Punjab — An Econometric Study', *Indian Journal of Agricultural Economics*, vol. XXVI, no. 4 (October–December).

Kmenta, J. (1986), *Elements of Econometrics*, Ch. 12, pp. 618–25, Second Edition, Macmillan Publishing Company, New York.

Krishna, R. (1963), 'Farm Supply Response in India — Pakistan: A Case Study of the Punjab Region', *The Economic Journal*, vol. LXXIII, no. 291 (September).

Krishna, R. and Raychaudhuri, G.S. (1980), *Some Aspects of Wheat and Rice Price Policy in India*, World Bank Staff Working Paper no. 381 (April), Washington D.C., International Bank for Reconstruction and Development.

Krishna, R., and Chibbar, A. (1983), *Policy Modeling of a Dual Grain Market : The Case of Wheat in India*, Research Report No. 38, International Food Policy Research Institute, Washington D. C., May.

Levy, A. (1982), *Efficiency and Equity in Agricultural Land Allocation*, unpublished PhD dissertation, University of California-Berkeley.

Levy, A., Justman, M. and Hochman, E. (1989), 'The Implications of Financial Cooperation in Isreal's Semi-Cooperative Villages', *Journal of Development Economics*, vol. 30, pp. 25–46.

Markowitz, H. (1952), 'Portfolio Selection', *Journal of Finance*, vol. 77–91.

Newberry, D.M.G. and Stiglitz, J.E. (1981), *The Theory of Commodity Price Stabilization*, Oxford University Press, New York.

Ray, S.K. and Subramanian, S. (1983), *Growth and Instability in Indian Agriculture*, (Mimeo) E/88/83, Institute of Economic Growth, Delhi, June.

Scandizzo, P., Hazell, P. and Anderson, J. (1984), *Risky Agricultural Markets*, Westview Press, Boulder and London.

Schultz, T.W. (1975), 'The Value of Ability to Deal with Disequilibria', *Journal of Economic Literature*, vol. 13, pp. 872–76.

Wright, B.D. (1979), 'The Effects of Ideal Production Stabilization: A Welfare Analysis Under Rational Behavior', *Journal of Political Economy*, vol. 87, pp. 1011–33.

Yassour, J.D., Zilberman, D. and Rausser, G.C. (1981), 'Optimal Choices Among Alternative Technologies with Stochastic Yield', *American Journal of Agricultural Economics*, vol. 63, pp. 718–24.

Zellner, A. (1962), 'An Efficient Method of Estimating Seemingly Unrelated Regressions and Tests for Aggregation Bias', *Journal of the American Statistical Association*, vol. 57, pp. 348–68.

Mathematical appendix

When only two crops are involved and the land constraint is binding, the objective function can be expressed as:

$$\max_{L_1} \{ E\,[u(y)\,] = [P_1^e\,\bar{y}_1 - c_1(w^e)]L_1 + [P_1^e\,\bar{y}_2 - c_2(w^e)]\,(1 - L_1)$$

$$-0.5R\,[P_1^{e^2}\,\sigma_1^2\,L_1^2 + P_2^{e^2}\,\sigma_2^2\,(1 - L_1)^2 + 2P_1^e\,P_2^e\,L_1\,(1 - L_1)\,\sigma_{12}]\,\}\,. \qquad \text{(A.1)}$$

The first-order condition for maximum expected utility is:

$$\frac{\partial E[u(y)]}{\partial L_1} = [P_1^e\,\bar{y}_1 - c_1(w^e)] - [P_2^e\,\bar{y}_2 - c_2(w^e)] - R[(P_1^{e^2}\,\sigma_1^e$$

$$- 2P_1^e\,P_2^e\,\sigma_{12} + P_2^{e^2}\,\sigma_2^2)L_1^* - P_2^{e^2}\,\sigma_2^2 + P_1^e\,P_2^e\,\sigma_{12}] = 0 \qquad \text{(A.2)}$$

and the second-order condition for maximum is

$$\frac{\partial^2 E[u(y)]}{\partial L_1^2} = -\,R(P_1^{e^2}\,\sigma_1^e + P_2^{e^2}\,\sigma_2^2 - P_1^e\,P_2^e\,\sigma_{12}) < 0. \qquad \text{(A.3)}$$

Equation 15 is obtained from A.2 and the inequality 16 from A.3.

For tractability, the proofs of the propositions summarizing the properties of the interior solution to the land allocation problem use the symbols N and D to denote the numerator and denominator on the right-hand side of equation 15, respectively.

Proof of Proposition 1: The perceived own price effect is found by differentiating equation 15 with respect to P_1^e:

$$\frac{\partial L_1^*}{\partial P_1^e} = \frac{(\bar{y}_1 - RP_1^e\,\sigma_{12})\,D - 2R(P_1^e\,\sigma_1^e - P_2^e\,\sigma_{12})N}{D^2}$$

$$= \frac{\bar{y}_1 - RP_2^e\,\sigma_{12} - 2R(P_1^e\,\sigma_1^2 - P_2^e\,\sigma_{12})L_1^*}{D}$$

$$= \frac{\bar{y}_1 - R[P_1^e \sigma_1^2 - (2L_1^* - 1) P_2^e \sigma_{12}]}{D}. \qquad \text{(A.4)}$$

By virtue of the second-order condition 16, D > 0 and hence

$$\frac{\partial L_1^*}{\partial P_1^e} \gtreqless 0 \text{ as } \bar{y}_1 \gtreqless R[P_1^e \sigma_1^2 - (2L_1^* - 1) P_2^e \sigma_{12}]. \textit{ QED}$$

Proof of Proposition 2: By differentiating equation 15 with respect to P_2^e we obtain

$$\frac{\partial L_1^*}{\partial P_2^e} = \frac{[-\bar{y}_2 + 2R(P_2^e \sigma_2^2 - P_1^e \sigma_{12})]D - 2R(P_2^e \sigma_2^2 - P_1^e \sigma_{12}) N}{D^2}$$

$$= \frac{-\bar{y}_2 + 2R(P_2^e \sigma_2^2 - P_1^e \sigma_{12}) (1 - L_1^*)}{D} \qquad \text{(A.5)}$$

and since D > 0

$$\frac{\partial L_1^*}{\partial P_2^e} \gtreqless 0 \text{ as } 2R(P_2^e \sigma_2^2 - P_1^e \sigma_{12}) (1 - L_1^*) - \bar{y}_2 \gtreqless 0. \textit{ QED}$$

Proof of Proposition 3: By differentiating equation 15 with respect to σ_2^2 we obtain

$$\frac{\partial L_1^*}{\partial \sigma_2^2} = \frac{RP_2^{e\,2} D - R P_2^{e\,2} N}{D^2}$$

$$= \frac{RP_2^{e2}[R(P_2^{e2}\sigma_1^2 - P_1^e P_2^e \sigma_{12}) - (P_1^e \bar{y}_1 - c_1(w^e)) + (P_2 \bar{y}_2 - c_2(w^e))]}{D^2} \qquad \text{(A.6)}$$

and hence

$$\frac{\partial L_1^*}{\partial \sigma_2^2} \gtreqless 0 \text{ as} [P_2\, \bar{y}_2 - c_2(w^e)] + R(P_1^{e2}\, \sigma_1^2 - P_1^e\, P_2^e\, \sigma_{12})$$

$$\gtreqless [P_1^e\, \bar{y}_1 - c_1\, (w^e)].\ \mathit{QED}$$

Proof of Proposition 4: By differentiating equation 15 with respect to σ_{12} we obtain

$$\frac{\partial L_1^*}{\partial \sigma_{12}} = \frac{RP_1^e\, P_2^e\, (D - 2N)}{D^2}$$

$$= \frac{R(P_1^e P_2^e[(P_1^e\, \bar{y}_1 - c_1\, (w^e)) - (P_2^e\, \bar{y}_2 - c_2(w^e)) + R(P_2^{e2}\, \sigma_2^2 - P_1^{e2}\sigma_1^2)])}{D^2}$$

(A.7)

and hence

$$\frac{\partial L_1^*}{\partial \sigma_{12}} \gtreqless 0 \text{ as } [P_1^e \bar{y}_1 - c_1(w^e)] - [P_2^e \bar{y}_2 - c_2\, (w^e)]$$

$$\gtreqless R(P_1^{e2}\, \sigma_1^2 - P_2^{e2}\, \sigma_2^2).\ \mathit{QED}$$

Part 3

SOVEREIGN EXTERNAL-DEBT CRISES: THE CASE OF THE DEVELOPING COUNTRIES

8 An overview of the developing countries' external-debt problem

While capital accumulation, per-capita income, and income inequality were the predominant issues of development economics in the post-Second World War era, it is the external debts of the less developed countries (LDCs) that have captured the attention of development economists as well as mainstream economists in the last decade. During the 1970s and the 1980s, the aggregate indebtedness of developing countries grew very rapidly, leading to a heightened concern about their ability to repay their debts. The growing debts also led to an increase in income inequality and poverty levels caused by the cuts in subsidies and wages prescribed by debt-relief programmes. According to Berg and Sachs' (1988) estimation results, this increase in the income inequality and poverty levels might raise the probability of insolvency and the need for debt rescheduling and discount, and hence intensify the already mounting tension between the developing countries and the industrialized countries even further.

Furthermore, the large external debts accumulated by the LDCs tended further to adversely affect their growth prospects. Thus, Krugman (1988, 1989) and Sachs (1988, 1989) have argued that high governmental debt-service payments require high tax rates that discourage capital formation and repatriation of flight capital. Similarly, Dornbusch (1988) has argued that the fact that the government is the main maker of debt-service payments in most of the heavily indebted countries moderates the improving effect of devaluation on the trade balance. The underlying rationale is that a devaluation raises the domestic-currency costs of servicing the foreign-currency debt. This in turn increases the budget deficit, raises the inflation rate, and reduces the competitiveness of the country's export. As a result, most of the LDCs have seen their growth rates slow, and many have seen living standards that were often already pitifully low fall even further. A more detailed discussion and empirical assessment of the possible simultaneous relationship between GNP and external debt is given in Chapters 9 and 10.

The major sources of continuous and rapid accumulation of external debts by the LDCs are: (1) inefficient allocation of resources stemming from an inward-looking trade policy of import substitution supported by subsidies, tariffs and licences; (2) the dramatic increase of oil prices in the 1970s followed by the rapid decline of these prices in the 1980s; and (3) the rise of the inflation rate in the US and Western Europe in the early 1980s that led to a hike of the interest rate. The prevailing view in the 1950s was that as the rich countries grew richer, they were bound to spend a smaller share of their incomes on basic and primary goods which were the developing countries' traditional exports. Due to this pessimistic expectation of declining volumes and prices of primary goods, many of the LDCs adopted an inward-looking trade strategy based on subsidies for domestic industries and import tariffs and licenses to keep out wasteful luxuries and to promote the sort of industrialization that would be necessary to escape from the poverty trap. However, this strategy inflicted an adverse effect on the functioning of the price system as a signalling device for obtaining an efficient allocation of domestic resources and led to a resource allocation that did not correspond to the developing countries' comparative advantage.

Furthermore, during the 1970s the oil prices had increased at an unprecedented rate leading to a sharp increase in the revenues of oil-exporting countries. A substantial portion of these revenues had been deposited in commercial banks of the industrialized countries. Facing large reserves, these banks, in turn, had been seeking demand for the excess supply of credit. They were willing to provide financial assistance to many developing countries endowed with large oil reserves (e.g., Mexico) and whose regimes were considered to be relatively stable (e.g., the Philippines) in a variable interest rate. Later, in the early 1980s, the interest rate on the loans extended to the LDCs had substantially risen by the inflationary process in the USA.

These events, coupled with the substantial dramatic fall of oil prices that had stemmed from the adjustment measures taken by the industrialized countries in both demand and supply of oil (the oil glut), have severely increased the developing countries' external debt burden and have led many of them to a stage of insolvency. Moreover, measures that have been taken by developing countries to alleviate the financial crisis, such as cuts in subsidies on basic consumption goods and freezing of nominal wages, were found insufficient and led to a further impoverishment of the middle and lower classes and to a higher level of social and political instability.

Developing countries are often affiliated to regional reference groups such as Latin America, Sub-Saharan Africa, and South-East Asia. The underlying rationale is that a greater geographical affinity facilitates transfer of both positive and negative externalities between countries. It is therefore possible that the well-being of an individual country is affected by the overall performances of its reference group. The identification of these external effects on the individual countries' costs of credit and borrowing behaviour is the subject of Chapter 11.

A statistical summary of the aggregate level of indebtedness of the aforementioned regional groups and the average interest rates paid on their external liabilities is given in Table 8.1. This table also presents the ratios of these levels of external debts to the regional groups' aggregate output as well as the regional groups' aggregate growth rates of gross product. These variables can be viewed as indicators of the external-debt burden and the regional groups' general ability to service their debts. The average annual real interest rates are proxied by the ratios of the interest payments (public and private) made by the regional groups during each year to the aggregate external debt levels at the beginning of the year. It is important to note that in many instances the actual interest payments were smaller than the due ones and therefore the ratio of interest payments to external debt level might understate the contracted interest rates.

Table 8.1
Total external debt (D, in billions of 1980 US dollars), debt burden (d), real interest rate (r) and growth rate (g) in Latin America and the Caribbean, Sub-Saharan Africa and Asia and the Pacific*

Latin America & the Caribbean

Year	ΣD	d	r	g
1971	60.6	0.182	0.052	0.070
1972	69.7	0.194	0.053	0.082
1973	77.2	0.180	0.063	0.194
1974	92.6	0.178	0.079	0.211
1975	101.5	0.199	0.076	-0.020
1976	117.9	0.220	0.066	0.050
1977	166.9	0.311	0.064	0.001
1978	191.9	0.329	0.051	0.086
1979	214.5	0.336	0.072	0.096
1980	242.7	0.348	0.081	0.093
1981	270.5	0.372	0.084	0.041
1982	285.8	0.469	0.087	-0.160
1983	297.9	0.584	0.074	-0.160
1984	300.1	0.593	0.076	-0.010
1985	300.8	0.602	0.073	-0.010
1986	308.1	0.613	0.063	0.006
1987	325.1	0.597	0.059	0.084
1988	302.1	0.488	0.052	0.135

Sub-Saharan Africa

Year	ΣD	d	r	g
1971	11.89	0.139	0.036	0.037
1972	13.05	0.143	0.034	0.073
1973	16.20	0.161	0.047	0.102
1974	18.96	0.148	0.038	0.274
1975	21.09	0.156	0.035	0.056
1976	24.28	0.167	0.032	0.073
1977	35.87	0.228	0.033	0.079

Table 8.1 (continued)

Year	ΣD	d	r	g
1978	44.67	0.271	0.030	0.049
1979	50.15	0.279	0.034	0.090
1980	54.93	0.278	0.043	0.102
1981	57.23	0.331	0.040	-0.130
1982	58.88	0.369	0.040	-0.080
1983	64.12	0.435	0.039	-0.080
1984	63.45	0.456	0.040	-0.060
1985	72.91	0.634	0.042	-0.020
1986	83.38	0.755	0.030	-0.190
1987	98.67	1.058	0.024	-0.160
1988	96.53	0.991	0.026	0.044
Asia and the Pacific				
1971	45.3	0.107	0.029	0.073
1972	49.8	0.113	0.031	0.035
1973	53.5	0.106	0.034	0.146
1974	59.9	0.112	0.033	0.065
1975	65.1	0.121	0.034	0.001
1976	72.3	0.140	0.038	-0.040
1977	93.3	0.165	0.039	0.093
1978	101.2	0.160	0.037	0.123
1979	110.1	0.162	0.044	0.073
1980	124.8	0.170	0.048	0.079
1981	131.5	0.191	0.048	-0.060
1982	146.9	0.224	0.049	-0.050
1983	157.8	0.241	0.045	-0.002
1984	160.4	0.248	0.046	-0.010
1985	180.0	0.282	0.046	-0.010
1986	196.7	0.314	0.048	-0.020
1987	213.7	0.317	0.047	0.074
1988	209.4	0.276	0.045	0.128

*** The computation of D (in billions of 1980 US dollars), d, r and g are based on data extracted from IBRD World Tables 1990 and World Debt Tables 1990.**

Table 8.1 reveals that between 1971 and 1988 the aggregate external debts of the developing countries in Latin America and the Caribbean and in Asia and the Pacific grew by about five times, and those of Sub-Saharan Africa by about nine times. This table also indicates that in the case of Sub-Saharan Africa, which as a region had the worst growth record, the ratio of the external debt to aggregate output converged to 1, indicating the enormous burden of the region's external liabilities. In addition, the chronic and substantial deficits in the current accounts of most of the Sub-Saharan African countries indicate these countries' inability to repay their external debts. During the period 1971 to 1981, the Latin American and the Caribbean external liabilities grew tremendously. Yet the rise of the external debt-output ratio in this region was moderated by the growth in the aggregate output. However, between 1982 and 1985 that region suffered from a substantial economic slow down that led to an accelerated rise in the external debt-output ratio to a peak of 0.613 in 1986. Subsequently, as a significant economic growth process was resumed in 1987, this ratio fell considerably to 0.488 in 1988. Nevertheless, the negative trade balance figures for this recovery period still indicate the region's severe problem in repaying its external debt. In the case of Asia and the Pacific, the accumulation of debt during the observed period was more evenly distributed over the years than in the case of Latin America and the Caribbean. Like the Latin American and the Caribbean countries, many countries in Asia and the Pacific suffered from economic slowdown and recession between 1981 and 1986. This slowdown was reflected in a hike in the external debt burden. But unlike the case of the Latin American and the Caribbean countries, the economic slowdown in Asia and the Pacific was much less severe and hence the external debt-output ratio remained relatively low in this region. The renewed output growth in the second half of the 1980s has further contributed to moderating this ratio.

Table 8.1 also indicates that the average interest rate paid by countries in Sub-Saharan Africa and Asia and the Pacific was considerably lower than that paid by the countries of Latin American and the Caribbean. These interest rate differentials might suggest that there were fundamental differences between the developing regions with regard to access to credit suppliers. Many of the countries in Sub-Saharan Africa and Asia and the Pacific have been classified as low-income countries, whereas many of the Latin American ones have been considered middle-income countries. Thus, while the former, and in particular the Sub-Saharan countries, were substantially restricted to official creditors such as the World Bank, the International Monetary Fund, and foreign governments, the latter also had access to dearer loans from profit-oriented commercial banks in the technologically advanced and rich countries. In 1982, the year in which the Mexican government was unable to service its debt and the external debt problem was recognized as a major international and financial crisis, the average interest rate paid by the Latin American and the Caribbean countries reached a peak of 8.7 per cent. Subsequently it was reduced by repudiation and debt restructuring and forgiveness.

It is important to note that a very large fraction of the developing countries' external debt is a public or a publicly guaranteed debt, i.e., a sovereign debt, and hence it is vulnerable to repudiation. Moreover, in the absence of effective retaliatory ability, repudiation might evolve as the most possible outcome of the debt crisis, leading in turn to intensified hostility between the technologically advanced economies and the developing countries. In order to alleviate the developing countries' debt burden and to reduce the risk for creditors, secondary markets for sovereign debts were created during the 1980s. In these markets, indebted countries could buy back their debts at a discount. Table 8.2 presents the total external debts and their secondary markets' price for a selected group of highly indebted developing countries. These secondary market prices reflect to a certain extent the creditors' reservation prices of various countries' debts. Berg and Sachs (1988), who estimated a tobit model of the size of the discount on each countries debt in the secondary market, have found that higher income inequality leads to a greater discount on debt, while higher outward orientation, agricultural share and GNP per capita squared tend to decrease the secondary market discount. A typical and basic explanation of creditors' reservation price is based on the distinction between a 'good' state of world in which the indebted country meets its liabilities fully and a 'bad' state of work in which the country will repudiate a certain portion of its external debt. In this setting, as long as the realization of the state of world is not certain and the

Table 8.2
External debt, debt burden, and secondary market prices for highly indebted countries

	Total External Debt (billions of US $)	*Total Debt -GNP ratio (1987)*	*Secondary Market Prices of Bank Debt (20 July 1989)*
Argentina	60	0.74	0.18
Brazil	114	0.39	0.11
Chile	19	1.25	0.64
Colombia	17	0.50	0.60
Costa Rica	5	1.16	0.14
Cote d'ivoire	14	1.44	0.06
Ecuador	10	1.07	0.14
Jamaica	4	1.76	0.42
Mexico	100	0.78	0.44
Morocco	21	1.32	0.44
Nigeria	30	1.23	0.24
Peru	19	0.40	0.04
Philippines	29	0.86	0.54
Uruguay	4	0.59	0.55
Venezuela	36	0.94	0.40
Yugoslavia	22	0.39	0.54

Source: The World Bank, *World Debt Tables, 1988–89*, ed. The World Bank, *Quarterly Review, June 1989*. Salomon Brothers, Indicative Prices for Developing Country Debt, July 1989.

perceived repudiation rate is positive, the creditors' reservation price is smaller than one dollar per each dollar of recycled debt. Furthermore, the greater the perceived repudiation rate and the perceived probability of a bad state of world, the lower the creditors' reservation price of recycling the indebted countries' liabilities. An elaboration and extension of this basic model of the secondary-market prices' determination to the more likely setting of Cournot-Nash equilibrium whereby both creditor and debtor have an aversion toward risk and set the repudiation and retaliation levels so as to maximize their expected utilities with consideration of each other's reaction is presented in Chapter 12. In addition, the strategic interaction between creditors and indebted sovereigns is analyzed within a game-theory framework in Chapter 13; and Chapter 14 analyzes the optimal accumulation of capital stock, external debt and reputation by incorporating the indebted country's inclination to service its external liabilities and the adverse effects of not meeting foreign loans' commitments on the country's trustworthy reputation. Repudiation and loss of reputation might limit a country's access to international markets of credit, consumer and capital goods and hence can lead to a higher average cost of servicing a country's new external loans, less favourable terms of trade with the rest of the world and accelerated depreciation of capital stock.

In view of the developing countries' high level of indebtedness, it has been argued by Krugman (1988) that those countries' external liabilities act like a high marginal tax rate, which discourages capital formation and deters their governments from taking painful, but necessary, measures to improve those countries' economic performance. Therefore, when an indebted country is on the downward sloping side of the 'debt relief Laffer curve', both debtor and creditor can benefit from a debt-reduction. This issue and the rescheduling of a sovereign debt is analyzed in Chapter 15.

Despite the worldwide economic recovery and the renewed sustainable growth of many developing countries in Asia and Latin America during the first half of the 1990s, the external debt crisis, which had started more than a decade ago when the Mexican government could not service its external liabilities, is far from being over. In January 1995, Mexico's foreign exchange reserves were almost halved to a mere $3.5 billion after a devaluation of the peso and a stock-exchange crush, making a default on short-term liabilities inevitable. A default has been prevented by a US-led rescue plan including fifty billion US dollars of loan guarantees. During the 1990s, many of the former centrally planned economies in East Europe have joined the club of highly indebted countries. By the mid-1990s, developing countries as a group have become more indebted than they were at any time during the 1980s, with Brazil and Mexico still leading the pack but followed more closely by India, Indonesia, China, Russia and Argentina. In 1993, the external debts of the developing countries as a proportion of their combined gross domestic product reached about 40 per cent and debt-service ratio (total interest and principal payments as a share of exports of goods and services) was at a crippling level for many of them (e.g., 77 per cent for Algeria, 64 per cent for Peru, and 41 per cent for Hungary).

References

Berg, A. and Sachs, J. (1988), 'The Debt Crisis: Structural Explanation of Country Performance', *Journal of Development Economics*, vol. 29, pp. 271–306.

Dornbusch, R. (1988), 'Our LDC Debts', in Feldstein, Martin, (ed.), *The United States in the World Economy,* University of Chicago Press for The National Bureau of Economic Research, Chicago.

Krugman, P.R. (1988), 'Financing vs. Forgiving a Debt Overhang', *Journal of Development Economics*, vol. 29, pp. 253–68.

—— (1989), 'Market-Based Debt-Reduction Schemes', in Frenkel, Jacob A., Michael P. Dooley and Peter Wickham (eds.), *Analytical Issues in Debt*, International Monetary Fund, Washington DC.

Sachs, J. (1988), 'Comprehensive Debt Retirement: The Bolivian Example', *Brookings Papers on Economic Activity*, vol. 2, pp. 705–13.

—— (1989), 'Conditionality, Debt Relief, and the Developing Country Debt Crisis', in Sachs, Jeffry (ed.), *Developing Country Debt and Economic Performance*, University of Chicago Press, Chicago.

9 Are the external debts of developing countries a symptom or a cause of economic slowdown?

Co-authored by Khorshed Chowdhury and Edgar Wilson

Our causality tests indicate that the external debts of developing countries are not a symptom of economic slowdown. They also indicate that external debts lead to economic slowdown in the cases of several Latin-American countries and Sudan. A feedback relationship between economic growth and external debt accumulation is not rejected for thirteen countries. These mixed results imply that there is no general coherent relationship between external debt and economic slowdown and hence there is no unique way to remedy the failing economies of the developing countries.

9.1 Introduction

Since the early 1980s, the external debt problem, its causes and implications for economic growth have become major concerns for many developing countries and international institutions for economic development such as the World Bank and the International Monetary Fund as well as for many academic economists. During the past decade, it has become apparent that

---

Reprinted with permission from the *Indian Economic Association Conference Volume*, Part III, 1991, pp. 57–72, with modifications.

there is a major controversy between two schools of thoughts about the effects of the external debt on economic growth and hence the necessity for an international facility for debt relief. This controversy is highlighted in the 'Symposium on New Institutions for Developing Country Debt' which appeared in the winter 1990 issue of the *Journal of Economic Perspectives*.

The first school of thought is represented by Kenen (1990) and Sachs (1990). They have argued that the external debt overhang is a primary cause of economic slowdown in the heavily indebted countries and hence there is an urgent need for an international debt relief facility. Their view is based on the underlying rationale given by Krugman (1989) that high government debt-service payments require high tax rates which in turn discourage capital formation and repatriation of flight capital. It is also supported by Dornbusch's (1988) argument that, since the government is the main maker of debt-service payments in most of the heavily indebted developing countries, the improving effects of devaluation on the trade balance are small. Devaluation raises the domestic currency costs of servicing the foreign-currency debt and, subsequently, increases the budget deficit, raises the growth rate of the money supply, raises the inflation rate, and deteriorates the country's terms of trade.

The second school of thought is represented by Bulow and Rogoff (1990) who have argued that the external debts of developing countries are a symptom of poor economic management and economic growth rather than a primary cause of economic slowdown. They have also argued that the presence of official creditors such as the International Monetary Fund and the World Bank ossified the negotiating position of the private banks in the industrialized countries and the indebted developing countries, and complicated the negotiations between them on debt rescheduling and relief. The presence of these institutions also creates a 'free-rider' problem whereby the indebted countries who negotiate the rescheduling of their external debts in later stages are likely to use the previous arrangements obtained with other indebted countries as a benchmark for obtaining better deals. Thus, enforcing the private banks to reveal a tougher attitude toward countries which negotiate the rescheduling of their debts earlier.

The purpose of this chapter is to test the aforementioned polar hypotheses about the causal relationship between the GNP's growth rate and the external debt's accumulation rate. The interpretation of causal relationships between economic growth and external debt accumulation is not simple and should be done with a great deal of caution. This is due to the possibility that economic growth and external debt accumulation rates are affected by common factors such as technological level, organizational structure, incentive scheme, compatibility of resource allocation to the country's comparative advantage, terms of trade, interest rate differential between the country and the rest of the world, etc. Nevertheless, in order to shed more light on the aforementioned controversy and the potential contribution of a new international institution for debt relief to the economic growth of the developing countries, it is useful to subject the issue to statistical tests.

The structure of the chapter is as follows. Granger causality tests are conducted for twenty-nine indebted developing countries located in Latin-America and the Caribbean, Asia and the Pacific, Sub-Saharan Africa, South Europe and the Mediterranean basin with annual data encompassing the nineteen-year period between 1970 to 1988. Among the countries analysed are those classified by the World Bank as the seventeen Highly Indebted Countries. Section 9.2 describes the conceptual framework adopted for conducting the causality tests. Section 9.3 reports the results of these tests and the long-term effects of the external debt accumulation rate and the GNP growth rate on each other. Finally, section 9.4 concludes the chapter with a brief summary of the main empirical findings and their implications.

9.2 Conceptual framework

A useful definition of causal relationship between time series has been suggested by Granger (1969). By this definition X causes Y if Y_t can be predicted better by using past X_t, than by not using it. That is, X causes Y if the prediction error is reduced by including lags of X in the regression equation of Y_t as well as lags of Y. A feedback exists between X and Y if X causes Y and Y causes X.

Following a widely accepted approach, we assume that the GNP's time series can be approximated by the exponential growth equation

$$GNP(t) = GNP_0 \exp(gt + \varepsilon_t) \tag{1}$$

where *g* denotes the GNP growth rate, and ε is a white noise (i.e., it is an identically and independently distributed random disturbance with zero mean and finite variance σ_1^2).

Similarly, we assume that the time series of the total external debt (TED) conforms to the exponential equation

$$TED(t) = TED_0 \exp(ht + u_t) \tag{2}$$

where *h* denotes the accumulation rate of TED, and *u* is a white noise with zero mean and finite variance σ_2^2.

Granger's causality test is based on the assumption that both time series under consideration are covariance-stationary. That is, the moments of their distributions are time invariant. Recalling equations 1 and 2, as long as g and h are significantly different from zero, the time series of the GNP and TED do not obey the covariance-stationarity assumption. Hence, a certain transformation of these series is required. By taking the logarithmic transformation of these exponential specifications, the following regression equations are obtained:

$$\ln GNP(t) = \ln GNP_0 + gt + \varepsilon_t \tag{3}$$

$$\ln TED(t) = \ln TED_0 + ht + u_t. \tag{4}$$

By taking the first difference of the natural logarithms of these variables, we obtain further the following pair of covariance-stationary series:

$$y_t \equiv \ln GNP_t - \ln GNP_{t-1} = g + \varepsilon'_t \tag{5}$$

$$x_t \equiv \ln TED_t - \ln TED_{t-1} = h + u'_t\ . \tag{6}$$

Here,

$$\varepsilon'_t \equiv \varepsilon_t - \varepsilon_{t-1} \tag{7}$$

is a white noise having zero mean and $2\sigma_2^1$ variance, and

$$u'_t \equiv u_t - u_{t-1} \tag{8}$$

is a white noise having zero mean and $2\sigma_2^2$ variance.

It is important to note that y_t and x_t denote the current annual growth rate of GNP and the current accumulation rate of TED, respectively. They fluctuate around the long-term annual growth rates *g* and *h* of the original time series GNP and TED. Thus, testing causality between *x* and *y* can be meaningfully interpreted as testing causality, in the Granger sense, between the current annual growth rate of GNP and the current annual accumulation rate of TED.

Following Granger's procedure and Akaike's (1969, 1970) final prediction error (FPE) criterion, the test of causal relationships between *y* and *x* comprises three stages.[1] The first stage is a search for the autoregressive equations of these variables which have the least FPE. The second stage selects the optimal number of lags of the other variable to be added to the autoregressive equation obtained in the previous stage in order to minimize the FPE. Finally, stage three conducts and F-test of the hypothesis that the set of all the additional lags introduced in the second stage has a significant contribution to predicting the value of the variable under consideration. As an alternative to the FPE criterion, the Hocking (1976) S_p criterion, which can provide an asymptotically optimal choice as to the number of regressors (Breiman and Freedman, 1983), is also applied.[2]

The estimation of the growth rate and the debt accumulation rate and the regression analyses in the various stages of the causality tests employ the logarithmic transformations of the time series data on GNP in domestic prices of 1980 and the total external debt in US dollars of 1980 for twenty-nine highly indebted countries in Latin America and the Caribbean, Asia-Pacific, Sub-Saharan Africa and South Europe and the Mediterranean basin during the period

1970–1988. The data are obtained from the *World Debt Tables 1990–91*, Vol. 2. In view of potential autocorrelation problems, the Cochrane-Orcutt estimation method is applied.

9.3 Empirical findings

Tables 9.1 to 9.4 summarize the estimated long-term growth rate of GNP (g) and long-term accumulation rate of external debt (h) and the causality tests' results for the twenty-nine developing countries by regional affiliation. These tables also present the long-term effects of the external debt accumulation rate and the GNP growth rate on each other for the cases in which the causal relationships between the current rates of growth and debt accumulation are not rejected.[3] The hypothesis that the accumulation rate of external debts affects the GNP growth rate is denoted by H_1 and the hypothesis that the GNP growth rate affects the accumulation rate of external debts by H_2. The results of these hypotheses tests are reported in the tables at the 1 per cent level of significance. These hypotheses are also tested at the 5 per cent level of significance. Any contradiction between the results obtained in the latter case and those obtained in the former is indicated by an asterisk. The results of the causality tests obtained with the S_p criterion coincide with those obtained with the FPE criterion and hence are not reported. Further information about the causality tests is provided in Table A.1 in the Appendix.

Tables 9.1 to 9.4 indicate that while the GNP long-term growth rates are low, the external debts' long-term accumulation rates are high for all the twenty-nine countries included in the analysis. In this group of developing countries, the average long-term annual growth rate is 3.14 per cent and its standard deviation is 2.01 per cent, whereas the average long-term annual accumulation rate of external debt is 9.80 per cent and its standard deviation is 3.89 per cent during the observed period 1970–88. These results are significant at the one per cent level in most cases. Moreover, the fact that the determination coefficients (R^2) are close to one in most cases lends support to the exponentional specifications of the GNP and TED time series underlying the definitions of the current annual growth and accumulation rates on which the tests of causal relationships are conducted. The computed correlation coefficient

(0.22), as well as the least-squares estimates of the second-order polynomial relationship, between the estimated long-term growth rates and debt accumulation rates indicate that there is no clear statistical association between these long-term rates.[4] The results of the causality tests are discussed below in a greater detail for the four regional groups of developing countries.

Findings for the Latin-American and Caribbean countries

The hypothesis that the accumulation rate of external debt affects the GNP growth rate (H_1) is not rejected for 83.33 per cent (at the 1 per cent level) to 91.67 per cent (at the 5 per cent level) of the countries in Latin America and the Caribbean. Among the countries in which this hypothesis is not rejected it is found that the long-term effect of the external debt accumulation rate on the GNP growth rate is negative in the cases of Bolivia, Brazil, Jamaica, Peru and Venezuela; and also for Argentina at the 5 per cent level of significance. The adverse effect of external debt on GNP is mostly noticeable in the case of Brazil where an increase of 1 per cent in the external debt leads to a decline of the GNP by 2.77 per cent in the long run. This finding lends support to Kenen-Sachs's argument in favour of the establishment of a new institution for debt relief. However, the long-term effect of the external debt accumulation rate on the GNP growth rate is found to be positive in the cases of Chile, Colombia, Costa Rica, Ecuador and Uruguay suggesting a trade off between GNP and level of indebtedness.

The hypothesis that the GNP growth rate affects the external debt accumulation rate (H_2) is not rejected in 50 per cent (at the 1 per cent level) to 58.33 per cent (at the 5 per cent level) of the countries in Latin America and the Caribbean. Among these countries, the long-term effect of the GNP growth rate on the external debt accumulation rate is found to be negative in the cases of Jamaica, Peru and Uruguay. The effect of GNP growth in alleviating the external debt burden is mostly noticeable in the case of Chile where an increase of one per cent in the GNP leads to a decline of the external liabilities by 8.45 per cent in the long run. However, in the cases of Brazil, Colombia, Costa Rica and Ecuador, the GNP growth rate has led to an increase in their levels of indebtedness.

The causality tests in the case of Latin America and the Caribbean do not support the Bulow-Rogoff proposition that the external debt is a symptom of economic slowdown rather than a cause of economic slowdown. This is because the requirements of Bulow-Rogoff's proposition — that H_1 is rejected, that H_2 is not rejected and that the GNP growth reduces the external liabilities — are not met by any of the Latin American and the Caribbean countries.

It is important to note that a feedback relationship between external debt accumulation rate and GNP growth rate is found for 58.33 per cent (at the 1 per cent level) to 66.67 per cent (at the 5 per cent level) of the Latin American countries including Brazil, Chile, Colombia, Ecuador, Jamaica, Peru, Uruguay and Costa Rica (only at the 5 per cent level).

Finally, the results for Mexico are interesting and unique. In the Mexican case, the tests trace no causal relationship between the GNP growth rate and the external debt accumulation rate.

Table 9.1
Long-term rates, causality test's results and long-term effects for countries in Latin America and the Caribbean

	Long-Term Rates of		*Reject at 1% Level of Significance*		*Long-Term Effects of*	
Country	GNP growth*	debt accum-ulation*	H_1	H_2	x on y	y on x
Argentina	0.00696	0.08095	Yes**	Yes	-0.088	—
	(1.821)	(5.535)				
	0.569	0.974				
Bolivia	0.01557	0.08048	No	Yes	-0.041	—
	(1.905)	(6.852)				
	0.880	0.963				

Table 9.1 (continued)

Country	GNP growth*	debt accumulation*	H_1	H_2	x on y	y on x
Brazil	0.05126	0.11368	No	No	-2.768	0.497
	(5.960)	(4.394)				
	0.966	0.968				
Chile	0.01813	0.05955	No	No	0.273	-8.446
	(2.758)	(4.476)				
	0.693	0.957				
Colombia	0.04335	0.08046	No	No	0.158	1.125
	(12.555)	(16.591)				
	0.992	0.961				
Costa Rica	0.03299	0.10393	No	Yes**	0.331	2.811
	(5.437)	(5.025)				
	0.938	0.980				
Ecuador	0.05814	0.15529	No	No	0.109	1.967
	(5.343)	(4.368)				
	0.956	0.957				
Jamaica	-0.01347	0.02542	No	No	-0.714	-2.631
	(3.093)	(2.668)				
	0.799	0.792				
Mexico	0.03821	0.10035	Yes	Yes	—	—
	(5.216)	(4.772)				
	0.970	0.977				
Peru	0.02114	0.04930	No	no	-0.007	-2.939
	(5.388)	(4.464)				
	0.825	0.906				
Uruguay	0.01432	0.09242	No	No	0.359	-1.707
	(2.329)	(13.023)				
	0.805	0.952				
Venezuela	0.0200	0.14902	No	Yes	-0.755	—
	(3.059)	(3.185)				
	0.895	0.921				

* The numbers in the parentheses are t-ratios and the numbers below the t-ratios indicate the determination coefficients (R^2).

** The opposite conclusion is obtained at the 5 per cent level of significance.

Findings for the Asia-Pacific countries

The hypothesis that the accumulation rate of external debt affects the GNP growth rate is not rejected for 60 per cent (at the 1 per cent level) to 80 per cent (at the 5 per cent level) of the countries in Asia-Pacific. It is interesting that among all the investigated Asia-Pacific countries in which this hypothesis is not rejected (Indonesia, Pakistan, South Korea and the Philippines), the long-term effect of the external debt accumulation rate on the growth rate is positive. This effect is mostly noticeable for Pakistan where an increase of 1 per cent in the external debt leads to an increase of the GNP by 0.92 per cent in the long run. This finding lends no support to the Dornbusch-Krugman proposition that the external debts of developing countries are a cause of economic slowdown.

The hypothesis that the GNP growth rate affects the external debt accumulation rate is not rejected in 40 per cent (at the 1 per cent level) to 60 per cent (at the 5 per cent level) of the investigated countries in Asia-Pacific. However, in all of the cases where this hypothesis is not rejected (Pakistan, Philippines and India), the long-term effect of the GNP growth rate on the external debt accumulation rate is positive and hence lends no support to the Bulow-Rogoff proposition. This effect is mostly noticeable in the case of the Philippines where a 1 per cent increase in the GNP leads to a 1.25 per cent increase of the external debt in the long run.

Finally, it is important to note that at the 1 per cent level of significance, the Indian case reveals no causal relationship between the GNP growth rate and the external debt accumulation rate. In contrast, the Pakistani case indicates that a feedback relationship between the rates of GNP growth and external debt accumulation is not rejected.

Findings for countries in Sub-Saharan Africa

The hypothesis that the accumulation rate of external debt affects the GNP growth rate is not rejected for 50 per cent (at the 1 per cent level) to 87.5 per cent (at the 5 per cent level) of the countries in Sub-Saharan Africa. Among the countries in which this hypothesis is not rejected, it is found that the long-term effect of the external debt accumulation rate on the growth rate is negative only in the

Table 9.2
Long-term rates, causality test's results and long-term effects for countries in Asia-Pacific

Country	*Long-Term Rates of* GNP growth*	debt accumulation*	*Reject at 1% Level of Significance* H_1	H_2	*Long-Term Effects of* x on y	y on x
India	0.04211 (16.748) 0.981	0.05068 (5.261) 0.965	Yes	Yes**	—	0.957
Indonesia	0.05911 (13.149) 0.995	0.09639 (7.280) 0.972	No	Yes	0.398	—
Pakistan	0.05325 (13.411) 0.995	0.03287 (7.276) 0.948	No	No	0.921	0.510
Philippines	0.03968 (4.965) 0.964	0.10619 (4.355) 0.968	Yes**	No	0.328	1.247
South Korea	0.08293 (19.345) 0.993	0.10473 (3.584) 0.964	No	Yes	0.712	—

* The numbers in the parentheses are t-ratios and the numbers below the t-ratios indicate the determination coefficients (R^2).

** The opposite conclusion is obtained at the 5 per cent level of significance.

case of Sudan. In this case, a 1 per cent increase in the external debt leads to a decline of the Sudanese GNP by 2.27 per cent in the long run. This finding is compatible with the Dornbusch-Krugman proposition. However, in all other cases (Ethiopia, Kenya and Tanzania, and also Zaire and Cote d'Ivoire at the 5 per cent level) an increase in the external debt accumulation rate leads to a modest rise in the GNP growth rate in the long run.

The hypothesis that the GNP growth rate affects the external debt accumulation rate is not rejected in 25 per cent (at the 1 per cent level) to 62.5 per cent (at the 5 per cent level) of the countries in Sub-Saharan Africa. Among these countries, the long-term effect of the GNP growth rate on the external debt accumulation rate is found to be positive and substantial in the cases of Nigeria, Sudan and Tanzania. This finding does not lend support to the Bulow-Rogoff proposition. The long-term effect of the GNP growth rate on the external debt accumulation is only slightly positive in the case of Kenya and substantially negative for Cote d'Ivoire.

It is important to note that the causality test's results for the Sub-Saharan countries do not lend support to the Bulow-Rogoff proposition. Even in the case of Nigeria, where H_1 is rejected and H_2 is not rejected, the long-term effect of a rise in the GNP growth rate on the external debt accumulation rate is substantially positive. In the cases of Cote d'Ivoire, Ghana and Zaire no causal relationships between the growth rate and the external debt accumulation rate are traced at the 1 per cent level of confidence. However, in these cases causal relationships cannot be ruled out at the 5 per cent level of significance. Finally, a feedback between the growth rate and the external debt accumulation rate is not rejected in the case of Kenya and also in the cases of Cote d'Ivoire, Sudan and Tanzania at the 5 per cent level of significance.

Findings for the South-European and Mediterranean countries

Among the South-European and Mediterranean countries, the hypothesis that the accumulation rate of external debt affects the GNP growth rate is not rejected except in the case of Yugoslavia. In contrast to the Dornbusch-Krugman proposition, the long-term effect of the external debt accumulation rate on the GNP growth rate of Yugoslavia is positive. Similarly, the hypothesis that the GNP growth rate affects the external debt accumulation rate is not rejected only in the case of Greece. In contrast to the Bulow-Rogoff proposition, the long-term effect of the GNP growth rate on the external debt accumulation rate in Greece is positive and large. Finally, it is important to note that no causal relationships between

Table 9.3
Long-term rates, causality test's results and long-term effects for countries in Sub-Saharan Africa

Country	*Long-Term Rates of* GNP growth*	debt accumulation*	*Reject at 1% Level of Significance* H_1	H_2	*Long-Term Effects of* x on y	y on x
Cote d'Ivoire	0.03307 (3.995) 0.935	0.16291 (6.663) 0.977	Yes**	Yes**	0.158	-0.843
Ethiopia	0.02240 (11.196) 0.939	0.10065 (24.395) 0.990	No	Yes	0.203	—
Ghana	0.00560 (1.097) 0.359	0.03654 (3.834) 0.800	Yes*	Yes	0.141	—
Kenya	0.05293 (13.349) 0.970	0.09016 (5.555) 0.959	No	No	0.452	0.137
Nigeria	0.02151 (2.373) 0.809	0.18119 (19.234) 0.940	Yes	No	—	5.507
Sudan	0.02850 (3.722) 0.849	0.14125 (5.911) 0.977	No	Yes**	-2.271	1.979
Tanzania	0.02253 (7.102) 0.965	0.10104 (5.156) 0.974	No	Yes**	0.290	2.779
Zaire	0.00407 (1.166) 0.341	0.12366 (3.880) 0.949	Yes**	Yes	0.018	—

* The numbers in the parentheses are t-ratios and the numbers below the t-ratios indicate the determination coefficients (R^2).

** The opposite conclusion is obtained at the 5 per cent level of significance.

Table 9.4
Long-term rates, causality test's results and long-term effects for countries in South Europe and the Mediterranean Basin

Country	*Long-Term Rates of* GNP growth*	debt accumulation*	*Reject at 1% Level of Significance* H1	H2	*Long-Term Effects of* x on y	y on x
Greece	0.02814 (5.040) 0.957	0.10328 (17.303) 0.978	Yes	No	—	9.146
Morocco	0.04423 (27.247) 0.984	0.12723 (5.416) 0.971	Yes	Yes	—	—
Portugal	0.03117 (9.373) 0.954	0.12014 (4.317) 0.965	Yes	Yes	—	—
Yugoslavia	0.03212 (4.218) 0.959	0.07209 (3.291) 0.950	No	Yes	0.324	—

* The numbers in the parentheses are t-ratios and the numbers below the t-ratios indicate the determination coefficients (R^2).
** The opposite conclusion is obtained at the 5 per cent level of significance.

the rate of growth of GNP and the external debt accumulation rate are traced in the cases of Morocco and Portugal.

9.4 Conclusion

The statistical tests of causal relationships between the GNP growth rate and the external debt accumulation rate and the computed long-term effects of the GNP growth rate on the external debt accumulation rate indicate that the Bulow-Rogoff proposition, that the external debt of the developing countries are just a symptom of economic slowdown, is rejected in all of the twenty-nine highly indebted countries in Latin America and the Caribbean, Asia and the Pacific, Sub-Saharan Africa, South Europe and the Mediterranean basin. However, the Dornbusch-Krugman proposition that the external debt leads to economic slowdown is not rejected only for 50 per cent of the investigated countries in Latin America and for Sudan. Moreover, among these countries, the long-term effect of the external debt accumulation rate on the GNP growth rate is substantially large (in absolute value) only in the cases of Brazil, Jamaica, Venezuela and Sudan. The results for thirteen countries out of the twenty-nine (44.83 per cent) indicate the existence of a feedback (bi-directional) relationship between the GNP growth rate and the external debt accumulation rate.

In view of these mixed causality-test results, it is inadequate to make any type of generalizations of the potential causal relationships between economic growth and external debt. Thus, in designing a recovery policy for alleviating the external debt burden and promoting economic growth, it is necessary to consider the case of each developing country separately. The recovery policy should be based on the country's interrelationships between its GNP and external debt. It should also incorporate the effects of other intervening macroeconomic variables within a system of simultaneous (recursive) equations whenever a feedback (uni-directional) relationship is found. In order to assess the potential long-term effects of external debt and GNP on each other, the system should incorporate dynamic elements.

Notes

1 The FPE is computed according to the following formula:

$$FPE = [(T + K) / (T - K)]SSR/T$$

where T is the number of observations, K is the number of variables on the right-hand side of the regression equation, and SSR is the sum of square residuals.

2 The S_p is computed according to the following formula:

$$S_p = [SSR/(T - K)] [1 + (K/(T - K - 1))].$$

3 The computation of the long-term effect of x on y (LTE_{xy}) is based on the regression equations selected in the second stage of the causality tests by the FPE of S_p criteria. For example, if the selected equation is of the form:

$$y_t = \sum_{i=1}^{I} a_i y_{t-i} + \sum_{j=1}^{J} \beta_j x_{t-j} + \text{residual}$$

then the long-term effect of x on y is given by

$$LTE_{xy} = \sum_{j=1}^{J} \beta_j / (1 - \sum_{i=1}^{I} a_i).$$

The long-term effect of y on x is computed in an analogous way.

4 The least-squares estimates of the parameters of the second-order polynomial relationship between the estimated long-term rates of growth and debt accumulation and their t-ratios are:

$$g_t = -0.37715 + 0.68453h_t - 0.28859h_t^2 + \text{residual}_t$$
$$(0.196) \quad (1.711) \quad (1.475)$$

$$F = 26.150 \text{ and } R^2 = 0.1204.$$

References

Akaike, H. (1969), 'Fitting Autoregressive Models for Prediction', *Annals of the Institute of Statistical Mathematics*, vol. 21, pp. 243–7.

—— (1970), 'Statistical Predictor Identification', *Annals of the Institute of Statistical Mathematics*, vol. 22, pp. 203–17.

Breiman, L. and Freedman, D. (1983), 'How many Variables Should Be Entered in a Regression Equation', *Journal of the American Statistical Association*, vol. 78, no. 381 (March), pp. 131–6.

Bulow, J. and Rogoff, K. (1990), 'Cleaning up Third World Debt Without Getting Taken to Cleaners', *The Journal of Economic Perspectives*, vol. 4, no. 1 (Winter), pp. 31–42.

Dornbusch, R. (1988), 'Our LDC Debts', in Feldstein, M. (ed.), *The United States in the World Economy*, University of Chicago Press for The National Bureau of Economic Research, Chicago.

Granger, C.W.J. (1969), 'Investigating Causal Relationships by Econometric Models and Cross Spectral Methods', *Econometrica*, vol. 37, pp. 425–35.

Hocking, R.R. (1976), 'The Analysis and Selection of Variables in Linear Regression', *Biometrics*, vol. 32, pp. 1–49.

IBRD (1990), *World Debt Tables 1990–91*, vol. 2, Washington DC.

Kenen, P.B. (1990), 'Organizing Debt Relief: The Need for a New Institution', *The Journal of Economic Perspectives*, vol. 4, no. 1 (Winter), pp. 7–18.

Krugman, P.R. (1989), 'Market-Based Debt-Reduction Schemes', in Frenkel, J.A., Dooley, M.P. and Wickham, P. (eds.), *Analytical Issues in Debt.*, International Monetary Fund, Washington DC.

Sachs, J.D. (1990), 'A Strategy for Efficient Debt Reduction', *The Journal of Economic Perspectives*, vol. 4, no. 1 (Winter), pp. 19–30.

Appendix: Table A.1
Summary of results of Granger causality tests for the twenty-nine countries

Country	Causality from *x* to *y*					Causality from *y* to *x*				
	m*	n*	F computed	F critical 1%	F critical 5%	n*	m*	F computed	F critical 1%	F critical 5%
Latin America & Caribbean										
Argentina	1	6	3.38	5.07	3.09	1	2	2.21	6.36	3.68
Bolivia	7	1	48.61	10.00	4.96	6	1	1.54	9.65	4.84
Brazil	1	7	104.77	5.20	3.14	7	1	31.54	10.00	4.96
Chile	7	1	2072.57	10.00	4.96	5	3	286.70	6.55	3.71
Colombia	1	7	27.71	5.20	3.14	4	4	266.04	5.99	3.48
Costa Rica	1	7	1447.00	5.20	3.14	1	7	468.11	10.00	4.96
Ecuador	1	6	1011.75	5.07	3.09	7	1	3065.96	10.00	4.96
Jamaica	2	5	281.74	5.64	3.33	1	7	126.24	5.20	3.14
Mexico	3	5	2.87	5.64	3.33	7	1	2.68	10.00	4.96
Peru	7	1	10.03	10.00	4.96	1	7	28.62	5.20	3.14
Uruguay	7	1	89.17	10.00	4.96	5	3	96.70	6.55	3.71
Venezuela	1	7	74.55	5.20	3.14	7	1	1.03	10.00	4.96

Asia-Pacific										
India	7	1	1.46	10.00	4.96	1	5	3.68	5.06	3.11
Indonesia	7	1	19.25	10.00	4.96	1	1	1.81	8.13	4.49
Pakistan	3	5	17.40	5.64	3.33	1	6	13.79	5.07	3.09
Philippines	7	1	5.82	10.00	4.96	7	1	25.16	10.00	4.96
South Korea	1	7	18.18	5.20	3.14	7	1	1.90	10.00	4.96
Sub-Saharan Africa										
Cote d'Ivoire	1	1	4.75	8.53	4.49	7	1	5.83	10.00	4.96
Ethiopia	7	1	215.14	10.00	4.96	1	4	2.82	5.21	3.18
Ghana	5	1	6.94	9.33	4.75	7	1	-0.32	10.00	4.96
Kenya	4	4	45.76	5.99	3.48	3	5	281.82	5.64	3.33
Nigeria	4	2	2.61	6.93	3.89	7	1	28.65	10.00	4.96
Sudan	6	2	241.58	7.56	4.10	4	4	5.91	5.99	3.48
Tanzania	2	5	31.25	5.32	3.20	6	2	6.96	7.56	4.10
Zaire	1	6	4.96	5.07	3.09	6	2	3.92	7.56	4.10
South Europe & Mediterranean										
Greece	7	1	0.18	10.00	4.96	1	7	81.27	5.20	3.14
Morocco	6	2	3.13	7.56	4.10	7	1	0.67	10.00	4.96
Portugal	6	1	0.76	9.65	4.84	7	1	-0.49	10.00	4.96
Yugoslavia	7	1	214.78	10.00	4.96	6	1	0.51	9.65	4.84

*Here, m and n denote the number of lags of y and x, respectively.

10 An integrative analysis of external debt, capital accumulation and production in Latin America, Asia-Pacific and Sub-Saharan Africa

Co-authored by Khorshed Chowdhury

This chapter estimates the nexus of inter-relationships between public and private external debts accumulation, capital accumulation and production with panel data for the period 1970–88 from highly indebted developing countries clustered into three distinct regions: Latin-America, Asia-Pacific and Sub-Saharan Africa. The simultaneous equations' estimation results indicate that the full effects of the public and private external debts on GNP are small and of an opposite sign, whereas an increase in the GNP level raises substantially the public and private external debts. These findings support the Bulow-Rogoff proposition that the external debts of developing countries are not a primary cause of economic slowdown.

10.1 Introduction

In order to supplement the study of the cause and effect relationships between GNP and external debt with more structural economic analysis, the present chapter assesses the direct, indirect and full effects of the external debt on GNP, and *vice versa*, by

Reprinted with permission from the *Journal of Economics and Finance*, vol. 17, no. 3 (Fall) 1993, pp. 105–119, with modifications.

estimating a system of simultaneous equations which displays the possible interactions between GNP, capital stock accumulation, public and publicly guaranteed external debt and private external debt accumulation. The simultaneous equation system also incorporates the effects of exogenous and lagged-dependent variables on the aforementioned endogenous variables. It is estimated with panel data for the period 1970–1988 on thirty-six highly indebted developing countries clustered into three distinct regions: Latin-America, Asia-Pacific and Sub-Saharan Africa.

The underlying conceptual framework, estimation procedure and results are given in the following sections. The simultaneous equation system of GNP, capital accumulation, and public and private external debt accumulation is presented in the next section. This is followed by a section that describes the estimation method, data sources and estimation results and a section that discusses and interprets the estimation results. The estimation results highlight the complexity of the interrelationships between GNP, public and publicly guaranteed external debt, private external debt and capital stock. They also indicate the important role of intervening socioeconomic factors, such as industrial structure, terms of trade, population size and income inequality, in the determination of the GNP level and the accumulation of capital and external debts. The chapter is concluded by a brief summary and policy implications.

10.2 Simultaneous equation system of output, capital and external debt accumulation

A country's GNP can affect its external borrowing by increasing imports and consequently the current account deficit. Moreover, by recalling the common practice of using the external debt-GNP ratio as a measure of the external debt burden, the larger the GNP, *ceteris paribus*, the lower the external debt burden, and consequently the smaller the country's financial leverage. Thus, a larger GNP can enhance the availability of external credit and at a lower cost. While the above-mentioned factors tend to increase the country's external liabilities, a larger level of GNP, *ceteris paribus*, can reduce a country's reliance on external sources for satisfying the domestic demand for consumer goods and financing investment in capital stock. Thus, the combined, or full, effect of GNP on the country's external debt can be positive, zero, or negative when the former factors overweigh, equal, or are overweighed by the latter.

In turn, one can also expect a reciprocal relationship as the country's level of indebtedness might affect the GNP level in the following ways. First, the higher the level of indebtedness, and in particular that of the business sector, *ceteris paribus*, the higher the country's leverage, the more limited the external sources of credit and the greater the number of instances of financial distress and liquidation, which, in turn, adversely affect the GNP level directly and indirectly by discouraging domestic investment. Second, as argued by Krugman (1989), Helpman (1989), Dooley and Helpman (1992) and Boyce (1992), an increase in the public and publicly guaranteed external debt might indirectly depress the level of GNP by discouraging capital formation and encouraging capital flight due to tax-increase expectations. However, if a significant portion of external borrowing is directed toward financing efficient investments in productive capital, a positive correlation between a country's GNP level and its external debt can be anticipated.

These relationships are summarized in a system of simultaneous equations of aggregate production, external debt accumulation, and capital accumulation. The proposed system distinguishes between public and publicly guaranteed external debt (EDPUB) and private external debt (EDPRIV), and thus comprises four equations. The system includes state-transition variables — the lags of capital stock, public external debt and private external debts (LCAPITAL, LEDPUB and LEDPRIV) — in order to incorporate the effects of capital depreciation and debt-servicing costs on the accumulation of capital stock (CAPITAL) and the external debt, respectively.

The system also includes some socioeconomic factors, such as the total labour force participating in production (LABOR), the percentage of the country's labour force in agriculture (PLFAG), population (POP) and a measure of income inequality — the income share accruing to the bottom 40 per cent of households (INSH40). Our attempt to incorporate into the analysis additional socioeconomic factors, such as the labour-force school years completed and poverty levels, have failed due to the unavailability of data for many countries for a substantial number of years.

The LABOR and PLFAG are introduced in the aggregate production equation. While LABOR is considered to have an effect on the GNP as a production input, the PLFAG is taken as an indicator of the level of modernization of the production process. It is expected that the higher the percentage of the labour force in agriculture the lower the aggregate product. PLFAG is also introduced in the accumulation equations of capital and public and private external debts as an indicator of the industrial structure of the economy. Thus, PLFAG might also have an indirect effect on GNP through its effect on CAPITAL, EDPUB and EDPRIV.

The socioeconomic variables POP and INSH40 are introduced in the capital-accumulation equation as indicators of the income distribution which, in addition to the GNP, can affect the domestic level of savings. It is hypothesized that, all other things remaining the same, the larger the population the lower the rate of savings and hence the smaller the capital accumulation. In contrast, the effect of INSH40 on capital accumulation is not clear, *a priori*. On the one hand, a higher level of income inequality (i.e., smaller value of INSH40) can lead to a higher propensity to save and consequently to a higher level of savings and investment. On the other hand, social and political dissatisfaction and instability stemming from a substantial degree of income inequality might adversely affect domestic investment and might also lead to a capital flight. Furthermore, social and political dissatisfaction and unrest might reduce a government's ability and commitment to implement unpopular fiscal measures such as subsidy and wage cuts, and the restrictive monetary policies which are necessary for alleviating the external-debt problem. Thus, INSH40 is also introduced in the public and the publicly guaranteed external-debt-accumulation equation.

The external-debt-accumulation equations also incorporate the effects of changes in the country's terms of trade (TOT). It is expected that an increase in TOT reduces the country's external liabilities. Finally, the aggregate-production equation includes the squares of capital and labour (CAPITALSQ and LABORSQ, respectively) in order to assess the properties of the marginal products of these production inputs.

Consistently with the aforementioned arguments, the simultaneous-equation system comprises the following linear equations:

The aggregate production function

$$GNP_{it} = a_o + a_1EDPUB_{it} + a_2EDPRIV_{it} + a_3CAPITAL_{it} + a_4CAPITALSQ_{it} + a_5LABOR_{it} + a_6LABORSQ_{it} + a_7PLFAG_{it} + \varepsilon_{1it}. \quad (1)$$

The capital accumulation equation

$$CAPITAL_{it} = b_o + b_1GNP_{it} + b_2EDPUB_{it} + b_3EDPRIV_{it} + b_4LCAPITAL_{it} + b_5PLFAG_{it} + b_6POP_{it} + b_7INSH40_{it} + \varepsilon_{2it}. \quad (2)$$

The public and publicly guaranteed external debt accumulation equation

$$EDPUB_{it} = c_o + c_1GNP_{it} + c_2LEDPUB_{it} + c_3PLFAG + c_4TOT_{it} + c_5INSH40_{it} + \varepsilon_{3it}. \quad (3)$$

The private external debt accumulation equation

$$EDPRIV_{it} = d_o + d_1GNP_{it} + d_2LEDPRIV_{it} + d_3PLFAG_{it} + d_4TOT_{it} + \varepsilon_{4it}. \quad (4)$$

Here, i and t are country and year indices, respectively; and ε_1, ε_2, ε_3, and ε_4 are random disturbances having zero means and finite variances and covariances.

10.3 Data, estimation method and estimation results

The simultaneous-equation system described above satisfied the order and the rank conditions for identification. It is estimated with annual observations for the period 1970–1988 on thirty-six countries clustered into three distinct regions: Latin America, Asia-Pacific, and Sub-Saharan Africa. The Latin American group comprises eighteen countries: Argentina, Bolivia, Brazil, Chile, Colombia, Costa Rica, Ecuador, El Salvador, Guatemala, Guyana, Honduras, Jamaica, Mexico, Nicaragua, Panama, Paraguay, Peru, and Uruguay. The Asia-Pacific group includes ten countries:

Bangladesh, Fiji, India, Indonesia, Malaysia, Pakistan, Philippines, South Korea, Sri Lanka, and Thailand. The Sub-Saharan African group includes eight countries: Cote D'Ivoire, Gabon, Ghana, Kenya, Nigeria, Sudan, Tanzania, and Zaire. The underlying rationale for clustering the countries into regional groups is as follows. On the one hand, the short time series does not enable a separate estimation of the simultaneous-equation system for each country. On the other hand, pooling all the countries together might lead to meaningless estimation results as substantial structural differences among them are not captured by the included country-specific variables. Since greater geographical affinity may be associated with a higher degree of similarity and may facilitate transfer of both positive and negative externalities between countries, clustering the countries into regional groups can be viewed as a reasonable compromise ensuring a higher likelihood that the observations considered in the econometric analysis are generated by a relatively similar process.

In order to obtain consistent and efficient estimates of the simultaneous-equation system's parameters, the three-stage least squares (3SLS) estimation method is applied to pooled annual observations on countries affiliated to a geographical region. The nominal variables GNP, EDPUB and EDPRIV are extracted from the *World Tables*, 1989–90 Edition, and from the *World Debt Tables 1990–91*. They are deflated by the US GNP deflator, and expressed in millions of 1980 US dollars. Correspondingly, the terms of trade index (TOT) is taken with 1980 as the base year (that is, 1980=100) and as reported in the *World Tables 1989–90*. The capital stock is also taken in millions of 1980 US dollars. Since this variable is not observed, it was approximated by using the gross domestic investment figures obtained from the *World Tables 1989–90* and a constant annual depreciation rate (0.1), as explained in the Appendix. Our sensitivity analyses reveal that the estimation results are not substantially changed when the depreciation rate is allowed to vary between 0.05 and 0.20. The population figures are also obtained from the *World Tables 1989–90* and presented in millions. The rest of the variables, including LABOR, PLFAG and INSH40, are extracted from the *Social Indicators of Development 1990*. LABOR is taken as the product of the total labour force and the overall participation rate, and is presented in millions. PLFAG and INSH40 are presented as percentages.

The estimation results of the simultaneous-equation system are summarized by region in Tables 10.1, 10.2 and 10.3 for Latin America, Asia Pacific, and Sub-Saharan Africa, respectively.

10.4 Interpretation of the estimation results

The empirical findings indicated by Tables 10.1–10.3 are as follows.

The effect of GNP on the public and private external debts

In the cases of Latin America, Asia Pacific and Sub-Saharan Africa, the GNP raises both the public and private external debts. An increase of 1 per cent in the GNP is likely to increase the public and publicly guaranteed external debt by 0.469, 0.415 and 1.450 per cent and the private external debt by 0.293, 0.072 and 0.269 per cent in the cases of Latin America, Asia-Pacific and Sub-Saharan Africa, respectively.

The effect of the public external debt on GNP

In the case of Latin America, the direct effect of the public and publicly guaranteed external debt on GNP is negative. Note, however, that in contrast to the capital-flight argument, the indirect effect of the public and publicly guaranteed external debt on GNP through increasing the capital stock is positive and larger in absolute terms than the direct effect. Thus, in the case of Latin America, the full effect of the public external debt on GNP is positive but small: an increase of 1 per cent in the public external debt is likely to increase the GNP by 0.158 per cent. Note, further, that the positive estimates of the indirect effects of the public external debt on GNP obtained in the cases of Asia-Pacific and Sub-Saharan Africa also indicate that the capital flight generated by tax-increase expectations is smaller than the contribution of the public external borrowing in financing investments in capital stock. Moreover, in these cases the direct effects, and hence the full effects, of the public external debt on GNP are positive and substantially larger than in the Latin American case: an increase of 1 per cent in

Table 10.1
3SLS estimation results for Latin-America*

Explanatory Variables	GNP	CAPITAL	EDPUB	EDPRIV
	Dependent variables			
Endogenous				
GNP	—	2.0084 (10.302)	0.1214 (14.824)	0.0216 (7.4589)
CAPITAL	0.7360 (11.6950)	—	—	—
EDPUB	-1.2378 (6.8979)	2.5063 (12.419)	—	—
EDPRIV	1.5378 (3.4459)	-4.4637 (3.8420)	—	—
Predetermined				
LEDPUB	—	—	0.5539 (18.441)	—
LEDPRIV	—	—	—	0.7035 (18.368)
LCAPITAL	—	0.0167 (1.1538)	—	—
LABOR	341.86 (0.2662)	—	—	—
CAPITALSQ	-5.0E-07 (2.5993)	—	—	—
LABORSQ	141.690 (2.0748)	—	—	—
PLFAG	-36.733 (0.6188)	254.60 (2.1152)	-48.680 (2.0577)	-2.9730 (0.5771)
TOT	—	—	-71.354 (7.3833)	0.3478 (0.1689)
POP	—	-914.67 (4.1129)	—	—
INSH40	—	162.89 (1.1382)	79.930 (0.8523)	—
CONSTANT	957.90 (0.3804)	-10754.0 (2.0596)	8101.1 (4.3728)	63.044 (0.2013)

* The t-ratios are indicated in the parentheses.

Table 10.2
3SLS estimation results for Asia-Pacific*

Explanatory Variables	GNP	CAPITAL	EDPUB	EDPRIV
	Dependent variables			
Endogenous				
GNP	—	3.1169 (6.2610)	0.0934 (11.337)	0.0021 (2.4975)
CAPITAL	0.2843 (3.7229)	—	—	—
EDPUB	0.5631 (2.6877)	1.7683 (2.4012)	—	—
EDPRIV	3.2594 (3.3068)	-15.3880 (2.3682)	—	—
Predetermined				
LEDPUB	—	—	0.4868 (11.503)	—
LEDPRIV	—	—	—	0.8509 (29.858)
LCAPITAL	—	0.0666 (1.2640)	—	—
LABOR	376.99 (1.0745)	—	—	—
CAPITALSQ	-2.0E-07 (1.1691)	—	—	—
LABORSQ	3.449 (1.1956)	—	—	—
PLFAG	-18.593 (0.1736)	575.22 (1.7242)	-86.805 (4.4611)	-8.1243 (2.6694)
TOT	—	—	-18.092 (2.1666)	2.4253 (1.9263)
POP	—	-358.61 (3.1891)	—	—
INSH40	—	-1316.30 (1.2954)	318.800 (4.0055)	—
CONSTANT	2506.60 (0.4026)	-18298.0 (1.2074)	2594.9 (1.8580)	809.690 (4.0133)

* The t-ratios are indicated in the parentheses.

Table 10.3
3SLS estimation results for Sub-Saharan Africa*

Explanatory Variables	GNP	CAPITAL	EDPUB	EDPRIV
	Dependent variables			
Endogenous				
GNP	—	2.0988	0.7081	0.0152
		(5.5768)	(9.1134)	(2.0527)
CAPITAL	0.5367	—	—	—
	(1.1383)			
EDPUB	0.2774	0.8488	—	—
	(1.6489)	(1.7509)		
EDPRIV	-1.1606	1.6235	—	—
	(2.8061)	(2.0683)		
Predetermined				
LEDPUB	—	—	0.1820	—
			(4.2212)	
LEDPRIV	—	—	—	1.0733
				(42.906)
LCAPITAL	—	0.0466	—	—
		(1.8074)		
LABOR	1970.10	—	—	—
	(6.0952)			
CAPITALSQ	-2.0E-05	—	—	—
	(0.7865)			
LABORSQ	-220.550	—	—	—
	(4.3492)			
PLFAG	-196.940	468.25	-25.905	-3.1608
	(3.8539)	(3.8132)	(1.4070)	(1.7688)
TOT	—	—	-20.586	-0.8684
			(4.2421)	(1.8442)
POP	—	-441.26	—	—
		(3.7055)		
ISNH40	—	-398.57	-10.850	—
		(4.0788)	(0.3209)	
CONSTANT	13649.00	-28881.0	2611.4	267.360
	(2.7586)	(2.7487)	(1.7175)	(1.7704)

*** The t-ratios are indicated in the parentheses.**

the public external debt is likely to directly and indirectly raise the GNP level by 0.240 per cent in the case of Asia-Pacific and by 0.358 per cent in the case of Sub-Saharan Africa.

The effect of the private external debt on the GNP

In the cases of Latin America and Asia Pacific, the direct effect of the private external debt on GNP is positive. However, in both cases the adverse indirect effects of the private external debt on GNP through lowering private investment and the overall level of capital stock are large in absolute value and substantially exceed the direct effects. Thus, the full effects of the private external debt on GNP are negative: an increase of 1 per cent in the private external debt is likely to reduce the GNP level by 0.129 per cent in the case of Latin America and by 0.033 per cent in the case of Asia Pacific. In the case of Sub-Saharan Africa, the direct effect of the private external debt on GNP is negative, whereas the indirect effect is positive. In this case, the direct effect dominates the indirect effect and hence the full effect of private external debt on GNP is also negative: an increase of 1 per cent in the private external debt is likely to reduce the GNP level by 0.016 per cent.

The effect of GNP and public and private external debt on capital stock

The GNP has a positive direct effect on the stock of capital in Latin America, Asia-Pacific and Sub-Saharan Africa. Moreover, in recalling the aforementioned positive effects of GNP on the public and private external debts, the effect of GNP on capital stock is indirectly amplified by the positive effect of the public external debt on capital stock in all of the three regions; but, excluding the case of Sub-Saharan Africa, it is indirectly moderated by the negative effect of the private external debt on capital stock. In the case of Sub-Saharan Africa, the positive effect of the private external debt on capital stock reinforces the positive effect of GNP on capital accumulation. In all of the three regions, the full effect of GNP on capital accumulation is positive and exceeds the direct effect.

The effect of capital on GNP

The marginal product of capital is significantly positive in the cases of Latin America and Asia-Pacific: an increase of 1 per cent in the capital stock is likely to raise the GNP level by 1.289 per cent in the case of Latin America and by 0.539 in the case of Asia-Pacific. The estimates associated with CAPITALSQ indicate further that these marginal products are diminishing. In the case of Sub-Saharan Africa, the marginal product of capital is positive but statistically insignificant. Also, in this case the marginal product of capital is found to be diminishing.

The effect of labour on GNP

Only in Sub-Saharan Africa was the marginal product of labour found to be significantly positive: an increase of 1 per cent in the labour force participating in production is likely to increase the GNP level by 0.941 per cent. In this case, the estimate associated with LABSQ indicates further that the marginal product of labour is diminishing. In the cases of Latin America and Asia-Pacific, the marginal product of labour is positive but statistically insignificant.

The effects of the lags of the public and private external debts

The motion equations of the public and the private external debts are expected to have positive state-transition parameters (c_2 and d_2) which are equal to one plus the accumulation rate of the public or the private external debt, respectively. The accumulation rates indicate the difference between the average real interest rate actually charged and the share of the forgiven debt. The estimates of these state-transition parameters are significantly positive in all cases, but, excluding the case of the private external debt of Sub-Saharan Africa, smaller than one. Thus, they indicate that, in all of the three regions, the shares of public and private external debts forgiven exceed the real interest rates actually charged on these debts, and/or that the contracted real interest rates are negative. In the case of the public external debt, the estimated coefficients reveal that in general Sub-Saharan African countries enjoyed better debt-repayment arrangements than the Asian-Pacific and Latin American countries, and that the Asia-Pacific countries enjoyed better debt-repayment terms than the Latin American countries. This result might reveal the more forgiving attitude of the official creditors toward the lower income countries. It is worth mentioning that in all cases the estimates of the state-transition parameters of the private external debt are substantially greater than those of the public debts and indicate, perhaps, the stricter repayment terms of credit extended to private firms. This finding can be explained by the following arguments: 1. the private sector is significantly more indebted to commercial banks than the public sector, 2. unlike the private external debt, the public external debt is a sovereign debt which can be repudiated and hence the bargaining position of a government is better than that of private debtors, and 3. debt discounts stem in part from altruism mixed with an awareness of equity considerations, and hence it is more likely that debt discounts would be directed toward relieving the public external debt burden. The estimation results indicate that the worst conditions on repaying a private external debt have been imposed on Sub-Saharan African countries where the average real interest rate actually charged is about 7.33 per cent per annum. The Asia-Pacific countries enjoyed a significant degree of forgiveness and/or negative real interest rate (about 0.15 per cent) and the Latin American countries enjoyed a more substantial private external debt relief (about 30 per cent).

The effect of the lag of capital stock

The state-transition parameter of the capital-stock's motion equation (b_4) is inversely related to the annual depreciation rate of capital. Thus, the estimated low values of these parameters can be seen as indicators of very high rates of capital depreciation in all three regions.

The effect of the industrial structure on GNP, capital stock and public and private external debts accumulation

The fact that the directions (i.e., signs) of the estimates associated with the industrial structure variable PLFAG are identical for the three investigated regions indicates the universality of the direct effects of the industrial structure on GNP, capital and public and private external debts accumulation. The estimated direct effects indicate that the greater the percentage of the labour force employed in agriculture : 1. the lower the GNP level (this result is statistically significant only for Sub-Saharan Africa), 2. the greater the accumulation of capital stock, 3. the smaller the accumulation of public and publicly guaranteed external debt, and 4. the smaller the accumulation of private external debt.

The effect of the terms of trade

In all three cases, it is found that the higher the value of the terms of trade index the lower the public and publicly guaranteed external debt. For Sub-Saharan Africa, it was also found that the private external debt decreases with the terms of trade. However, in Asia-Pacific, the private external debt increases with the terms of trade. The ineffectiveness of the increase in the terms of trade in reducing the private external debt is also evident in the case of Latin America.

The effect of population and income inequality on the accumulation of capital stock

As expected, in all the regions the accumulation of capital stock is adversely affected by the size of the population. The underlying rationale is that, *ceteris paribus*, the larger the population the smaller the share of income allocated to saving. The effect of income inequality on capital accumulation is statistically significant only for Sub-Saharan Africa, where a larger income share accruing to the bottom 40 per cent of households is associated with a lower level of capital accumulation. This result probably illustrates the aforementioned positive relationship between income inequality and the propensity to save. A similar result is obtained for Asia-Pacific, but it was not found to be statistically significant at the 5-per-cent level. In contrast, an opposite, but statistically insignificant, result is found for Latin America. In view of the very high degree of income inequality prevailing in the Latin American countries, the adverse effect of any further deterioration of income distribution on investment through an increase in social and political instability will exceed the potential increase in domestic savings.

The effect of income inequality on the accumulation of public external debt

Income inequality might intensify feelings of relative deprivation and hence increase social and political tension (Sen, 1973; Yitzhaki,

1979). This, in turn, reduces the government's commitment and ability to implement drastic measures such as subsidy and wage cuts and the strict monetary and fiscal policy necessary for restoring efficiency in resource allocation, curbing the inflation and improving the terms of trade, and subsequently reducing the country's external-debt burden. However, it is not clear, *a priori*, whether income inequality is positively associated with public external debt. In certain cases, wage and subsidy cuts aimed at reducing the current account deficit might come at the expense of a further deterioration in the level of income inequality. The estimation results are quite diversified in that respect. Sub-Saharan Africa shows a negative, but statistically insignificant, relation between the public external debt and the income share accruing to the bottom 40 per cent of the households, whereas in Asia-Pacific and Latin America, a positive (though insignificant in the case of Latin America) relation is found.

10.5 Summary and conclusion

To supplement the controversy about the cause and effect relationships between GNP and external debt in developing countries with empirical evidences, this study estimated the mutual direct and indirect effects of these variables within a simultaneous-equation framework.

With regard to the aforementioned controversy, the estimates of the simultaneous-equation system indicate that the full (direct plus indirect) effect of GNP on public and private external debts is positive: an increase of 1 per cent in the GNP level is expected to raise the public and publicly guaranteed external debt level by 0.469, 0.415 and 1.450 per cent and the private external-debt level by 0.293, 0.072 and 0.269 per cent in Latin-America, Asia-Pacific and Sub-Saharan Africa, respectively. In contrast to Kenen and Sachs' assertion, it is found that the effects of the public and private external debts on the GNP level in those regions is small: a 1 per cent rise in the public and the publicly guaranteed external debt level is likely to increase the GNP level by 0.158, 0.240 and 0.358 per cent in Latin-America, Asia-Pacific and Sub-Saharan Africa, respectively; whereas a rise of 1 per cent in the private external debt is expected to reduce the GNP level by only 0.129, 0.033 and 0.016

per cent in the cases of Latin America, Asia-Pacific and Sub-Saharan Africa, respectively. These magnitudes and the directions of the estimated elasticities lend support to the first half of Bulow-Rogoff's claim that the external debts of the developing countries are not a primary cause of economic slowdown and that there is no urgent need to establish an international institution for organizing debt-relief and debt-rescheduling negotiation between indebted developing countries and their private creditors. Moreover, the estimation results indicate that an economic slowdown (that is, a decrease in the GNP level) is accompanied by lower external liabilities on behalf of the developing countries.

The other findings of the chapter are as follows. The GNP has a positive direct effect on the stock of capital in Latin America, Asia-Pacific and Sub-Saharan Africa. Moreover, the effect of GNP on capital stock is indirectly amplified by the positive effect of the public external debt on capital stock in these regions; but, excluding Sub-Saharan Africa, it is indirectly moderated by the negative effect of the private external debt on capital stock. In the case of Sub-Saharan Africa, the positive effect of the private external debt on capital stock reinforces the positive effect of GNP on capital accumulation. In all of the three regions, the full effect of GNP on capital accumulation is positive.

In general, Sub-Saharan African countries enjoyed better terms for repaying their public and publicly guaranteed external debt than the Asian-Pacific and Latin-American countries; and the Asia-Pacific countries enjoyed better debt repayment terms than the Latin-American countries. However, this order is reversed when examining the private external debt: the toughest repayment terms have been imposed on Sub-Saharan African countries, whereas the Asia-Pacific countries enjoyed a significant degree of forgiveness and/or negative real interest rate, and the Latin-American countries enjoyed the most substantial private external-debt relief.

It is found that the greater the percentage of the labour force employed in agriculture, the lower the GNP level, the greater the accumulation of capital stock, the smaller the accumulation of public and publicly guaranteed external debt, and the smaller the accumulation of private external debt. In all of the three investigated regions, a negative association is found between the public and the publicly guaranteed external debt and the terms of trade. In Sub-Saharan Africa, the private external debt decreases with the terms of trade. However, the private external debt increases with the terms of trade in Asia-Pacific. The ineffectiveness of the terms of trade in reducing the private external debt is also evident in Latin-America. This ineffectiveness might be a reflection of the continuous and severe deterioration in the terms of trade caused by the very high rates of inflation that had prevailed in many of the Latin-American countries during the observed period. It also may indicate that price stabilization is a pre-requisite for an improvement in the current account.

Finally, a negative, but statistically insignificant, association between the public external debt and the income share accruing to the bottom 40 per cent of the households is found for Sub-Saharan Africa, whereas in Asia-Pacific and Latin America a positive (though insignificant in the case of Latin America) association is found. The statistically insignificant association between the public external debt and income inequality in Latin America might be explained by the severity of income inequality in that region and hence the insufficiency of small changes in income inequality levels to alter the problematic social and political situation which hampers the commitment of governments in that region to deal effectively with their external-debt problem. In contrast, in the Asia-Pacific region, where income is substantially more equally distributed and populist policy is less dominant, it is evident that an improvement in the public external-debt problem occurs at the expense of equality in the distribution of income.

References

Boyce, J. K. (1992), 'The Revolving Door? External Debt and Capital Flight: A Philippine Case Study', *World Development*, vol. 20, no. 3, pp. 335–49.

Dooley, M.P. and Helpman, E. (1992), 'Tax Credits for Debt Reduction', *Journal of International Economics*, vol. 32, pp. 165–77.

Helpman, E. (1989), 'Voluntary Debt Reduction: Incentives and Welfare', in Frenkel, J.A., Dooley, M. and Wickham, P. (eds.),

Analytical Issues in Debt, International Monetary Fund, Washington DC, pp. 279–310.

IBRD (1990), *World Debt Tables 1990–91*, vol. 2, Washington DC.

—— (1990), *World Tables 1989–90*, Washington DC.

—— (1990), *Social Indicators of Development 1990*, Washington DC.

Krugman, P.R. (1989), 'Market-Based Debt-Reduction Schemes', in Frenkel, Jacob A., Dooley, Michael and Wickham, Peter (eds.), *Analytical Issues in Debt*, International Monetary Fund, Washington DC, pp. 258–78.

Sen, A. (1973), *On Economic Inequality*, Clarendon Press, Oxford.

Yitzhaki, S. (1979), 'Relative Deprivation and the Gini Co-efficient', *Quarterly Journal of Economics*, vol. 93, pp. 321–4.

Appendix

Reproduction of the capital stock's time-series

In order to reproduce the unobserved capital stock's time-series from the documented gross investment (I) time-series, it is assumed that the motion equation of capital stock is given by

$$K_t = I_t + (1-\delta)K_{t-1} \qquad \text{(A.1)}$$

where δ denotes a constant annual depreciation rate. Of course, if the initial capital stock (K_o) were known, the time-series of capital stock could be easily computed for a predetermined value of δ by virtue of equation A.1. In the absence of such information, the following procedure was used to assess K_o. By assuming further that

$$K_t = K_o g^t \qquad \text{(A.2)}$$

and then substituting A.2 into A.1 for K_t and K_{t-1} we obtained

$$K_o = \frac{I_t}{g^{t-1}\,[g - (1 - \delta)]} \qquad (A.3)$$

where g is equal to 1 plus the unknown accumulation rate of capital stock. By recalling that A.3 holds for t as well as for t-1

$$\frac{I_t}{g^{t-1}} = \frac{I_{t-1}}{g^{t-2}} \qquad (A.4)$$

and hence

$$g = \frac{I_t}{I_{t-1}}\,. \qquad (A.5)$$

Since different values of *g* are likely to be obtained for any arbitrary choice of two consecutive values of *I*, we considered the sample average of the right-hand side of A.5, which is an unbiased estimator of *g*:

$$g = \frac{1}{T}\sum_{t=1}^{T} \frac{I_t}{I_{t-1}}\,. \qquad (A.6)$$

We substituted t=1 into A.3 to obtain

$$K_o = \frac{I_1}{g - (1 - \delta)} \qquad (A.7)$$

and computed K_o for each country with the first (1970) observed value of gross investment, the estimated value of *g* from A.6, and a predetermined value of δ. Subsequently, we substituted the computed initial capital stock in A.1 to find the projected level of capital stock for the following year; and by subsequent substitutions, the time-series of capital stock was produced.

11 An analysis of the potential externalities affecting the borrowing behaviour of developing countries

This chapter deals with the externalities associated with the individual developing country's cost of credit and borrowing level. As long as the supply curve of credit is positively sloped, the interest rate charged on credit extended to a particular developing country is affected by the aggregate borrowing level of the rest of the countries. Moreover, the relatively high level of indebtedness of big developing countries and their problems to service their external debts, might adversely affect the reputation of the developing countries as a whole and reduce their financial credibility. In addition, the individual country's information about the borrowing of the other debtor countries is not perfect and hence it perceives the interest rate on loans taken as a random variable and might suffer from substantial costs of risk bearing.

11.1 Introduction

The interest rate charged on an individual developing country's liabilities might reflect its financial position in the credit market. However, there might be other factors, that are external to the individual developing country, affecting the cost of credit and providing further explanation for the rapid growth of the country's level of indebtedness. As long as the supply curve of credit is positively sloped, the interest rate charged on credit extended to a

---

Reprinted, in part, with permission from *Australian Economic Papers* vol. 31, no. 58, June 1992, 164–176.

country should be affected by the aggregate borrowing level of the rest of the countries. Moreover, the relatively high level of indebtedness of large developing countries, such as Brazil and Mexico in Latin America and Nigeria and Zaire in Sub-Saharan Africa, and their difficulties in servicing their external debts, might adversely affect the reputation of the developing countries as a whole and reduce their financial credibility.

The purpose of this chapter is to explore, test, and quantify the effects of the aforementioned external factors on the cost of credit for the individual developing country and its level of borrowing. The assessment of the role of these external factors is carried out in the following sections. Section 11.2 takes into account credit-supply's considerations, and estimates the external effects of the regions' level of indebtedness and borrowing on the interest rate charged on credit extended to each individual country.

Furthermore, since the individual country does not have full information about the borrowing of its counterpart debtors, it perceives the interest rate on loans taken as a random variable, and hence might suffer from substantial costs of risk bearing. Section 11.3 analyses the implications of this type of externality, as well as the implications of the aforementioned externalities associated with the cost of credit, on the borrowing behaviour of developing countries within the context of a stochastic framework, in which countries borrowing large amounts of money behave like Stackelberg leaders. That is, they maximize expected utility from consumption subject to their resource constraint while taking into account the reaction of the following smaller borrowing countries. The parameters of the resultant Stackelberg equilibrium borrowing equations for leading and following developing countries are estimated for each region, and the existence of external effects on their borrowing behaviour is tested in Section 11.4.

Finally, a conceptual framework of a jointly co-ordinated credit system, which takes into account global welfare considerations as well as the individual country's welfare, and which is capable of moderating the potential adverse effects of the aforementioned externalities, is outlined in Section 11.5.

11.2 Externalities, credit supply's considerations, and the estimation of the interest rate equation

Under the assumption that a greater geographical affinity tends to facilitate the transfer of both positive and negative externalities between countries, it is reasonable to hypothesize that the cost of credit for any country might be directly related to the current borrowing and initial levels of indebtedness of the group of countries with which it is associated, as well as to its own current borrowing and initial level of indebtedness. There are two ways by which developing countries belonging to a common regional group inflict such external effects on one another:

1. Given that the credit supply curve is positively sloped, the greater the group's aggregate borrowing, the higher the cost of credit to the individual country.
2. The greater the indebtedness level of the rest of the countries, the greater their incentive to repudiate and hence the lower the expected debt repayment. The decline in the group's overall credibility leads creditors to charge higher interest rates on new loans extended to the country in order to accommodate the excessive risk.

In view of the aforementioned externalities and credit supply's considerations, it is suggested that the average interest rate (r) charged on the i-th country's borrowing at period *t* can be expressed in mathematical notations by the following ad-hoc equation:

$$r_{it} = r_1 D_{i\,t-1} + r_2 \frac{1}{N-1} \sum_{j \neq i}^{N} D_{j\,t-1} + r_3 B_{it} + r_4 \sum_{j \neq i}^{N} B_{jt} \qquad (1)$$

where, j = 1,...,N denotes the countries belonging to the regional group which the i-th country is affiliated to; D_{it-1} and D_{jt-1} are the i-th and the j-th countries' external debts at the end of the previous period, respectively; B_{it} is the i-th country's borrowing at period *t*; B_{jt} is the j-th country's borrowing at period *t*; and r_1,r_2,r_3, and r_4 are parameters representing the effects of these factors, respectively, on the i-th country's anticipation of the average cost of its new borrowing.

The purpose of this section is to estimate the unknown parameters of equation 1 in order to provide a preliminary assessment of the external effect of the regional reference group's aggregate level of indebtedness and borrowing on the cost of credit for the individual country member. The estimation of the interest rate equation is carried out with annual observations on countries listed in Table 11.1 and classified in the aforementioned regional groups for the period 1975–1986. All of the explanatory variables are expressed in millions of 1985 US dollars. The estimation results are summarized in Table 11.1. An alternative specification of the interest-rate equation, in which the debt-output ratios of the regional group and the individual country replace the respective absolute levels of debts, leads to significantly less satisfactory estimation results.

Table 11.1
The estimated interest rate equation's coefficients for Latin America, Sub-Saharan Africa and Asia-Pacific*

Explanatory variables	*Estimated parameters for three reference groups* Latin America	Sub-Saharan Africa	Asia -Pacific
D_i	0.9991398E-06 (6.579)	0.4317022E-05 (5.476)	0.1771181E-06 (0.764)
$\frac{1}{N-1}\sum_{j\neq 1}^{N} D_j$	0.2764420E-06 (14.038)	0.6253893E-06 (10.898)	0.5774115E-06 (15.470)
B_i	-0.8877093E-06 (0.784)	-0.490653OE-05 (1.954)	0.3498145-05 (1.474)
$\sum_{j\neq 1}^{N} B_j$	0.4149293E-06 (2.405)	-0.2749078E-06 (0.657)	0.2003761E-06 (0.498)
R^2	0.250	0.017	0.022
F-test	293.201	138.354	121.854
d.f.	260	314	122

* The t-ratios are indicated in parentheses.

As indicated by the F-test values, the estimation results of the interest rate equation's parameters as a whole are statistically significant for the three regional groups of developing countries. Most particularly, the t-ratios show that for all of the three regional groups the initial level of indebtedness of a country as well as the initial level of indebtedness of the regional group to which the country is affiliated have, as expected, significant positive effects on the interest rate on that country's current borrowing. Only in the case of Asia-Pacific this effect of the individual country's level of indebtedness is statistically insignificant. Moreover, in the case of Asia-Pacific, the effect of an infinitesimal increase in the affiliation group's level of indebtedness on the interest rate on the individual country's liabilities exceeds the effect of an infinitesimal increase in that country's own liabilities. If the likelihood of repudiation rises with the level of indebtedness, these findings imply that an increase in the level of indebtedness of a country and/or in the level of indebtedness of the rest of the countries affiliated to the same regional group reduce that country's reputation in the credit market and hence raise the cost of its current borrowing.

A further indication of negative external effects among countries belonging to a regional group is that in the case of Latin America the aggregate current borrowing level of the rest of the countries significantly increases the cost of credit for the individual country member. The existence of this source of external effect was rejected in the cases of Sub-Saharan Africa and Asia-Pacific. A possible explanation to this variation in the estimation results is that, due to their low levels of per-capita income, a major part of the Sub-Saharan and Asia-Pacific countries' credit is provided by non-profit international funds, whereas the medium-income countries of Latin America rely more heavily on credit supplied by commercial banks. This distinction may also explain the significantly negative effect of the country's current borrowing on the interest rate for Sub-Saharan countries.

The existence of structural differences in the credit supply across the three regional groups is indicated further by Chow tests. These tests check how well each of the three regional groups' credit-supply equation conforms to the other two groups' credit-supply schedule under various sets of restrictions embedded in the null hypothesis of no structural changes including: (1) the whole set of the credit-supply equation's coefficients is not different for the three regional groups, (2) the coefficient associated with the individual country's initial level of indebtedness and current level of borrowing are not different for the three regional groups, and (3) the coefficients associated with the aggregate initial level of indebtedness and aggregate current level of borrowing of the rest of the countries affiliated to the same regional group are not different for the three regional groups. The computed values of the corresponding F-test statistics are presented in Table 11.2 below. These values indicate that the three versions of the null hypothesis of no structural differences in the credit supply schedule across the three regional groups are rejected at the 5 per cent level of confidence.

Table 11.2
Tests of structural differences in the credit supply equations across regional groups

Null hypothesis	*F-test statistics when the unrestricted regression analysis excludes* Latin America	Sub-Saharan Africa	Asia-Pacific
Version 1	34.315	25.341	11.078
Version 2	3.132	6.367	4.198
Version 3	56.290	15.044	18.242

11.3 Uncertainty, risk aversion, and the borrowing behaviour of LDCs in a Stackelberg equilibrium

While the previous section's ad-hoc analysis of the supply of credit lends support to the hypothesis that the greater the reference group's aggregate borrowing and level of indebtedness, the higher the cost of credit to the individual country; this section considers the implications of these external factors with a broader and more elaborate framework that also takes into account credit-demand's considerations. In this framework, each individual country maximizes expected utility from consumption and investment and takes into account the external effect inflicted by the rest of the countries' financial position and borrowing behaviour on its consumption possibilities. Moreover, it is assumed that the individual country does not have full information about the borrowing of its counterpart debtor countries. Instead, it perceives the interest rate on loans taken during the present period as a random variable, and thus might suffer from substantial costs of risk bearing.

The following analysis is based on the assumption that the i-th country forms its expectations about the interest rate (r_{it}^e) rationally by incorporating the credit-supply's considerations according to equation 1 and its assessment of the borrowing level of the rest of the countries. It is postulated that the i-th country's borrowing at *t* is chosen to maximize the country's (or the representative agent's) expected utility from private consumption and investment and government spending (C) subject to its perceived resource constraint:

$$C_{it} = \alpha_i B_{it} y_{it} + NIM_{it} - RPM_{it} - IPL_{it} - r_{it}^e B_{it}. \qquad (2)$$

In this formulation y_i denotes the average productivity of a borrowed dollar directed to a production activity, and α_i is the proportion of the borrowing abroad directed to financing domestic production activities. The rest, $(1 - \alpha_i)B_{it}$, helps in financing the net import of consumption and investment goods (NIM), repayments of principal that matured (RPM), interest payments on liabilities accumulated previously (IPL) and on current borrowing.

The model refers to two sub-groups of countries in a given reference group distinguished by the scale of their borrowing abroad — the big borrowers vis-a-vis the smaller borrowers. In which case it seems reasonable to say that the sub-group of the big borrowers is behaving as a leader (L) in a Stackelberg setting and the sub-group of the smaller borrowers is behaving as a follower (F). The Stackelberg equilibrium is found by computing the follower's reaction to a given borrowing level of the leader. This reaction is incorporated, in turn, into the leader's decision about the optimal borrowing level.

The computation of the follower's reaction function assumes that the follower does not have full information about the leader's borrowing level, but that the follower's expectations about the leader's borrowing level are unbiased and normally distributed with finite variances σ^2_{Lt}:

$$B_{Lt}^e \sim N(B_{Lt}, \sigma^2_{Lt}). \quad (3)$$

This assumption and equations 1 and 2 imply that the follower's private and public consumption and investment (C_{Ft}) is normally distributed with mean and variance equal to:

$$E(C_{Ft}) = \alpha_F B_{Ft} y_{Ft} + NIM_{Ft} - RPM_{Ft} - IPL_{Ft}$$
$$- [r_1 D_{Ft-1} + r_2 D_{Lt-1} + r_3 B_{Ft} + r_4 B_{Lt}]B_{Ft} \quad (4)$$

$$VAR(C_{Ft}) = r_4^2 \sigma_{Lt}^2 B_{Ft}^2 . \quad (5)$$

Assuming for tractability that the follower's preferences over C_{Ft} can be represented by a negative exponential utility function reflecting constant absolute risk aversion, the follower's current borrowing is found by maximizing the difference between the mean of C_{Ft} and the costs of risk-bearing that are equal to half the product of the variance of C_{Ft} and the follower's degree of absolute risk aversion (R_F):

$$\max_{B_{Ft}} [E(C_{Ft}) - 0.5R_F \, VAR\,(C_{Ft})] \quad (6)$$

(See Freund, 1956, for a rigorous development of the mean-variance expected utility function, and Hammond, 1974, Meyer, 1987, and Hlawitschka, 1994, for a discussion of the generality and suitability of this framework.)

The first-order condition for maximum implies that the expected increase in the Follower's private and public consumption and investment from an additional dollar borrowed abroad (i.e., the marginal product of credit minus the marginal interest payment on credit) is offset by the rise in its costs of risk bearing stemming from the uncertainty about the leader's borrowing level :

$$\alpha_F y_{Ft} - [r_1 D_{Ft-1} + r_2 D_{Lt-1} + 2r_3 B_{Ft} + r_4 B_{Lt}] = R_F r_4^2 \sigma_{Lt}^2 B_{Ft}. \qquad (7)$$

The second-order condition for maximum

$$-2r_3 - R_F r_4^2 \sigma_{Lt}^2 < 0 \qquad (8)$$

is satisfied as long as the marginal costs of credit for the follower are increasing.

The necessary condition for maximum implies that the reaction of the follower's borrowing to the leader's borrowing is given by:

$$B_{Ft} = \beta(\alpha_F y_F - r_1 D_{Ft-1} - r_2 D_{Lt-1} - r_4 B_{Lt}) \qquad (9)$$

where

$$\beta = 1/(2r_3 + R_F r_4{}^2 \sigma_{Lt}^2) \qquad (10)$$

is by the second-order condition for maximum a positive term. Equations 9 and 10 imply that for any given leader's borrowing level, the follower's demand for credit is equal to the difference between the marginal product of a dollar borrowed abroad and the marginal cost stemming from the follower's and leader's initial levels of indebtedness and the leader's current borrowing, divided by twice the marginal cost stemming from the follower's own borrowing and risk bearing.

The computation of the leader's borrowing level assumes that the leader maximizes utility from private and public consumption and investment subject to the follower's reaction function specified above. Given that the parameters of the follower's reaction function and the follower's initial level of indebtedness are known to the leader, the leader's costs of risk bearing are nil. This implies in turn that, in view of the mean-variance expected utility specification and equations 1, 2 and 9, the leader's decision problem can be rendered as:

$$\max_{B_{Lt}} \{\alpha_L B_{Lt} y_{Lt} + MIN_{Lt} - RPM_{Lt} - IPL_{Lt}$$

$$- [r_1 D_{Lt-1} + r_2 D_{Ft-1} + r_3 B_{Lt} + r_4 \beta(\alpha_F y_{Ft}$$

$$- r_1 D_{Ft-1} - r_2 D_{Lt-1} - r_4 B_{Lt})] B_{Lt}\}. \quad (11)$$

The resultant necessary condition for maximum implies that the leader's borrowing in a Stackelberg equilibrium (B_{Lt}*) is given by:

$$B_{Lt}^* = \gamma[(\alpha_L y_{Lt} - r_4 \beta\alpha_F y_{Ft}) - (r_1 - r_2 r_4\beta) D_{Lt-1} - (r_2 - r_1 r_4\beta) D_{Ft-1}] \quad (12)$$

where

$$\gamma = 1/(2r_3 - 2r_4^2\beta). \quad (13)$$

Correspondingly, the follower's borrowing level in a Stackelberg equilibrium (B_{Ft}*) is found by substituting equation 12 for B_{Lt} in equation 9:

$$B_{Ft}^* = \beta(1 - r_4^2\beta\gamma)\alpha_F y_{Ft} - r_4 \beta\gamma\alpha_L y_{Lt} - \beta[(r_1 - r_2 r_4 \gamma$$

$$+ r_1 r_4^2 \beta\gamma)] D_{Ft-1} - \beta[(r_2 - r_1 r_4 \gamma + r_2 r_4^2 \beta\gamma)] D_{Lt-1} \quad (14)$$

Equations 12 and 14 imply the following propositions about the leading and following sub-groups' borrowing behaviour in a Stackelberg equilibrium.

Proposition 1: (the effect of D_{Lt-1} on B_{Lt})*

$$\frac{dB_{Lt}^*}{dD_{Lt-1}} \gtreqless 0$$

$$\text{as } \frac{r_1}{r_2} \lesseqgtr \frac{r_4}{2r_3 + R_F r_4^2 \sigma_{Lt}^2}.$$

Proposition 1 implies that the likelihood that the leader's initial debt level deters its borrowing at present:

a. rises with the follower's costs of risk bearing stemming from the uncertainty about the leader's borrowing at present ($R_F \sigma_{Lt}^2$),

b. rises with the effect of the leader's initial debt level on the interest rate charged on its own borrowing at present (r_1), and
c. declines with the effect of the follower's initial debt level on the interest rate charged on the leader's borrowing at present (r2) through a decline in the credibility of the reference group to which the leader and the follower are affiliated.

Proposition 2: (the effect of D_{Ft-1} on B_{Lt})*

$$\frac{dB_{Lt}^*}{dD_{Ft-1}} \gtreqless 0$$

$$\text{as} \quad \frac{r_2}{r_1} \lesseqgtr \frac{r_4}{2r_3 + R_F r_4^2 \sigma_{Lt}^2}.$$

Proposition 2 implies that the likelihood that the follower's initial debt level deters the leader's borrowing at present:

a. rises with the follower's costs of risk bearing stemming from the uncertainty about the leader's borrowing at present ($R_F \sigma_{Lt}^2$),
b. declines with the effect of the leader's initial debt level on the interest rate charged on its own borrowing at present (r_1), and
c. rises with the effect of the follower's initial debt level on the interest rate charged on the leader's borrowing at present (r_2) through a decline in the credibility of the reference group to which the leader and the follower are affiliated.

Proposition 3: (the effect of D_{Ft-1} on B_{Ft})* If $\gamma > 0$, then

$$\frac{dB_{Ft}^*}{dD_{Ft-1}} \gtreqless 0$$

$$\text{as} \quad \frac{r_2}{r_1} \gtreqless \frac{r_4(1-2r_4)}{2r_3 + R_F r_4^2 \sigma_{Lt}^2} + \frac{2r_3}{r_4}.$$

(A proof is provided in the Appendix.)

Proposition 3 implies that, given that $\gamma > 0$, the likelihood that the follower's initial debt level deters its borrowing at present:

a. declines with the follower's costs of risk bearing stemming from the uncertainty about the leader's borrowing at present ($R_F\sigma_{Lt}^2$), as long as $r_4<0.5$,
b. rises with the effect of the follower's initial debt level on the interest rate charged on its own borrowing at present (r_1), and
c. declines with the effect of the leader's initial debt level on the interest rate charged on the follower's borrowing at present (r_2) through a decline in the credibility of the reference group to which the leader and the follower are affiliated.

Proposition 4: (the effect of D_{Lt-1} on B_{Ft})* If $\gamma > 0$, then

$$\frac{dB_{Ft}^*}{dD_{Lt-1}} \gtreqless 0$$

as $\frac{r_1}{r_2} \gtreqless \frac{r_4(1-2r_4)}{2r_3 + R_F r_4^2 \sigma_{Lt}^2} + \frac{2r_3}{r_4}$.

Proposition 4 implies that, given that $\gamma>0$, the likelihood that the leader's initial debt level deters the follower's borrowing at present:

a. declines with the follower's costs of risk bearing stemming from the uncertainty about the leader's borrowing at present ($R_F\sigma_{Lt}^2$), as long as $r_4<0.5$,

b. declines with the effect of the follower's initial debt level on the interest rate on its own borrowing at present (r_1), and

c. rises with the effect of the leader's initial debt level on the interest rate charged on the follower's borrowing at present (r_2) through a decline in the credibility of the reference group to which the leader and the follower are affiliated.

Propositions 1 to 4 indicate that the leader's and follower's initial levels of indebtedness affect the leader's and follower's current borrowing levels in several ways and directions, and hence their total effects are not clear *a priori*. It is important to note that if $\gamma<0$, the inequalities indicated by propositions 3 and 4 are reversed.

However, equations 10 and 13 indicate that the greater the followers' degree of absolute risk aversion and level of uncertainty about the leaders borrowing level, the greater the likelihood that γ is positive.

11.4 Leaders and followers' estimated borrowing equations

The leaders and followers' borrowing equations developed above are estimated in this section in order to quantify and test further the hypothesized financial interdependencies between developing countries affiliated to a common reference group summarized by propositions 1 to 4. The estimation utilizes annual observations on the external debts and borrowing of developing countries in millions of US dollars at 1985 prices for the period 1975 to 1986. The countries included in the empirical analysis are classified according to regional affiliation into three general groups — Latin America, Sub-Saharan Africa and Asia-Pacific. The leaders in each of the regional groups are identified by their outstanding high level of annual borrowing: Brazil and Mexico in Latin America; Nigeria, Sudan, and Zaire in Sub-Saharan Africa; and India and Indonesia in Asia-Pacific. The rest of the countries are classified as followers. The estimation is performed with annual observations on the aggregate borrowing and initial indebtedness levels of the two types of countries in each of the regional groups. The estimation results are obtained by the Cochrane-Orcutt iterative procedure that minimizes the sum of squares of the transformed residuals, and are summarized in Table 11.3.

In general, the estimation results of the leaders and followers' borrowing equations are statistically significant in the cases of Latin America and Asia-Pacific, but are not significant in the case of Sub-Saharan Africa. The lack of statistically significant estimation results in the latter case is probably due to the fact that most of the credit extended to the Sub-Saharan countries was from non-profit international funds. The significant findings are as follows.

While the effect of the leading countries' absolute initial level of indebtedness on their current annual borrowing is significantly positive in the case of Latin America, it is significantly negative in

Table 11.3
The estimated borrowing equations' coefficients for leaders and followers in Latin America, Sub-Saharan Africa and Asia-Pacific 1975–86*

Explanatory variables	Latin America	Sub-Saharan Africa	Asia-Pacific
	Leaders' Borrowing Equation		
constant	463.5705 (0.124)	-999.55998 (0.402)	19341.38 (2.602)
The leaders' aggregate level of indebtedness (D_L)	0.7994862 (3.361)	-0.06111733 (0.281)	-0.5722540 (2.412)
The followers ' aggregate level of indebtedness (D_F)	0.6445407 (1.549)	0.1729466 (0.738)	0.1653956 (1.748)
R^2	0.964	0.163	0.319
F-test statistic	681.6729	4.970476	2.926900
Durbin-Watson test statistic	1.736	1.596	1.955
	Followers' Borrowing Equation		
constant	23272.287 (4.031)	3089.440 (0.847)	31261.98 (2.354)
The leaders' aggregate level of indebtedness (D_L)	-0.1244822 (2.895)	0.1127531 (0.390)	-0.8408428 (2.294)
The followers' aggregate level of indebtedness (D_F)	0.2554852 (3.494)	-0.1365340 (0.420)	0.1941243 (1.274)
R^2	0.461	0.135	0.226
F-test statistic	51.54835	2.508637	2.356048
Durbin-Watson test statistic	2.035	1.884	2.188

* The t-ratios are indicated in the parentheses.

the case of Asia-Pacific and deterring further borrowing. Recalling proposition 1, these findings might indicate that while the underlying factor 'c' dominates factors 'a' and 'b' in the former case, the underlying factors 'a' and 'b' dominate factor 'c' in the latter.

In both the Latin American and Asia-Pacific cases the effect of the following countries aggregate initial level of indebtedness on the leading countries borrowing is significantly positive. In view of proposition 2, this finding might indicate that the underlying factor 'b' dominates the underlying factors 'a' and 'c'.

In contrast, in both the Latin American and the Asia-Pacific cases the leading countries' aggregate level of indebtedness significantly deter the following countries' aggregate borrowing. Recalling proposition 4, this finding might indicate that the underlying factor 'c' dominates factors 'a' and 'b'.

In both the Latin American and the Asia-Pacific cases the following countries initial aggregate level of indebtedness does not deter their current borrowing. Moreover, in the case of Latin America, the following countries level of borrowing significantly increases with their initial level of indebtedness. In view of proposition 3, this finding might indicate that the underlying factors 'a' and 'c' dominate factor 'b'.

11.5 Global welfare considerations and a jointly coordinated credit system

The adverse effects of the externalities described and assessed in the previous sections on the global welfare level of the developing countries can be moderated by a jointly coordinated borrowing. The general framework of a jointly coordinated borrowing is based on the maximization of a Bergson-Samuelson global welfare function defined on the individual countries' utilities from consumption, where each country's consumption possibilities depend upon its borrowing level, and where the global borrowing level is constrained:

$$\max_{B_{1t},\ldots,B_{Nt}} W[U^1(C_{1t}),\ldots,U^N(C_{Nt})] \tag{15}$$

subject to

$$C_{it} = \alpha_i B_{it} y_{it} + NIM_{it} - RPM_{it} - IPL_{it}$$

$$- [r_1 D_{it-1} + r_2 \frac{1}{N-1} \sum_{j \neq 1}^{N} D_{jt-1} + r_3 B_{it} + r_4 \sum_{j \neq i}^{N} B_{jt}] B_{it} \quad (16)$$

for every i = 1,...,N, and

$$\sum_{j=1}^{N} B_{jt} = \bar{B}. \quad (17)$$

The necessary condition for maximum global welfare implies

$$\frac{\partial W}{\partial U^i} \frac{\partial U^i}{\partial C_i} [\alpha_i y_i - (r_i + r_3 B_i)] = \mu \quad (18)$$

for every country i = 1,...,N; where μ is the shadow value of the global credit constraint.

As can be seen from the necessary condition for maximum, such a coordinated credit system leads to the following globally desired properties:

1. The net marginal benefits from extending credit to either country i = 1,...,N (i.e., the marginal product of credit minus the marginal factor cost of credit) are the same in terms of global welfare units.
2. The uncertainty about the borrowing levels of the rest of the countries and the accompanying costs of risk bearing for the individual country are eliminated.

Although from a global welfare perspective there is a need for a higher degree of co-ordination in order to moderate the adverse effects of the externalities existing in the credit market and the segmentation of this market, the design and application of such co-ordination is very difficult. The Bergson-Samuelson welfare function is nothing but a very general way to describe global welfare and hence it is not much use in deciding what kind of ethical judgement might be reasonable in allocating credit to developing countries. This problem is, of course, the major obstacle in establishing a jointly co-ordinated credit system.

11.6 Conclusion

This chapter was concerned with the potential transfer of externalities among highly indebted developing countries that might affect the cost of credit to the individual debtor country. These externalities stem from the 'free-rider' problem characteristic to price pooling. That is, as long as the supply curve of credit is positively sloped, the interest rate charged on credit extended to a particular country is affected by the aggregate borrowing level of the rest of the countries. Moreover, the relatively high level of indebtedness of big developing countries and their difficulties in servicing their external debts, might adversely affect the reputation of the developing countries as a whole and reduce their financial credibility. The estimation of the interest rate equations lent support to the significant role of these externalities in explaining the cost of credit to individual countries in the three distinct developing regions of Latin America, Sub-Saharan Africa, and Asia-Pacific.

This chapter considered further the external effect on the individual country's cost of credit imposed by uncertainty about the rest of the countries' borrowing behaviour. Since the individual country does not have full information about the borrowing of its counterparts debtors, it perceives the interest rate on loans taken during the present period as a random variable, and hence might suffer from substantial costs of risk bearing. The implications of this type of externality on the borrowing behaviour of developing countries were analysed within the context of a stochastic Stackelberg-type model, in which big-borrowing countries maximizes expected utility from consumption subject to their resource constraint while taking into account the reaction of the following smaller borrowing countries. The estimation results of the derived borrowing equations were found to be statistically significant in the cases of Latin America and Asia-Pacific. The empirical findings indicate that in the Latin American and Asia-Pacific cases the initial levels of indebtedness of the relatively small-borrowing countries raise the borrowing levels of the big-borrowing countries. In contrast, the small-borrowing countries demand for credit is deterred by the big-borrowing countries initial level of indebtedness. In terms of the conceptual model, this decline in the demand for credit by small-borrowing countries corresponds to the rise in the interest rate stemming from the adverse effect of the big-borrowing countries' initial level of indebtedness on the credibility of the regional group as a whole. It is also aimed at lowering the small-borrowing countries costs of risk bearing generated by the uncertainty about the big-borrowing countries demand for credit. This empirically indicated asymmetry reveals the role that the externalities embedded in the international credit market play to the disadvantage of the small-borrowing developing countries.

Appendix

Proof of Proposition 3

The differentiation of equation 14 with respect to D_{Ft-1} implies

$$\frac{dB_{Ft}^*}{dD_{Ft-1}} = -\beta(r_1 - r_2r_4\gamma + r_1r_4^2\beta\gamma) \gtreqless 0$$

as $r_4^2\,\beta\gamma - r_2r_4\,\gamma/r_1 \lesseqgtr -1$. And given that $\gamma>0$,

$$\frac{dB_{Ft}^*}{dD_{Ft-1}} \gtreqless 0 \text{ as } r_4(r_2/r_1 - r_4\beta) \gtreqless 1/\beta.$$

By substituting equations 10 and 13 for β and γ, respectively

$$\frac{dB_{Ft}^*}{dD_{Ft-1}} \gtreqless 0$$

as $\frac{r_2}{r_1} \gtreqless \frac{r_4(1-2r_4)}{2r_3 + R_Fr_4^2\sigma_{Lt}^2} + \frac{2r_3}{r_4}$. *QED*

Proof of Proposition 4

The differentiation of equation 14 with respect to D_{Lt-1} implies

$$\frac{dB_{Ft}^*}{dD_{Lt-1}} = -\beta(r_2 - r_1r_4\gamma + r_2r^2{}_4\beta\gamma) \gtreqless 0$$

as $r_4^2\beta\gamma - r_1 r_4\gamma/r_2 \gtreqless -1$.

Given that $\gamma>0$,

$$\frac{dB_{Ft}^*}{dD_{Lt-1}} \gtreqless 0$$

as $r_4\,(r_1/r_2 - r_4\beta) \gtreqless 1/\beta$.

By substitution equations 10 and 13 for β and γ, respectively,

$$\frac{dB_{Ft}^*}{dD_{Lt-1}} \gtreqless 0$$

as $\dfrac{r_1}{r_2} \gtreqless \dfrac{r_4(1-2r^2{}_4)}{2r_3 + R_F r^2{}_4 \sigma_{Lt}{}^2} + \dfrac{2r_3}{r_4}$. *QED*

References

Freund, R.J. (1956), 'An Introduction to Risk into a Risk-Programming Model', *Econometrica*, vol. 24, pp. 253–63.

Hammond, S. (1974), 'Simplification of Choice under Uncertainty', *Management Science*, vol. 20.

Hlawitschka, W. (1994), 'The Empirical Nature of Taylor-Series Approximations to Expected Utility', *American Economic Review*, vol. 84, pp. 713–9.

Meyer, J. (1987), 'Two-Moment Decision Models and Expected Utility Maximization', *American Economic Review*, vol. 77.

12 Repudiation, retaliation and the secondary market price of sovereign debts

This chapter is concerned with the relationship between the secondary-market price of sovereign debts and the possibility of repudiation and retaliation. Using the distinction between 'good' and 'bad' states of world, the indebted countries optimal repudiation rate as well as the creditor's optimal retaliation and reservation price for any repudiation rate are analyzed under the assumption that the debtor and creditor are risk averse and expected-utility maximizers. Matching both debtor and creditor's considerations, the chapter analyzes the Cournot-Nash equilibrium repudiation and retaliation rates and the secondary market price of a sovereign debt.

12.1 Introduction

A country's external debt is a sovereign debt. Hence, a rise in a country's level of indebtedness increases its incentive to repudiate (Kenen, 1990). The secondary market for sovereign debts has been a mechanism for alleviating countries' external-debt burden and increasing the expected debt repayments. In this market, an indebted country expects to buy back its debt at a discount, reflecting the creditors' belief that the country will not meet its external obligations fully. In this respect, Berg and Sachs (1988), who fitted a tobit model to developing countries' debt discounts, have concluded that higher income inequality leads to a greater discount, while higher outward orientation, agricultural share, and GNP per capita squared tend to decrease the secondary market discount. Other market-based debt-reduction schemes have been discussed by Krugman (1989) and non-market-based debt-relief arrangements by Sachs (1989).

The simplest conceptual approach for explaining the secondary prices of sovereign debts is based on the notion of the *Debt-Laffer Curve* (Krugman, 1988) and the distinction between 'good' and 'bad' states of world implying that the sovereign debt repayment has the following binomial distribution:

$$DR = \begin{cases} D & 1-p \\ (1-r)D & p \end{cases} \qquad (1)$$

where,

D = the book value of the sovereign debt,

p = the probability of a 'bad' state of world, and

r = the rate of repudiation.

Consequently, that approach suggests that the price of a sovereign external debt (P) in the secondary market can be approximated by the ratio of the expected debt repayment to the book value of the debt:

$$P = \frac{E(DR)}{D} = 1 - rp. \qquad (2)$$

That is, the discount on a dollar of debt is equal to the repudiation rate times the probability of a 'bad' state of world in which the country's revenues are too small for servicing its external liabilities.

The drawbacks of the approach described above are that it does not provide an explanation for the rate of repudiation and does not take into account creditors' retaliation as well as risk aversion of both the indebted sovereign and creditor. The purpose of this chapter is to provide a conceptual analysis of the relationship between the secondary-market price of sovereign debt and the possibility of repudiation and retaliation under the assumption that both creditor and debtor are risk averse, maximize expected utility and take each other's reaction into account. The analysis assumes that the creditor's retaliation is limited to seizing the debtor's assets abroad and restrained from escalation to a trade warfare. It also assumes that the indebted country is relatively small and facing competitive foreign lenders so that the creditor and debtor should not be viewed as being engaged in an implicit reputation contract. As has been argued by Bulow and Rogoff (1989):

> [a] good reputation for repaying foreign loans does not enhance a small country's ability to borrow abroad. As long as the country faces competitive foreign investors, then any service provided by the current lender can equally well be provided by a new investor. (p. 47)

Using the distinction between 'good' and 'bad' states of world, the creditor's optimal retaliation and reservation price for any repudiation rate as well as the indebted country's optimal repudiation rate for any level of retaliation are analyzed in the following sections. The Cournot-Nash equilibrium repudiation and retaliation rates and the secondary market price of sovereign debts are found subsequently by matching both debtor's and creditor's considerations under the assumption of symmetric information about the state of the world.

12.2 The creditor's optimal seizure rate for a given repudiation rate

The formulation of the creditor's behaviour is based on the belief that in a 'good' state of world the indebted country enjoys relatively high revenues and is able to repay its liabilities; whereas in a 'bad' state of world the indebted country's revenues are moderate and consequently it repudiates part or all of its external debts. Using this distinction between 'good' and 'bad' states of world, the returns for the creditor, y, are perceived to have the following distribution:

$$y = \begin{cases} D & 1 - p \\ (1 - r)D + sA & p \end{cases} \tag{3}$$

where,

A = the indebted country's assets abroad (e.g., public assets on which the sovereign has a direct control, such as embassies and consulates, and private assets on which the sovereign has only an indirect control);

p = the creditor's assessment of probability of a 'bad' state of world;

r = the creditor's assessment of the indebted country's repudiation rate; and

s = the share of the debtor's assets holding abroad seized by the creditor.

Given that the creditor's subjective distribution of returns is as displayed by equation 3, the mean and variance of y are perceived by the creditor to be:

$$E(y) = (1 - rp)\,D + psA \tag{4}$$

and

$$\begin{aligned} var(y) &= (1 - p)D^2 + p[(1 - r)\,D + sA]^2 - [(1 - rp)D + psA]^2 \\ &= p\,(1 - p)\,[r^2 D^2 - 2rsAD + s^2A^2]. \end{aligned} \tag{5}$$

It is postulated that the creditor's preferences over the random returns can be represented by the mean-variance expected utility function:

$$E[u\,(y)] = E(y) - 0.5R_c var\,(y) \tag{6}$$

where R_c denotes the creditor's degree of absolute risk aversion.

(See Hlawitschka, 1994, for a recent discussion of the generality and suitability of this framework.)

The substitution of equations 4 and 5 into equation 6 implies that the creditor's expected utility from the debt-repayment and seizure of the sovereign's assets can be rendered as:

$$E[u(y)] = (1 - rp)D + psA - 0.5R_c\, p(1 - p)[r^2D^2 - 2rsAD + s^2A^2]. \tag{7}$$

Note that by delaying the decision about the retaliation level on future repudiation until realization of the state of the world, the creditor is running a risk of losing a collateral once a 'bad' state of world is realized, as such a delay might give the indebted country and its citizens an opportunity to liquidate and repatriate their assets abroad. Therefore, it is optimal for the creditor to chose the seizure rate in advance so as to maximize the above expected utility. This choice is made subject to the collateral constraint that $s \leq 1$.

The Kuhn-Tucker conditions for maximum constrained-expected utility from debt repayment and seizure of the indebted country's foreign assets are

$$pA + R_c\, p(1 - p)(rAD - sA^2) - \Gamma \leq 0 \tag{8a}$$

$$s[pA + R_c\, p(1 - p)(rAD - sA^2) - \Gamma] = 0 \tag{8b}$$

$$s \leq 1 \tag{8c}$$

$$\Gamma \geq 0 \tag{8d}$$

where Γ is the Lagrange multiplier representing the shadow value of the collateral constraint.

These conditions imply that the optimal seizure rate is given by

$$s^* = \begin{cases} [(1 - p)R_cA]^{-1} + (D/A)r & \text{if } \Gamma = 0 \quad (9a) \\ 1 & \text{if } \Gamma > 0\,. \quad (9b) \end{cases}$$

When the collateral constraint is not binding (i.e., A is relatively large in comparison to D and hence $\Gamma=0$), the creditor's best policy is to adopt a 'tit for tat' rule by which the seizure rate is smaller than unity and linearly increases with the perceived debtor's repudiation rate proportionally to the debtor's effective leverage (D/A). In this case, the optimal seizure rate also rises with the creditor's subjective probability of default, and declines with the creditor's degree of absolute risk aversion. Obviously, when the collateral constraint is binding, the creditor's best policy is a complete seizure of the indebted country's assets abroad.

12.3 Creditor's secondary market reservation price for a given repudiation rate

The creditor's reservation price (P_c) of recycling the indebted country's debt can now be found by substituting the optimal seizure rate into equation 7 and dividing the resultant expected utility by the debt level.

When the collateral constraint (i.e., A>D), the creditor's reservation price of recycling the indebted country's debt is

$$P_c = 1 + \left[(1 - \frac{D}{A^2})r + \frac{0.5}{(1\text{-}p)R_cD} \right] p. \tag{10}$$

Here, the creditor enjoys a retaliatory edge over the indebted country and hence his reservation price is greater than one and rises with the debtor's asset holding abroad, the perceived probability of default and the repudiation rate. However, the creditor's reservation price of the sovereign bonds is lowered by the creditor's degree of risk aversion and the sovereign's debt level.

It is more likely that the indebted country's foreign assets are significantly smaller than its external liabilities. In which case, the collateral constraint is binding and the creditor's reservation price is found by substituting a unit seizure rate in the creditor's expected utility and dividing the resultant by D:

$$P_c = 1 - \{r + 0.5R_c\,(1 - p)\,[r^2 - 2rA/D + (A/D)^2]D - A/D\}p \tag{11}$$

where A/D can be interpreted as the inverse of the indebted country's effective leverage. Note that in this case,

$$\frac{\partial P_c}{\partial \frac{A}{D}} = \{1 - 0.5R_c(1\text{-}p)\left[\frac{A}{D} - r \right]\}p. \tag{12}$$

Consequently, as long as A/D is larger than the repudiation rate perceived by the creditor, an increase in the effective leverage raises the creditor's reservation price of the sovereign external bonds proportionally to his degree of risk aversion and perception of the probability of default. Furthermore, in this case P_c declines with the perceived repudiation rate (r) as long as

$$r - A/D < 1/R_c\,(1 - p). \tag{13}$$

That is, the likelihood that a rise in the perceived repudiation rate reduces the creditor's reservation price declines with the indebted country's effective leverage and the creditor's assessment of the probability of 'bad' state of world, but increases with the creditor's degree of absolute risk aversion.

12.4 The indebted country's optimal repudiation rate

The indebted country's decision problem is postulated as setting the repudiation rate as to maximize expected utility from the returns on domestic assets and asset holding abroad, taking into account, on the one hand, that loan repayments reduce the consumption and investment budget; but on the other hand, that in the case of a default, the creditor retaliates by seizing part or all of the asset holding abroad. The analysis of the indebted country's behaviour is also based on the distinction between 'good' and 'bad' states of world. In a 'good' state of world the indebted country enjoys relatively high revenues and can repay its liabilities; whereas in a 'bad' state of world the indebted country's revenues are moderate and consequently it cannot repay its external debt fully. It is assumed that the creditor provides signals about the potential retaliation for any level of repudiation. These signals enable the indebted country to assess accurately the seizure rate function $0 \leq s(r) \leq 1$. It is also assumed that the rates of return on domestic assets and asset holding abroad are identical.

In this setting the distribution of the indebted country's consumption and investment budget, x, is given by

$$x = \begin{cases} (K + A)v - D & 1 - p \\ [K + (1 - s(r))A]\delta v - (1 - r)D & p \end{cases} \tag{14}$$

where,

K = the indebted country's domestic assets;

p = the debtor's assessment of the probability of a 'bad' state of world;

v = the rate of return on assets under a 'good' state of world; and

δ = the ratio of the indebted country's revenues under a 'bad' state of world to those attainable under a 'good' state of world ($0 < \delta < 1$).

The distribution of x implies that the mean and variance of the indebted country's consumption and investment budget are

$$E(X) = [(K + A)v - D]\,(1 - p) + \{[K + (1 - s\,(r))\,A]\,\delta v - (1 - r)\,D\}p \qquad (15)$$

and

$$var(x) = E(x^2) - (E(x))^2$$

$$= (1 - p)\,[(K + A)v - D]^2 + p\{[K + (1 - s\,(r))\,A]\,\delta v - (1 - r)\,D\}^2$$

$$+ \{[K + A)v - D]\,(1 - p) + \{(K + (1 - s\,(r))\,A)\,\delta v - (1 - r)D]p\}^2. \qquad (16)$$

Suppose that the indebted country's preferences on consumption and investment can be represented by the following mean-variance expected utility function:

$$E[u\,(X)\,] = E(X) - 0.5R_d\,var(X) \qquad (17)$$

where R_d is the indebted sovereign's degree of absolute risk aversion. Then, by substituting equations 15 and 16 into equation 17, the indebted country's decision problem can be rendered as

Maximizing $\{[(K + A)\, v - D]\,(1 - p) + \{[K + (1 - s\,(r))\, A]\, \delta v - (1 - r)\, D\}p$

$$-0.5R_d\, \{(1 - p)\, [(K + A)\, v - D]^2 + p\{[K + (1 - s(r))A]\, \delta v - (1 - r)\, D\}^2$$

$$+ \{[(K + A)\, v - D](1 - p) + \{(K + (1 - s\,(r))\, A)\, \delta v - (1 - r)\, D]p\}^2\}.$$

with respect to r and subject to the repudiation constraint

$$r \leq 1. \tag{18}$$

The Khun-Tucker conditions for maximum expected utility from consumption and investment are:

$$p[D - s'\,(r)\, \delta vA]\{1 - R_d\, [(K + (1 - s\,(r))A)\delta v - (1 - r)D]\,(1 + p)$$

$$- R_d\, [(K + A)v - D](1 - p)\} - \mu \leq 0 \tag{19a}$$

$$r\{p\, [D - s'\,(r)\, \delta vA]\{1 - R_d\, [(K + (1 - s(r))A)\delta v - (1 - r)D]\,(1 + p)$$

$$- R_d\, [(K + A)\, v - D]\,(1 - p)\} - \mu\} = 0 \tag{19b}$$

$$r \leq 1 \tag{19c}$$

$$\mu \geq 0 \tag{19d}$$

where μ is the Lagrange multiplier representing the shadow price of the repudiation constraint.

Suppose now that the indebted country's asset holding abroad is sizeable and/or the returns on these assets are sufficiently large, and the penalty for repudiation is perceived to increase substantially with the repudiation rate so that the indebted country refrains from practising a complete repudiation and repays a part of its loans (i.e., $\mu=0$ and hence $r<1$). Under this assumption, the optimal repudiation rate from the indebted country's perspectives should obey the following equality:

$$1 - R_d\, \{[(K + (1 - s\,(r))A)\delta v - (1 - r)D](1 + p)$$

$$- [(K + A)\, v - D](1 - p)\} = 0. \tag{20}$$

That is, a change in the costs of risk bearing stemming from an infinitesimal increase in the repudiation rate should be offset by the change in the expected consumption and investment.

12.5 Equilibrium rate of repudiation and the secondary market price

When the collateral constraint is binding and the probability of a 'bad' state of world is perceived by the creditor to be high, the creditor exercises a complete seizure of the indebted country's asset holding abroad before these assets would be liquidated by the indebted sovereign. In turn, it is optimal for the indebted country to repudiate fully its external debt, and consequently, by virtue of equation 11, the value of the sovereign external bonds in the secondary-market is smaller than one as indicated by the following expression:

$$P^* = 1 - \{1 + 0.5R_c\,(1 - p)\,[1 - 2A/D + (A/D)^2]D - A/D\}p. \qquad (21)$$

Note that since in this case $A/D<1$, an increase in A/D would raise the price of the sovereign external bonds in the secondary market. This effect is amplified by the creditor's degree of absolute risk aversion.

In contrast, in the less likely case where the indebted country's asset-holding abroad is sufficiently large so that the collateral constraint is not binding, the Cournot-Nash equilibrium secondary-market price of the sovereign external bonds is greater than one. Under the assumption that the indebted sovereign and the creditor have identical assessment of the distribution of the state of the world (i.e., p) and that they fully know each other's considerations, this equilibrium price can be found as follows. First, the substitution of the optimal seizure rate indicated by equation 9a into the debtor's optimality condition 20 implies that in equilibrium the debtor's optimal repudiation rate is:

$$r^* = \frac{[(1-p) - (1+p)\delta]v(K+A) + 2pD + \dfrac{(1+p)\,\delta v}{(1-p)R_c} + \dfrac{1}{R_d}}{(1-dv)(1+p)D} \qquad (22)$$

Subsequently, the substitution of r^* into equation 10 gives the equilibrium price of the sovereign external bonds in the secondary market:

$$P^* = 1 + \frac{0.5p}{(1-p)R_cD} + (1 - \frac{D}{A^2})pr^* \tag{23}$$

Equations 22 and 23 indicate that the effect of the probability of a 'bad' state of world on both the equilibrium repudiation rate and secondary-market price is not clear and straightforward as suggested by equation 2. These equations lead to the following propositions:

i. If $\delta < \frac{1-p}{1+p}$ (i.e., the ratio of rate of return on assets in a 'bad' state of world to that in a 'good' state of world is sufficiently small), the larger the sovereign domestic assets and asset-holding abroad the higher the equilibrium rate of repudiation and the secondary market price.

ii. If $\delta < \frac{1-p}{1+p}$, the higher the rate of return on the sovereign assets in a 'good' state of world the higher the equilibrium rate of repudiation and the secondary market price.

iii. The higher the creditor's and debtor's degree of absolute risk aversion the lower the equilibrium repudiation rate and secondary-market price of the sovereign external bonds.

References

Berg, A. and Sachs, J. (1988), 'The Debt Crisis: Structural Explanation of Country Performance', *Journal of Development Economics,* vol. 29, pp. 271–306.

Bulow, J. and Rogoff, K. (1989), 'Sovereign Debt: Is to Forgive to Forget?', *American Economic Review,* vol. 79, no. 1, pp. 43–50.

Hlawitschka, W. (1994), 'The Empirical Nature of Taylor-Series Approximations to Expected Utility', *American Economic Review,* vol. 84 (June), pp. 713–9.

Kenen, P.B. (1990), 'Organizing Debt Relief: The Need for a New Institution', *Journal of Economic Perspectives,* vol. 4, pp. 7–18.

Krugman, P.R. (1988), 'Financing vs. Forgiving a Debt Overhang', *Journal of Development Economics*, vol. 29, pp. 253–68.

—— (1989), 'Market-Based Debt-Reduction Schemes,' in Frenkel, J.A., Dooley, M.P. and Wickham, P. (eds.), *Analytical Issues in Debt*, International Monetary Fund, Washington DC.

Sachs, J. (1989), 'Conditionality, Debt Relief, and the Developing Country Debt Crisis', in Sachs, J. (ed.), *Developing Country Debt and Economic Performance*, University of Chicago Press, Chicago.

13 Repudiation, seizure and reputation within a game theoretic framework

The strategic interaction between a creditor and a sovereign debtor is analyzed as a 'one-shot' game with common knowledge where each player chooses an action as to maximize his expected payoff given his beliefs about the other player's action and the implications of those actions on the players' trustworthy reputation.

13.1 Introduction

As indicated in the previous chapter, a country's public external debt is a sovereign one and hence is not subject to bankruptcy law. However, repudiation of this debt might be costly. Creditors (in particular, official creditors such as lending governments or a syndicate of such lenders) might respond by seizing the indebted country's asset holding abroad (e.g., embassies, consulates, real properties and other investment assets owned by the indebted country's government and citizens). Other responses, such as trade sanctions, are possible but more difficult to enforce. Their implications will be analyzed in the next chapter. As in the previous chapter, the indebted sovereign and the creditor are assumed to decide on their repudiation and seizure strategies simultaneously. Unlike the previous chapter, in which partial repudiation and seizure were possible outcomes, the strategies available to the indebted sovereign in the game considered hereafter are either complete repayment of the debt or total repudiation; and the strategies available to the creditor are either complete seizure of the indebted country's asset holding abroad or no seizure of any of these assets. In view of the severe implications of strategies such as debt repudiation or asset seizure on the continuation of the relationship between the parties involved, it is reasonable to analyze the interaction between a particular indebted sovereign and a particular creditor within the framework of a 'one-shot game' rather than a repeated one. However, the description of the payoffs for each of the players takes into account the adverse effects of playing non-cooperatively and the benefits from playing cooperatively on future interactions of the creditor and the indebted sovereign with different players. This is done by rewarding the player who acted cooperatively while his counterpart was defecting with reputation gains and subjecting the defecting player to a loss of reputation, as suggested by Eaton and Gersovitz (1981), Kletzer (1984), and Grossman and Van Huyck (1988), to mention a few. For instance, in a case of repudiation the losses for the creditor from not seizing the indebted country's assets abroad when he could do so are moderated by the gain of trustworthy reputation from acting cooperatively and non-aggressively toward the indebted country, which may improve his bargaining power in the international credit market. In such a case, the unprovoked defaulting debtor is likely to suffer from a loss of trustworthy reputation. Similarly, seizure of an indebted country's asset holding abroad when the indebted country repays its debt can adversely affect the trustworthy reputation of a creditor while enhancing the trustworthy reputation of the 'innocent' debtor who was acting cooperatively.

The analysis of the strategic interaction between a creditor and an indebted country is organized in the following manner. Section 13.2 describes the strategy combinations available to the indebted sovereign and the creditor, the payoffs associated with these strategies and the criteria of choosing among them. The Nash-equilibrium solution to these problems in mixed strategies and in pure strategies are presented and discussed in sections 13.3 and 13.4, respectively. Section 13.5 extends the analysis of the interaction between the creditor and the indebted country to the case of two-way seizure of asset holding abroad. Section 13.6 concludes the chapter.

13.2 Description of the game and the players' decision problems

Using the notations from the previous chapter and denoting the reputation gains (*RG*) and reputation losses (*RL*) for the indebted country by RG_d and RL_d, and those for the creditor by RG_c and RL_c, the possible strategy combinations available to the indebted sovereign and the creditor and the associated payoffs are as summarized in Table 13.1. In each cell of this table, the entry on the left-hand side describes the payoff for the creditor whereas that on the right-hand side represents the payoff for the indebted sovereign country. A special feature of this payoff matrix is that when both players act cooperatively (i.e., repaying and not seizing), or non-cooperatively, there are no reputation gains or losses to be made. In contrast, reputation gains (losses) are accruable to a player acting cooperatively (non-cooperatively) while his opponent is playing non-cooperatively (cooperatively). Note that the incorporation of reputation gains or losses, when both players act cooperatively or non-cooperatively, will not change the results of the analysis significantly as long as these gains and losses are substantially smaller than those obtained when one player cooperates while the other is defecting.

Table 13.1
The debtor-creditor's payoff matrix

Creditor	Sovereign Debtor: Repay (L)	Sovereign Debtor: Repudiate (R)
Not seize (T)	$D,[v(K + A) - D]$	$RG_c,[v(K + A) - RL_d]$
Seize (B)	$[(D + A) - RL_c],[vK - D + RG_d]$	A,vK

The payoff matrix indicates that when both players cooperate (T,L) the creditor is fully repaid and the indebted sovereign's payoff includes the returns on both domestic assets and asset holding abroad. In contrast, when both players act non-cooperatively (B,R) the creditor's payoff is equal to the value of the seized assets, and the indebted sovereign enjoys only the returns on his domestic assets. When the creditor plays cooperatively and the indebted sovereign repudiates (T,R) the creditor's payoff consists of reputation gains whereas the benefit from non-repayment for the creditor is moderated by a loss of reputation. Finally, if the creditor seizes while the indebted sovereign is not defaulting (B,L), the payoff for the creditor includes the debt repayment and the value of the assets seized minus the loss of trustworthy reputation. In this case, the payoff for the indebted sovereign consists of the return on his domestic assets minus the debt repayment and plus the gains of trustworthy reputation. Note that it is not essential to include the returns on domestic assets for the indebted sovereign in this payoff matrix. The exclusion of these returns will not change the results of the analysis.

Each player chooses an action that maximizes his expected payoff given his beliefs about the other player's action and the implications of those actions on the players' trustworthy reputation. This payoff-maximizing behaviour, as well as the strategies available to the players and their associated payoffs, are considered to be common knowledge. The mathematical description of the creditor's and the indebted country's decision problems employs the following additional notations:

p_t = the probability that the creditor will not seize the indebted country's asset holding abroad;

p_b = the probability that the creditor will seize the indebted country's asset holding abroad;

p_l = the probability that the indebted sovereign will repay its external liabilities;

p_r = the probability that the indebted sovereign will repudiate his external liabilities;

π_t = the indebted sovereign's subjective assessment of the probability that the creditor will not seize his asset holding abroad;

π_b = the indebted sovereign's subjective assessment of the probability that the creditor will seize his asset holding abroad;

π_l = the creditor's subjective assessment of the probability that the indebted country will repay its debt; and

π_r = the creditor's subjective assessment of the probability that the indebted country will repudiate its debt.

Using these notations and the above definition of the game, the creditor's problem can be portrayed as

$$\max_{(p_t,\, p_b)} \{p_t[\pi_t D + \pi_r RG_c] + p_b[\pi_t(D + A - RL_c) + \pi_r A]\}$$

such that $p_t + p_b = 1$, $p_t \geq 0$ and $p_b \geq 0$.

Similarly, the indebted sovereign problem can be rendered as

$$\max_{(p_l,p_r)} \; p_l\{\pi_t[v(K+A) - D] + \pi_b[vK - D + RG_d]\} + p_r\{\pi_t[v(K+A) - RL_d] + \pi_b vK\}$$

such that $p_l + p_r = 1$, $p_l \geq 0$ and $p_l \geq 0$.

13.3 Nash equilibrium in mixed strategies

In addition to the assumption that both the creditor and the indebted sovereign choose p_t, p_b, p_l and p_r so as to maximize their expected payoffs given their beliefs about each other's actions, a Nash equilibrium consists of probability beliefs over strategies that are correct.

The Lagrangian associated with the creditor's constraint maximization problem can be expressed as

$$L = p_t[\pi_l D + \pi_r RG_c] + p_b[\pi_l(D + A - RL_c) + \pi_r A] + \lambda(1 - p_t - p_b) - \mu_t p_t - \mu_b p_b \quad (1)$$

where λ, μ_t and μ_b denote the Kuhn-Tucker multipliers on the constraints. By differentiating with respect to p_t and p_b we obtain that the Kuhn-Tucker conditions are

$$\pi_l D + \pi_r RG_c = \lambda + \mu_t \quad (2)$$

and

$$\pi_l(D + A - RL_c) + \pi_r A = \lambda + \mu_b. \tag{3}$$

The existence of a mixed strategy solution implies that μ_l and μ_b are equal to zero and hence the above conditions can be rendered as

$$\pi_l D + \pi_r RG_c = \pi_l(D + A - RL_c) + \pi_r A. \tag{4}$$

Recalling that $\pi_l + \pi_r = 1$, the creditor will find it optimal to play a mixed strategy when

$$\pi_l = \frac{RG_c - A}{RG_c - RL_c} \tag{5}$$

and

$$\pi_r = \frac{A - RL_c}{RG_c - RL_c}. \tag{6}$$

Similarly, the Lagrangian associated with the indebted sovereign's problem is

$$L = p_l\{\pi_t[v(K + A) - D] + \pi_b[vK - D + RG_d]\} + p_r\{\pi_t[v(K + A) - RL_d] + \pi_b vK\} + \phi(1 - p_l - p_r) - \mu_l p_l - \mu_r p_r \tag{7}$$

and the Kuhn-Tucker conditions are

$$\pi_t[v(K + A) - D] + \pi_b[vK - D + RG_d] = \phi + \mu_l \tag{8}$$

and

$$\pi_t[v(K + A) - RL_d] + \pi_b vK = \phi + \mu_r. \tag{9}$$

It is optimal for the indebted sovereign to play a mixed strategy when $\mu_l = \mu_r = 0$. In which case the above conditions can be rendered as

$$\pi_t[v(K + A) - D] + \pi_b[vK - D + RG_d] = \pi_t[v(K + A) - RL_d] + \pi_b vK. \tag{10}$$

Recalling that $\pi_t + \pi_b = 1$, the indebted country will find it optimal to play a mixed strategy when

$$\pi_t = \frac{D - RG_d}{RL_d - RG_d} \tag{11}$$

and

$$\pi_b = \frac{RL_d - D}{RL_d - RG_d}. \tag{12}$$

Since in a Nash equilibrium $p_t = \pi_t$, $p_b = \pi_b$, $p_l = \pi_l$ and $p_r = \pi_r$, the Nash equilibrium in mixed strategies consists of the following probabilities of response:

$$p_t = \frac{D - RG_d}{RL_d - RG_d} \tag{13a}$$

$$p_b = \frac{RL_d - D}{RL_d - RG_d} \tag{13b}$$

$$p_l = \frac{RG_c - A}{RG_c - RL_c} \tag{13c}$$

$$p_r = \frac{A - RL_c}{RG_c - RL_c}. \tag{13d}$$

In view of this equilibrium solution, the following conclusions about the way the creditor and the indebted sovereign can optimally play mixed strategies are drawn.

1. The probability that the creditor will not seize the indebted country's asset holding abroad should be equal to the difference between the debt and the potential reputation gains for the indebted country stemming from repayment, divided by the discrepancy between the potential reputation loss and reputation gains for the indebted country stemming from repudiation and repayment, respectively.

2. The probability that the creditor will seize the indebted country's asset holding abroad should be equal to the difference between the potential reputation loss for the indebted country from repudiation and the debt, divided by the discrepancy between the potential reputation loss and reputation gains for

the indebted country stemming from repudiation and repayment, respectively.

3. The probability that the indebted sovereign will repay the debt should be equal to the discrepancy between the potential reputation gains for the creditor from not seizing the indebted country's asset holding abroad and the value of these assets, divided by the difference between the potential reputation gains and losses for the creditor from not seizing and seizing the indebted country's asset holding abroad, respectively.

4. The probability that the indebted sovereign will repudiate its debt should be equal to the discrepancy between the value of the indebted country's asset holding abroad and the potential reputation loss for the creditor from seizing these assets, divided by the difference between the potential reputation gains and losses for the creditor from not seizing and seizing the indebted country's asset holding abroad, respectively.

Obviously, this Nash equilibrium in mixed strategies is meaningful only when interpreted as the frequencies of the various actions to be found optimally (in the Nash context) within the population of pairs of creditors and indebted sovereign countries.

13.4 Nash equilibria in pure strategies

It is important to note that since the Lagrangians associated with the players' constrained-maximization problems are linear in the control variables, both the creditor and the indebted sovereign should prefer a Nash equilibrium in pure strategies to the aforementioned Nash equilibrium in mixed strategies. The possible Nash equilibria in pure strategies can be identified in the payoff matrix by examining the best response of each player to what he believes would be the other player's strategy choice. The results of such an examination are summarized by the following propositions.

Proposition 1: If $D > RL_d$ (which is probably the case for most of the developing countries) and $RG_c > A$ (which is probably the case for a combination of a large creditor and a small indebted country), the combination of repudiation and non-seizure is a Nash equilibrium in pure strategies.

Proof: Given that the indebted sovereign's liabilities exceed the trustworthy reputation loss stemming from repudiation (i.e., $D > RL_d$), if the indebted sovereign thinks that the creditor will not seize his asset holding abroad, then the indebted sovereign's best response is to repudiate. On the other hand, when the indebted sovereign repudiates it is optimal for the creditor not to seize the indebted country's liabilities as long as his trustworthy reputation gains exceed the value of the indebted country's asset holding abroad (i.e., $RG_c > A$).

Proposition 2: If $D > RL_d$ and $A > RG_c$, the combination of repudiation and seizure is a Nash equilibrium in pure strategies.

Proof: If the debtor believes that the creditor would seize his asset holding abroad then, given that the amount of the sovereign's debt exceeds his trustworthy reputation gains from not repudiating (i.e., $D > RG_d$), it would be optimal for the indebted sovereign to repudiate his debt. Note further that when the indebted sovereign repudiates it is optimal for the creditor to seize the indebted country's asset holding abroad as long as the value of these assets exceeds the reputation gains accruable for the creditor from not doing so (i.e., $A > RG_c$).

Proposition 3: If $D < RL_d$ and $RL_c > A$ (which is the case for some developing countries with relatively small external debt and small asset holding abroad), the combination of repayment and non-seizure is a Nash equilibrium in pure strategy.

Proof: When the trustworthy reputation losses for the indebted sovereign from repudiation exceed the gains from doing so (i.e., $D < RL_d$) and the indebted sovereign believes that the creditor would not seize his asset holding abroad then the indebted sovereign's best choice is to repay his debt. Obviously, when the indebted sovereign repays it is optimal for the creditor not to seize the indebted country's asset abroad as long as his loss of trustworthy reputation exceeds the gains from doing so (i.e., $RL_c > A$).

Proposition 4: If $RG_d > D$ and $A > RL_c$, the combination of repayment and seizure is a Nash equilibrium in pure strategies.

Proof: When the indebted sovereign believes that the creditor would seize his asset holding abroad but the trustworthy reputation gains generated from repaying the debt are substantial and larger than the debt repayment amount (i.e., $RG_d > D$), it would be optimal for the indebted sovereign to repay its external liabilities. Note that when the indebted sovereign repays his debt it is optimal for the creditor to seize the indebted country's asset holding abroad as long as the value of these assets exceeds the loss of trustworthy reputation for the creditor from the unprovoked seizure (i.e., $A > RL_c$).

13.5 Extension of the game to a two-way seizure

The previous sections' analysis of the strategic interaction between the indebted sovereign and the creditor highlighted the role of seizing the indebted country's assets holding abroad in deterring repudiation of external debts. However, when the creditors' asset holding in the indebted country is large and important, it is possible for the indebted sovereign to harm the creditor significantly by confiscating, or eliminating, these assets. In this case, seizure should be viewed as a two-edge sword. The game considered in this section deals with this possibility and extends the previous game by taking into account that the strategies available to the indebted sovereign are: (I) repayment of the debt, (II) repudiation of the debt, or (III) both repudiation of the debt and seizure of the creditor's asset holding in the indebted country; while the strategies available to the creditor are: (a) no seizure of the indebted country's asset holding in the creditor country, or (b) seizure of these assets. As in the previous game, reputation gains and losses are accruable to both players and vary according to the nature of interaction between the players. That is, the description of the players' payoffs takes into account the costs of being perceived as a villain when acting non-cooperatively as well as the benefits of being perceived righteous, or even a victim, when playing cooperatively, for future interactions of the creditor and the indebted sovereign with other players.

The aforementioned strategies can generate any of the following six types of interaction between the indebted sovereign and the creditor.

(I,a) Mutual Cooperation: If both players acted cooperatively, they would be entitled to some reputation gains. In this case, the indebted sovereign's payoff would be equal to some reputation gains minus the debt repayment and the creditor's payoff would be equal to the sum of the debt repayment and some reputation gains.

(I,b) Repayment/Seizure: If the indebted sovereign repaid his debt while the creditor was seizing the debtor's asset holding abroad, the cooperating indebted sovereign would enjoy relatively high reputation gains whereas the creditor would suffer from relatively high reputation loss. In this case, the payoff to the indebted sovereign is equal to the reputation gains minus the debt repayment and the assets seized by the creditor, and the creditor's payoff would be equal to the debt repayment and the indebted countries' assets seized minus a loss of reputation.

(II,a) Repudiation/Non-Seizure: If the indebted sovereign repudiated while the creditor was not seizing his asset holding abroad, the indebted sovereign would face high reputation loss, while the creditor's payoff would consist of some considerable reputation gains.

(II,b) Repudiation/Seizure: If the indebted sovereign repudiated while the creditor was seizing his assets holding abroad, both would suffer from reputation loss. In this case, the payoff for the indebted sovereign is negative and consists of the loss of both reputation and asset holding abroad and the creditor's payoff is equal to the difference between the value of the debtor's assets seized and the reputation loss.

(III,a) Repudiation & Seizure/Non-Seizure: If the indebted sovereign acted aggressively and in addition to repudiating his debt also seized the creditor's assets while the creditor refrained from seizing the indebted sovereign assets abroad, the indebted sovereign would

suffer very high loss of reputation from being perceived as the villain, whereas the creditor would be entitled to very high reputation gains from being perceived as the victim. In this case, the indebted country's payoff is equal to the difference between the creditor's assets seized and the loss of reputation and the creditor's payoff consists of the difference between the reputation gains and his assets seized by the indebted sovereign.

(III,b) Repudiation and Mutual Seizure: If both players act aggressively, they would both face reputation losses and the indebted sovereign's payoff would be equal to the creditor's assets seized minus the assets seized by the creditor and the reputation loss, and similarly the creditor's payoff would be equal to the indebted sovereign's assets seized minus the assets seized by that sovereign and the reputation loss.

Let,

A_d = the indebted country's asset-holding in the creditor country;

A_c = the creditor's asset holding in the indebted country;

RG_d = reputations gains for the indebted country from acting cooperatively, with $RG_d^h > RG_d^l$;

RG_c = reputation gains for the creditor from acting cooperatively, with $RG_c^h > RG_c^m > RG_c^l$;

RL_d = repudiation loss for the indebted country from not acting cooperatively, with $RL_d^{vh} > RL_d^h > RL_d^m > RL_d^l$); and

RL_c = repudiation loss for the indebted country from not acting cooperatively, with $RL_c^h > RL_c^m > RL_c^l$.

Then the aforementioned types of interaction and their associated payoffs can be formulated as displayed in Table 13.2. In each cell of this table, the entry on the left-hand side indicates the indebted country's payoff whereas that on the right-hand side represents the creditor's payoff.

Table 13.2
The debtor-creditor's payoff matrix in the extended game

Debtor \ Creditor	(a) Not Seize	(b) Seize
(I) Repay	$(RG_d^h - D),(A_c + A_d + D - RL_c^h)$	$(A_d - D + RG_d^l),(A_c + D + RG_c^l)$
(II) Repudiate	$(A_d - RL_d^h),(A_c + RG_c^m)$	$(-RL_d^l),(A_c + A_d - RL_c^m)$
(III) Repudiate & Seize	$(A_c - RL_d^m),(A_d - RL_c^l)$	$(A_d + A_c - RL_d^{vh}),(RG_c^h)$

The possible Nash equilibria in pure strategies that can be identified in this payoff matrix are described in the following propositions.

Proposition 5: **If (i) $RG_d^l - D > -RL_d^h$, (ii) $RG_d^l - D > A_c - RL_d^{vh}$, and (iii) $RG_c^l > A_d - RL_c^h$, then the cooperative combination of repayment and non-seizure (I,a) is a Nash equilibrium in pure strategies.**

Proof: **If the inequalities (i) and (ii) hold and the indebted sovereign thinks that the creditor will not seize his asset holding abroad, the indebted sovereign's best response is to repay his debt. When the indebted sovereign repays his debt, it is optimal for the creditor not to seize the indebted country's asset holding abroad as long as inequality (iii) holds.**

Proposition 6: **If (i) $-RL_d^h > RG_d^l - D$, (ii) $-RL_d^h > A_c - RL_d^{vh}$, and (iii) $RG_c^m > A_d - RL_c^m$, then the combination of repudiation and non-seizure (II,a) is a Nash equilibrium in pure strategies.**

Proof: **If the inequalities (i) and (ii) hold and if the indebted sovereign thinks that the creditor will not seize his asset holding abroad, the indebted sovereign's best response is to repudiate. Note further that when the indebted sovereign repudiates it is optimal for the creditor not to seize the indebted country's liabilities as long as inequality (iii) holds.**

Proposition 7: If (i) $A_c - RL_d^{vh} > -RL_d^h$, (ii) $A_c - RL_d^{vh} > RG_d^l - D$, and (iii) $RG_c^h > A_d - RL_c^l$, then the combination (III,a), in which the indebted sovereign repudiates his debt and seizes the creditor's assets in his territory while the creditor refrains from seizing the indebted sovereign asset holding abroad, is a Nash equilibrium in pure strategies.

Proof: If the inequalities (i) and (ii) hold and if the indebted sovereign thinks that the creditor will not seize his asset holding abroad, the indebted sovereign's best response is to repudiate the debt and to seize the creditor's assets held in his territory. When the indebted sovereign repudiates and seizes, it is optimal for the creditor not to seize the indebted country's liabilities as long as inequality (iii) holds.

Proposition 8: If (i) $RG_d^h - D > -RL_d^l$, (ii) $RG_d^h - D > A_c - RL_d^m$, and (iii) $A_d - RL_c^h > RG_c^l$, then the combination (I,b), in which the indebted sovereign repays his debt and the creditor seizes the indebted country's asset holding abroad, is a Nash equilibrium in pure strategies.

Proof: If the inequalities (i) and (ii) hold and if the indebted sovereign thinks that the creditor will seize his asset holding abroad, the indebted sovereign's best response is to repay its debt. When the indebted sovereign repays his debt, it is optimal for the creditor to seize the indebted country's liabilities as long as inequality (iii) holds.

Proposition 9: If (i) $-RL_d^l > RG_d^h - D$, (ii) $-RL_d^l > A_c - RL_d^m$, and (iii) $A_d - RL_c^m > RG_c^m$, then the combination (II,b), in which the indebted country repudiates its debt and the creditor seizes the indebted country's asset holding abroad, is a Nash Equilibrium in pure strategies.

Proof: If the inequalities (i) and (ii) hold and if the indebted sovereign thinks that the creditor will seize his asset holding abroad, the indebted sovereign's best response is to repudiate its debt. When the indebted sovereign defaults, it is optimal for the creditor to seize the indebted country's liabilities as long as inequality (iii) holds.

Proposition 10: If (i) $A_c - RL_d^m > RG_d^h - D$, (ii) $A_c - RL_d^m > -RL_d^l$, and (iii) $A_d - RL_c^l > RG_c^h$, then the combination (III,b), in which the indebted country repudiates its debt and also seizes the creditor's assets held on its territory while the creditor is seizing the indebted country's asset holding abroad, is a Nash Equilibrium in pure strategies.

Proof: If the inequalities (i) and (ii) hold and if the indebted sovereign thinks that the creditor will seize his asset holding abroad, the indebted sovereign's best response is to repudiate its debt and to seize the creditor's assets held in its territory. When the indebted sovereign does so, it is optimal for the creditor to seize the indebted country's liabilities as long as inequality (iii) holds.

13.6 Conclusion

This chapter analyzed the interaction between the creditor and the indebted sovereign and identified and described the possible Nash equilibria in pure strategies within a framework of a 'one-shot game'. The payoffs of both the basic game and the extended game included reputation gains and losses for the players as their present behaviour might affect their future payoffs from dealing with other lenders or borrowers in the international credit market. It was shown that the possibility that any strategy combination will be a Nash equilibrium in pure strategies depends on the trustworthy reputation gains and losses for the players, the size of the debt and the asset holding of each of the players in the other player's country. In general, the analysis indicated that the larger the asset holding of any of the players in the opponent's country and the smaller the reputation gains, or losses, from acting cooperatively or non-cooperatively, respectively, the more likely it is that the players will choose non-cooperative and aggressive strategies. The exact intensity of their aggression, or cooperation, in each possible case was described by propositions.

References

Eaton, J. and Gersovitz, M. (1981), 'Debt with Potential Repudiation: Theoretical and Empirical Analysis', *Review of Economic Studies*, vol. 48, pp. 289–309.

Grossman, H. and Van Huyck, J. (1988), 'Sovereign Debt as a Contingent Claim: Excusable Default, Repudiation, and Reputation', *American Economic Review*, vol. 78, pp. 1088–87.

Kletzer, K.M. (1984), 'Asymmetries of Information and the LDC Borrowing with Sovereign Risk', *Economic Journal*, vol. 94, pp. 287–307.

14 The role of repudiation and trade and credit sanctions in the accumulation of sovereign debt, capital and reputation

This chapter analyzes the optimal accumulation of capital stock, external debt and reputation by incorporating explicitly the inclination of a sovereign country to service its external liabilities and the adverse effects of not meeting foreign loans' commitments on the country's trustworthy reputation. Repudiation and loss of reputation might limit the country's access to international markets of credit, consumer and capital goods; and subsequently might result in a higher average cost of servicing the country's future external liabilities, less favourable terms of trade with the rest of the world and accelerated depreciation of capital stock.

14.1 Introduction

Since 1973, the external debts of the developing countries have been growing at an unprecedented rate which have led to a heightened concern about these countries' ability and commitment to service and repay their liabilities. This concern is rooted in the fact that a country's external debt is a sovereign debt and unlike a private debt it is not subject to laws regarding bankruptcy and enforcement of collateral. Thus, when the potential penalties on default are insufficient, a rise in the country's degree of indebtedness increases the country's inclination to repudiate some, or all, of its external liabilities. While the previous chapters considered the indebted country's asset holding abroad as a deterrent to repudiation, this chapter refers to a case where those assets are negligible. Nevertheless, as has been suggested by Eaton and Gersovitz (1981) and Kletzer (1984), it is possible that the extent of repudiation is limited by the country's concern about the adverse effect of a default on its trustworthy reputation and, subsequently, on its access to foreign loans. The role of reputation, in conjunction with the desire for continued access to external loans, as a deterrent for repudiation have been analyzed further by Grossman and Van Huyck (1988) who distinguished between justifiable and excusable defaults and unjustifiable and inexcusable defaults and derived a reputation equilibrium in which the lenders' expectations about contingent debt servicing are validated. By assuming that small countries face competitive foreign investors, Bulow and Rogoff (1989) have disputed the role of the 'reputation for repayment' as a support for extending loans to small countries and have argued that lending to these countries should be supported by direct sanctions.

The present chapter incorporates both the reputational argument and the possibility of an implementation of trade sanctions against a defaulting country into the analysis of external debt and capital accumulation within an intertemporal utility maximization framework. In this framework, the indebted country chooses the paths of consumption, import, export and repudiation of external liabilities as to maximize the sum of the discounted utilities from consumption over an infinite planning horizon while taking into account the evolution of its production capacity, external debt and reputation. In addition to the potentially adverse effect of a deterioration in its trustworthy reputation on access to foreign loans, the motion equations of the indebted country's capital stock and external debt also incorporate the possibility of lenders' retaliation by limiting the country's access to international markets. Trade sanctions against the defaulting country are likely to reduce the revenues from export, increase the price of imports and accelerate the depreciation of capital items whose maintenance depends on foreign spare parts and skill.

The details of this analysis are presented in the following sections. Section 14.2 displays the indebted country's intertemporal utility maximization as an optimal control problem in which the control variables are consumption, import, export and rate of repudiation;

and the state variables are capital, external debt and reputation. It also derives the necessary conditions for maximum. Section 14.3 analyzes the characteristics of the optimal trajectories of the control and state variables. Section 14.4 describes the steady-state levels of repudiation, reputation, import, capital, output and external debt.

14.2 Dynamic model of optimal debt accumulation and repudiation with consideration for retaliation

The analysis of capital, external debt and reputation accumulation is based on the assumption that the indebted country chooses the paths of consumption, import, export and the rate of repudiation of external liabilities as to maximize the sum of the discounted utilities from consumption during an infinite horizon while taking into account the effects of repudiation and retaliatory sanctions on the country's capital stock, external debt and reputation. The choice of infinite time interval is to enable the assessment of long-run (steady state) effects.

In mathematical notations the sovereign's decision problem is portrayed as

$$\underset{(c,m,x,v)}{\text{maximizing}} \int_0^{\infty} e^{-\rho t} u(c_t)dt \tag{1}$$

subject to the state-transition equations:

$$\dot{K}_t = f(K_t, m_t) - c_t - x_t - \delta(R_t)K_t \tag{2}$$

$$\dot{D}_t = q(R_t)m_t - p(R_t)x_t + r(R_t)(1 - v_t)\, D_t \tag{3}$$

$$\dot{R}_t = -\beta\,(v_t - v^*). \tag{4}$$

Here,

u = the sovereign's instantaneous utility,
ρ = the sovereign's rate of time preference, $\rho \geq 0$,

K = the country's capital stock in physical units,
D = the country's amount of external debt in dollars,
R = the sovereign's trustworthy reputation — $R \geq 0$, and larger values of R indicate higher reputation,
c = the country's consumption level in physical units,
m = the country's import level in physical units,
x = the country's export level in physical units,
v = the rate of repudiation of external liabilities, $0 \leq v \leq 1$,
v* = the excusable rate of repudiation,
β = the reputational loss' parameter, $\beta > 0$,
δ = the rate of capital's depreciation,
f = the aggregate production function (aggregate production is measured in physical units),
q = the aggregate price of imported goods in dollars,
p = the aggregate price of exported goods in dollars,
r = the average cost of servicing the external debt, and
t = the time index.

It is assumed that:

1. The instantaneous utility is a concave function of consumption: $u' > 0$ and $u'' < 0$, $u'(0) = \infty$ and $u'(\infty) = 0$.
2. The aggregate production is a concave function of capital and imported inputs: $f_K > 0$, $f_m > 0$, $f(0,m) = f(K,0) = 0$, $f_{KK} < 0$, $f_{mm} < 0$ and $f_{KK}f_{mm} - f_{Km}f_{mK} > 0$.
3. The average cost of servicing the external debt rises as the indebted country's reputation declines, that is, $r_R < 0$.
4. The rate of capital depreciation increases as the country's trustworthy reputation declines due to retaliatory measures implemented by lending countries including a spare-part embargo, i.e., $\delta_R < 0$;
5. Due to a greater degree of isolation and loss of access to world markets, the prices of imported goods rise and the prices of exported goods fall as the indebted country's reputation declines, i.e., $q_R < 0$ and $p_R > 0$.
6. There exists an interior solution to the optimal-control problem. This assumption is compatible with the empirical evidence that, in most cases, repudiation is partial and retaliatory sanctions are limited rather than total or nil.

In this optimal-control problem, c(t), m(t), x(t) and v(t) are the control functions; and K(t), D(t) and R(t) are the state variables. The maximum principle developed by Pontryagin *et al.* (1962) implies that if the control functions and the corresponding trajectories of the state variables maximize the objective function 1 subject to the state-transition equations 2–4, there exist continuously differentiable co-state functions $\lambda_1(t)$, $\lambda_2(t)$ and $\lambda_3(t)$ such that the optimal control functions and the corresponding state and co-state functions simultaneously satisfy the state-transition equations, the co-state transition (or adjoint) equations and the optimality conditions. These transition equations and optimality conditions can be derived by considering the Hamiltonian (H) associated with the constrained intertemporal decision problem described by equations 1 to 4:

$$H = e^{-\rho t}u(c) + \lambda_1[f(K,m)-c-x-\delta(R)K]+\lambda_2[q(R)m-p(R)x$$
$$+r(R)(1-v)D]-\lambda_3\beta(v-v^*) \qquad (5)$$

where, for convenience, the time index *t* is omitted. In this context, the co-state variables λ_1, λ_2 and λ_3 can be interpreted as the shadow values (in utiles) of infinitesimal increments in the country's capital stock, amount of external debt and level of international reputation, respectively. The first term on the right-hand side (r.h.s.) indicates the direct contribution of current consumption to the overall level of utility, whereas the second, third and fourth terms on the r.h.s. display the indirect contributions of current net investment, borrowing and repudiation of external liabilities, respectively, to the sovereign's overall utility level through altering future consumption possibilities.

In addition to the state-transition equations, the necessary conditions include the adjoint equations

$$\dot{\lambda}_1 = -\lambda_1 [f_K (K,m) - \delta(R)] \qquad (6)$$

$$\dot{\lambda}_2 = -\lambda_2 r(R)(1-v) \qquad (7)$$

$$\dot{\lambda}_3 = \lambda_1 \delta_R K - \lambda_2 [q_R - p_R x + r_R(1 - v)D] \quad (8)$$

and the optimality conditions

$$H_c = e^{-\rho t} u'(c) - \lambda_1 = 0 \quad (9)$$

$$H_m = \lambda_1 f_m(K,m) + \lambda_2 q(R) = 0 \quad (10)$$

$$H_x = -\lambda_1 - \lambda_2 p(R) = 0 \quad (11)$$

$$H_v = -\lambda_2 r(R) D - \lambda_3 \beta = 0. \quad (12)$$

Finally, the transversality conditions require that, from the sovereign's perspectives, there is no value to the terminal levels of capital, external debt and reputation. As long as the sovereign's rate of time preference is positive, these conditions are also satisfied in the case where the terminal levels of the state variables are positive.

The time differentials of the optimality conditions 9-12 yield singular-control equations describing the transitions of the control variables. The singular-control equations, the adjoint equations 6-8 and the state-transition equations 2-4 constitute a system of non-linear differential equations. Due to its size and complexity, it is impossible to solve this system and identify its asymptotic properties without additional strong assumptions and a substantial loss of generality. Thus, the following sections present only some essential features of the optimal paths of the control and state variables and the steady-state levels of these variables.

14.3 Characteristics of the optimal trajectories

The adjoint equation 6 requires that, along the optimal path, the rate of change in the shadow price of capital is equal to the difference between the capital's rate of depreciation and the marginal product of capital. The optimality condition 9 indicates that at any instance within the planning horizon the shadow price of capital should be equal to the marginal utility from current consumption and thus reflects the trade-off between current consumption and future consumption.

The adjoint equation 7 requires that along the optimal path the rate of change in the shadow value of external debt is equal, in absolute terms, to the repudiation-free interest rate (1 - v)r. Furthermore, the optimality condition 11 implies that the ratio of the shadow prices of capital and external debt should be equal to the price of the country's export, and in recalling the optimality condition 9:

$$\lambda_2 = - e^{-\rho t} u'(c)/p(R). \tag{13}$$

By substituting 13 and 9 into the optimality condition 10 for λ_1 and λ_2 we obtain further that along the optimal path the marginal product of the imported inputs should be equal to the country's import-export price ratio:

$$f_m(K,m) = q(R)/p(R). \tag{14}$$

Note further that since the country's import-export price ratio declines with R and since the marginal product of imported inputs is diminishing, the greater the country's trustworthy reputation the larger the amount of imported goods along the optimal path.

The optimality condition 12 implies that along the optimal path the rate of repudiation of external liabilities is such that the marginal gains (in utiles) from lowering the costs of servicing the country's external debt are offset by the adverse effect of the loss of reputation on present and future consumption and utility levels. By substituting equation 13 into the optimality condition 12, the shadow value of an infinitesimal increase in the country's reputation can be expressed as

$$\lambda_3 = r(R)De^{-rt} u'(c)/\beta p(R). \tag{15}$$

By differentiating the optimality condition 9 with respect to *t*, it can be shown that

$$-\rho e^{-\rho t} u'(c) + e^{-\rho t} u''(c) \dot{c} - \dot{\lambda}_1 = 0 \tag{16}$$

and in recalling conditions 6 and 9 we obtain that

$$\dot{c} = -[f_K(K,m) - \delta(R) - \rho]u'(c)/u''(c). \tag{17}$$

Similarly to the optimal growth theory's proposition (e.g, Cass, 1965), equation 17 implies that, given that the sovereign's marginal utility is diminishing, consumption increases, remains the same, or decreases over time if the marginal product of capital is greater, equal to, or smaller than the rental (or user) cost of capital ($\delta + \rho$). This effect of the marginal net return on capital is amplified by the degree of concavity of the sovereign's utility function. Note that in this framework, the marginal product of capital increases (decreases) with the amount of the imported inputs when K and m are complementaries (substitutes) in production, and the rental cost of capital declines with the country's level of reputation.

By taking the time differential of the optimality condition 11

$$-\dot{\lambda}_1 - \dot{\lambda}_2\ p(R) - \lambda_2 p(R)\ \dot{R} = 0 \tag{18}$$

and in recalling conditions 6, 7, 9 and 11 it can be shown that the transition of the country's international trustworthy reputation is given by

$$\dot{R} = \{(1 - v)r(R) - [f_K(K,m) - \delta(R)]\ p(R)\}/p_R(R). \tag{19}$$

Since p_R is assumed to be positive, whenever the repudiation-free interest rate is greater, equal to, or smaller than the foreign exchange receipts from exporting the net marginal product of capital, the country's reputation increases, remains the same, or decreases, respectively. The change in the country's reputation is amplified by the vulnerability of the country's export to retaliatory measures implemented by the lending countries as indicated by the export price's derivative with respect to R. Note that for given levels of K and m, the higher the country's reputation the lower the repudiation-free interest rate and the greater the foreign exchange receipts from exporting the net marginal product of capital and hence the greater the country's inclination to repudiate and lower its reputation.

The time differential of the optimality condition 12 implies

$$-\dot{\lambda}_2 r(R)D - \lambda_2 [r_R(R)D\dot{R} + r(R)\dot{D}] - \dot{\lambda}_3 \beta = 0 \quad (20)$$

and by substituting conditions 7 and 8 into equation 20 for $\dot{\lambda}_2$ and $\dot{\lambda}_3$, respectively, and in recalling that along the optimal path λ_1 and λ_2 behave in accordance with condition 11, it can be shown that

$$r(R)^2(1-v)D - r_R(R)D\dot{R} - r(R)\dot{D} + \beta[q_R m - p_R x + r_R(1-v)D + p(R)\,\delta_R(R)K] = 0. \quad (21)$$

By dividing both sides of equation 21 by r(R)D and rearranging terms, it can be shown that along the optimal path the instantaneous rate of change in the country's external debt is given by

$$\frac{\dot{D}}{D} = \frac{\beta}{r(R)}[(1-v)r_R + p(R)\,\delta_R\,(K/D) + (q_R m - p_R x)/D - r_R\dot{R}/\beta] + (1-v)\,r(R). \quad (22)$$

Equation 22 and the assumptions that $\delta_R < 0$, $q_R < 0$ and $p_R > 0$ indicate that the higher the country's leverage (D/K) and the lower the sensitivity of the country's import and export prices to changes in trustworthy reputation, the higher the optimal rate of external debt accumulation.

14.4 Steady-state levels of repudiation, reputation, import, capital stock output and external debt

By setting $\dot{R}=0$ in equations 4,19 and 22, $\dot{c}=0$ in equation 17, and $\dot{D}=0$ in equation 22, we obtain that in steady state (ss):

$$V_{ss} = v^* \quad (23)$$

$$(1 - v_{ss})\,r(R_{ss}) - [f_K(K_{ss}, m_{ss}) - \delta(R_{ss})]p(R_{ss}) = 0 \quad (24)$$

$$f_K(K_{ss}, m_{ss}) = \delta(R_{ss}) + \rho \quad (25)$$

$$\frac{\beta}{r(R_{ss})}[(1 - v_{ss})r_R(R_{ss}) + p(R_{ss})\delta_R(R_{ss})(K_{ss}/D_{ss}) + (q_R(R_{ss})m_{ss} - p_R(R_{ss})x_{ss})/D_{ss}] + (1 - v_{ss})\, r(R_{ss}) = 0. \tag{26}$$

The steady-state levels of repudiation and reputation

Equation 23 indicates that in steady state the country's rate of repudiation of external debt should be equal to the excusable rate. The substitution of 23 and 25 into equation 24 implies that the steady-state level of the country's reputation should be such that the repudiation-free interest rate is equal to the sovereign's rate of time preference times the stationary price of the country's export:

$$(1 - v^*)\, r(R_{ss}) = \rho p(R_{ss}) \tag{27}$$

By taking the total differential of equation 27 and in recalling that $0 \leq v^* \leq 1$, $r_R < 0$ and $p_R > 0$ we obtain that the higher the excusable repudiation rate and the rate of time preference, the lower the country's reputation in steady state:

$$\frac{dR_{ss}}{dv^*} = \frac{r(R_{ss})}{(1 - v^*)\, r_R(R_{ss}) - \rho p_R(R_{ss})} < 0 \tag{28}$$

and

$$\frac{dR_{ss}}{d\rho} = \frac{p(R_{ss})}{(1 - v^*)\, r_R(R_{ss}) - \rho p_R(R_{ss})} < 0\,. \tag{29}$$

The above derivatives suggest further that the more sensitive the average cost of servicing the external debt and the price of export to changes in the country's reputation, the smaller the effect of an increase in either the excusable repudiation rate or the rate of time preference on the steady-state level of the country's trustworthy reputation.

In order to explore further the effects of the responses of r and p to changes in R on the country's reputation in steady state let us consider the following linear forms:

$$r = r_{max} - r_1 R \qquad r_{max}, r_1 > 0 \tag{30}$$

and

$$p = p_{min} + p_1 R \qquad p_{min}, p_1 > 0 \tag{31}$$

where r_{max} and p_{min} are the average cost of servicing the external debt and the aggregate price of export when the country's reputation reaches the lowest level (that is, $R = 0$), respectively, and r_1 and p_1 indicate the sensitivities of the average contracted interest rate and price of export to changes in the country's reputation, respectively. The substitution of these forms into equation 27 leads to the following close-form solution to the country's stationary level of trustworthy reputation:

$$R_{ss} = \frac{(1 - v^*)r_{max} - \rho p_{min}}{\rho p_1 + r_1(1 - v^*)}. \tag{32}$$

This solution implies

$$\frac{dR_{ss}}{dr_{max}} = \frac{(1 - v^*)}{\rho r_1 + r_1(1 - v^*)} > 0 \tag{33}$$

$$\frac{dR_{ss}}{dp_{min}} = \frac{-\rho}{\rho r_1 + r_1(1 - v^*)} < 0 \tag{34}$$

$$\frac{dR_{ss}}{dr_1} = \frac{-(1-v^*)\,[(1-v^*)r_{max} - \rho p_{min}]}{[\rho p_1 + r_1(1 - v^*)]^2} \lesseqgtr 0 \text{ as } (1-v^*)r_{max} \gtreqless \rho p_{min} \tag{35}$$

$$\frac{dR_{ss}}{dp_1} = \frac{-\rho[(1 - v^*)r_{max} - \rho p_{min}]}{[\rho p_1 + r_1(1 - v^*)]^2} \lesseqgtr 0 \text{ as } (1-v^*)r_{max} \gtreqless \rho p_{min}. \tag{36}$$

The steady-state levels of import, capital and production

In order to find the steady-state levels of import (m_{ss}), capital (K_{ss}) and production (y_{ss}), consider the following Cobb-Douglas aggregate production function

$$y = K^{\alpha_1} m^{\alpha_2} \quad 0 < \alpha_1, \alpha_2 < 1 \tag{37}$$

Then, in recalling equations 14 and 25 it can be shown that the marginal products of imported inputs and capital in steady state should be equal to:

$$\alpha_2 K_{ss}^{\alpha_1} m_{ss}^{\alpha_2 - 1} = q(R_{ss})/p(R_{ss}) \tag{38}$$

$$\alpha_1 K_{ss}^{\alpha_1 - 1} m_{ss}^{\alpha_2} = \delta(R_{ss}) + \rho. \tag{39}$$

Equations 38 and 39 indicate that the steady-state levels of import and capital are such that:

$$\frac{K_{ss}}{m_{ss}} = (\alpha_1/\alpha_2)\frac{q(R_{ss})/p(R_{ss})}{\delta(R_{ss}) + \rho} \tag{40}$$

$$m_{ss} = \left(\frac{\delta(R_{ss}) + \rho}{\alpha_1}\right)^{\frac{\alpha_1}{1-\alpha_2+\alpha_1\alpha_2}} \left(\frac{q(R_{ss})}{\alpha_2\, p(R_{ss})}\right)^{\frac{1-\alpha_1}{1-\alpha_2+\alpha_1\alpha_2}} \tag{41}$$

$$K_{ss} = \left(\frac{\delta(R_{ss}) + \rho}{\alpha_1}\right)^{\frac{1-\alpha_2}{1-\alpha_2+\alpha_1\alpha_2}} \left(\frac{q(R_{ss})}{\alpha_2\, p(R_{ss})}\right)^{\frac{2(1+\alpha_1\alpha_2)-\alpha_1}{\alpha_1(1-\alpha_2+\alpha_1\alpha_2)}}. \tag{42}$$

The steady-state level of output can be found by substituting equations 41 and 42 in the aggregate production function.

Equation 40 implies that, for a given level of reputation, the steady-state ratio of capital to imported inputs in production:

1. increases with the capital-import's production elasticities ratio,
2. increases with the import-export price ratio in steady state,
3. decreases with the rate of depreciation of capital in steady state, and
4. decreases with the sovereign's rate of time preference.

Moreover, equations 41 and 42 indicate that, for a given level of trustworthy reputation, K_{ss}, m_{ss}, and subsequently y_{ss}, increase with: 1. the depreciation rate of capital, 2. the rate of time preference, and 3. the import-export's price ratio.

Note, however, that the effect of the country's steady-state trustworthy reputation level on the capital-import ratio is not clear, since both the import-export's price ratio and the capital's depreciation rate; appearing in the numerator and denominator of equation 40, respectively; decline with R_{ss}. Therefore, if the import-export's price ratio is more (less) sensitive than the capital's depreciation rate to changes in R, the lower the country's trustworthy reputation the more (less) capital intensive the country's production process in steady state.

Note further that the effect of the rate of time-preference (that is, the degree of myopia) on the capital-import ratio in steady state is not obvious once the country's reputation is not held constant. On the one hand, and as indicated above, an increase in the rate of time-preference raises *directly* the rental costs of capital and hence moderates the steady-state's capital-import ratio. On the other hand, and in view of equation 32, an increase in the rate of time preference lowers the country's reputation and hence affects *indirectly* the capital-import ratio in accordance with the relative sensitivity of the capital's depreciation rate and the import-export's price ratio. Thus, the *full* effect of the rate of time preference is clear only in the case where the import-export price ratio is less sensitive than the rate of capital depreciation to changes in the country's trustworthy reputation. In this case, both the direct and indirect effects of an increment in the rate of time preference are negative and hence reduce the stationary capital-import ratio. When the import-export's price ratio is more sensitive than the depreciation rate to changes in the country's trustworthy reputation, the indirect effect of an increment in the rate of time preference on the stationary capital-import ratio in the production process is positive and offsets the direct effect.

The steady-state level of external debt

By setting $\dot{D}$ and $\dot{R}$ to be equal to zero in equation 21 the country's external debt in steady state (D_{ss}) is given by

$$D_{ss} = \frac{[p_R(R_{ss})x_{ss} - q_R(R_{ss})m_{ss}] - p(R_{ss})\,\delta_R(R_{ss})\,K_{ss}}{(1 - v^*)\,[r_R(R_{ss}) + r(R_{ss})^2/\beta]}. \tag{43}$$

In recalling the assumptions that p_R is positive and q_R and δ_R are negative, it is clear that the numerator is positive. However, in view of the assumption that the contracted interest rate declines as the country's reputation rises (i.e., $r_R < 0$), the sign of the denominator of the term on the right-hand side of equation 43 is not clear and hence

$$D_{ss} \gtreqless 0 \text{ as } r(R_{ss}) \gtreqless \frac{\beta E_{ss}}{R_{ss}} \tag{44}$$

where E_{ss} is the stationary elasticity (in absolute terms) of the contracted interest rate with respect to the indebted country's trustworthy reputation. As can be expected, the more sensitive the country's trustworthy reputation to repudiation (i.e., the larger the β) the smaller the country's external liabilities in steady state, and for a sufficiently large β and contracted interest rate elasticity it is possible that the initially indebted country will be a net creditor in steady state, provided that the steady-state is reached. Equation 43 indicates further that the size of D_{ss}, in absolute terms, increases with: 1. the country's steady-state levels of import, export, capital stock and the price of export; and 2. the sensitivity of the export's price, import's price and capital depreciation rate to changes in the country's trustworthy reputation. It is important to note further that an increment in the excusable rate of repudiation increases directly the stationary level of external debt if $r_{ss} > bE/R_{ss}$. However, in recalling equation 28, the direct effect of v^* on D_{ss} is likely to be moderated indirectly by the deterioration in the country's stationary level of trustworthy reputation.

References

Bulow, J. and Rogoff, K. (1989), 'Sovereign Debt: Is to Forgive to Forget?', *American Economic Review*, vol. 79, pp. 43–50.

Cass, D. (1965), 'Optimum Growth in an Aggregative Model of Capital Accumulation', *Review of Economic Studies*, vol. 32, pp. 233–40.

Eaton, J. and Gersovitz, M. (1981), 'Debt with Potential Repudiation: Theoretical and Empirical Analysis', *Review of Economic Studies*, vol. 48, pp. 289–309.

Grossman, H. and Van Huyck, J. (1988), 'Sovereign Debt as a Contingent Claim: Excusable Default, Repudiation, and Reputation', *American Economic Review*, vol. 78, pp. 1088–97.

Kletzer, K.M. (1984), 'Asymmetries of Information and the LDC Borrowing with Sovereign Risk', *Economic Journal*, vol. 94, pp. 287–307.

Pontryagin, L.S., Boltyanskii, V.G., Gamkrelidze, R.V. and Mishchenko, E.F. (1962), *The Mathematical Theory of Optimal Process*, Wiley, New York.

15 Rescheduling a sovereign debt: Expected repayment, risk and time preference

By assuming that the probability of default increases with the debt-service burden, it is shown that the set of admissible rescheduling schemes of a sovereign debt to a private creditor can be depicted by a U-shaped curve in the plane spanned by the renegotiated annual debt repayment and the renegotiated length of the repayment period. By classifying creditors and debtors by risk and time preference, the choice of a rescheduling scheme from this set and the likelihood of agreement is analyzed for eighty-one possible combinations of creditors and debtors.

15.1 Introduction

In view of the developing countries' high level of indebtedness, it has been argued by Krugman (1988) that a country's financial obligations act like a high marginal tax rate which deters governments from taking painful measures to improve a country's economic performance and discourages capital formation. Thus, when an indebted country is on the downward sloping side of the 'debt relief Laffer curve', both debtor and creditor can benefit from a debt-reduction. Krugman (1989) has also argued that the basic approach for solving the developing countries' debt problem is rescheduling and concerted lending.

The purpose of this chapter is twofold: first, to identify the set of sovereign-debt rescheduling schemes which are admissible for both creditor and debtor for negotiation; and second, to analyze the creditor's and debtor's risk and time preference over the feasible set and to assess the prospects for agreement. Assuming that a country's inclination to repay its liabilities decreases with its debt burden, but that the costs of repudiation are substantial, and recognizing that a short-term illiquidity does not necessarily lead to a long-term insolvency, this chapter analyzes the set of debt-rescheduling schemes which are admissible for both the debtor and the creditor. It is shown that this set can be depicted by a U-shaped curve in the plane spanned by the renegotiated annual debt repayment and period of repayment. The location of the preferred rescheduling scheme on this curve is identified for eighty-one possible combinations of creditors and debtors classified by their attitude toward risk and rate of time preference.

The structure of the chapter is as follows. Section 15.2 analyzes the probability of default and the expected annual debt repayment and constructs the 'debt Laffer curve'. Section 15.3 presents the debt repayment constraint and constructs the admissible rescheduling curve. Section 15.4 describes the effects of risk and time preference on the creditor's and debtor's choices of an admissible rescheduling scheme. Section 15.5 presents the possible combinations of creditors and debtors and indicates the likelihood of agreement between them about a rescheduling scheme. The degree of similarity between the creditor's choice and the debtor's choice is discussed further in the concluding remarks in section 15.6.

15.2 Probability of default, expected annual debt repayment and the 'debt Laffer curve'

Consider a situation in which a sovereign country is liable to a single private creditor, or to a well-coordinated syndicate of private creditors, and cannot service its external liabilities in accordance with the originally contracted terms, and in which both the indebted country and its creditor have a sufficient incentive for rescheduling the country's liabilities over a T-year period in equal (in constant prices) annual repayments of principal and interest. Dealing with a sovereign country whose asset holdings abroad are negligible, the creditor is aware of the fact that his or her control over the rescheduled repayment is limited. Nevertheless, assume that the probability of default perceived by the creditor is smaller than one due to substantial costs that can be inflicted directly by retaliatory sanctions, such as a ban on trade and credit, and indirectly through a loss of trustworthy reputation. Assume further that the perceived probability of default: 1. rises with the burden of servicing the debt, measured by the ratio of the renegotiated annual repayment to the indebted country's level of gross national product (GNP), as public pressure against tax-increase and subsidy-cuts mounts; and 2. decreases with the creditor's ability to retaliate by limiting the country's access to the international credit market proportionately to the creditor's market share.

These assumptions are incorporated into the following linear expression:

$$p = \alpha(M/Y) - \lambda s \qquad (1)$$

where,

p	=	the probability of default,
M	=	a constant renegotiated annual repayment of principal and interest in constant prices,
Y	=	the indebted country's GNP in constant prices,
s	=	the creditor's share in the international credit market,
α	=	a positive scalar indicating the marginal effect of the debt burden on the country's inclination to default,[1] and
λ	=	a positive scalar indicating the deterrent effect of the creditor's power in the international credit market.

In accordance with the debt-overhang hypothesis, assume that the indebted country's investment is adversely affected by the annual debt repayments through a decline in the government budget for investment and through an (expected and actual) increase in tax rates, which, in the presence of capital mobility, discourages capital formation and repatriation of flight capital (Krugman, 1989; Helpman, 1989; Dooley and Helpman, 1992; and Boyce, 1992).[2] Since the country's GNP is directly related to investment, this assumption implies that the indebted country's GNP is adversely affected by the annual debt repayment as indicated, for convenience, by the following linear equation:

$$Y = \bar{Y} - \delta M, \delta \geq 1 \quad (2)$$

where $\bar{Y}$ is the highest level of GNP attainable had the annual debt-repayments been nil, and δ is a positive scalar indicating the potentially adverse marginal effect of the renegotiated annual debt-repayment on the country's GNP. Equation 2 also indicates that the renegotiated debt-repayment cannot exceed $\bar{Y}/\delta$.

The substitution of equation 2 into equation 1 for Y implies that the probability of default perceived by the creditor is given by

$$p = \alpha[M / (\bar{Y}-\delta M)] - \lambda s \quad (3)$$

which, by differentiation, indicates that

$$p_M = \frac{\alpha \bar{Y}}{(\bar{Y} - \delta M)^2} > 0 \quad (4)$$

and

$$p_{MM} = \frac{2\, \delta\, \alpha\, \bar{Y}}{(\bar{Y} - \delta M)^3} > 0. \quad (5)$$

Obviously, the creditor requires that $0 \leq p < 1$. Since p rises with M, this requirement implies that the renegotiated annual debt repayment lies within the interval $M_{min} \leq M < M_{max}$, where $p(M_{min}) = 0$ and $p(M_{max}) = 1$. The substitution of these boundary conditions into equation 3 yields:

$$M_{min} = \left(\frac{\lambda s}{\alpha + \delta \lambda s}\right)\bar{Y} \quad (6)$$

and

$$M_{max} = \left(\frac{1+\lambda s}{\alpha + \delta(1+\lambda s)}\right)\bar{Y}. \quad (7)$$

Note that since $\alpha > 0$, $M_{max} < \overline{Y}/\delta$. Note further that the feasible interval $M_{max} - M_{min}$ is shifted rightward by larger values of $\overline{Y}$ and λs and by smaller values of α and δ. This interval is also enlarged by higher values of $\overline{Y}$.

In view of the above arguments, the annual debt-repayment (ADR) is perceived by the creditor to be distributed as follows:

$$ADR = \begin{cases} M & 1-\alpha M/(\overline{Y}-\delta M) + \lambda s \\ 0 & \alpha M/(\overline{Y}-\delta M) - \lambda s.^{3} \end{cases} \tag{8}$$

Consequently, the expected annual debt repayment (EADR) is:

$$EADR = [1 - \alpha M/(\overline{Y} - \delta M) + \lambda s]M \tag{9}$$

and by differentiation

$$\frac{\partial EADR}{\partial M} = 1 - [p(M) + p_M(M)M] \gtreqless 0 \text{ as } M \lesseqgtr \tilde{M} \tag{10}$$

where

$$\tilde{M} = \left[1 - \sqrt{\frac{\alpha}{\alpha+\delta(1+\lambda s)}}\right]\frac{\overline{Y}}{\delta}. \tag{11}$$

Intuitively, an increase in the renegotiated annual debt repayment reduces the probability of payment each year and hence the expected annual debt repayment is subject to a 'debt Laffer curve'. That is, beyond the critical level $\tilde{M}$ an increase in the payment due causes the probability of default to go up so much that expected payment falls. Thus, EADR rises and then falls with M as illustrated in Figure 15.1.

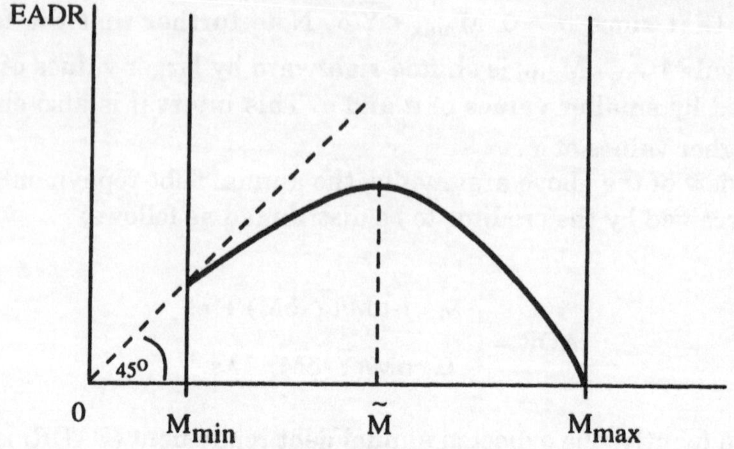

Figure 15.1 The 'debt Laffer curve'

15.3 Debt repayment constraint and the 'admissible rescheduling curve'

Suppose that the distribution of the actual annual debt-repayment is perceived by the creditor to be stable over the repayment period.[4] In view of equation 9, the present value (PV) of the stream of the expected annual debt-repayments (SEADR) over a T-year period is given by:

$$PV(SEADR) = \sum_{t=0}^{T} [1-\alpha M/(\bar{Y}-\delta M)+\lambda s]M/(1+r)^t$$

$$= [1-\alpha M/(\bar{Y}-\delta M)+\lambda s]M[\beta(1-\beta^T)/(1-\beta)] \quad (12)$$

where

$$\beta = 1/(1+r) \quad (13)$$

and r is a constant, real, interest rate per annum.

Suppose that equation 3 and the values of its right-hand-side variables and coefficients are common knowledge in the sense that the debtor knows that the creditor uses equation 3 and relevant data and that the creditor knows that he or she (the debtor) uses the same equation and data in assessing the probability of default, and *vice versa.* Suppose that the creditor is aware of the possibility that, due to a domestic pressure, the sovereign might not always be able to raise taxes and reduce other spending (e.g., subsidies) for servicing the country's external liabilities. Suppose further that the creditor's profits from retaliation are small and that the creditor believes that the sovereign is reliable in the sense that a short-term, or current, illiquidity does not necessarily lead to a long-term insolvency. In which case, the creditor prefers to tolerate the uncertainty about future repayments and negotiates new debt-repayment's terms which implicitly incorporate episodes of temporary illiquidity. In this setting, and in view of equation 12, it is suggested that the rescheduling schemes (M,T) which are admissible for negotiation by both the creditor and debtor should obey the following 'debt-repayment constraint':

$$[1 - \alpha M/(\bar{Y}-\delta M)+\lambda s]M[\beta(1-\beta^T)/(1-\beta)] = D_0 \tag{14}$$

where D_0 denotes the country's external debt, after discount, at the beginning of the rescheduling horizon. This constraint can be equivalently rendered as

$$T = \{\log\{\beta-(1-\beta)D_0/[1-\alpha M/(\bar{Y}-\delta M)+\lambda s]M\}/\log\beta\} - 1. \tag{15}$$

The set of all the admissible rescheduling schemes can be depicted by a curve in the M-T plane, which is referred to hereafter as the 'admissible rescheduling curve'. By totally differentiating equation 14 and by recalling that the probability of default rises with M, it can be shown that along the 'admissible rescheduling curve' of a sovereign debt the period of repayment is initially shortened but later lengthened as the renegotiated annual repayment rises.

Proposition: Along the admissible rescheduling curve

$$\frac{dT}{dM}\begin{cases} <0 \text{ for } & M_{min} \leq M < \tilde{M} \\ =0 \text{ for } & M = \tilde{M} \\ >0 \text{ for } & \tilde{M} < M < M_{max}. \end{cases} \tag{16}$$

The proof of this proposition is given in the Appendix. Intuitively, note that $1-\beta^T$ rises as T rises. Hence, EADR must fall as T rises to satisfy the debt repayment constraint 14. This requires M initially to fall and then to rise as T rises. If M is small, the 'debt-Laffer curve' is upward sloping. Thus, for small values of M, a higher M means a higher EADR and subsequently a shorter period of repaying D_0. At some point, however, EADR begins to fall as M continues to rise. At this point, T must be raised to maintain D_0 constant as M rises.

Figure 15.2 illustrates the above-mentioned proposition by displaying the set of all the rescheduling schemes which are admissible for negotiation by both the debtor and the creditor, $\Omega = \{(M,T) \in R_+^2: [1-\alpha M/(\bar{Y}-\delta M)+\lambda s]M[\beta(1-\beta^T)/(1-\beta)]=D_0\}$, as a U-shaped curve in the plane spanned by M and T.[5] Equation 14 indicates further that an increase in the debtor's initial liabilities and an increase in the international interest rate shift the 'admissible rescheduling curve' upward, whereas an increase in the country's potential GNP level and an increase in the creditor's market share in the international credit market shift the curve downward by reducing the probability of default.

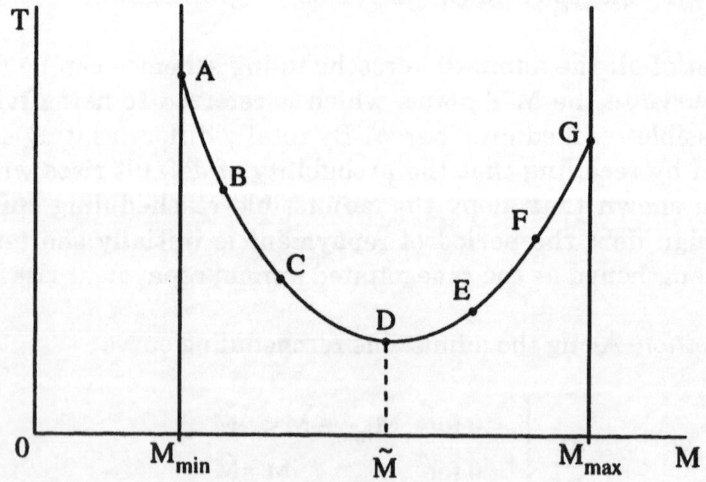

Figure 15.2 **The 'admissible rescheduling curve'**

15.4 Risk, time preference and the creditor's and debtor's choices

The 'admissible rescheduling curve' developed above is the locus of all combinations of M and T yielding a constant sum of discounted expected annual repayments which is equal to the remaining external debt after an initial and predetermined discount. Attitude toward risk and time preference, which may affect the creditor's and debtor's choice of a rescheduling scheme, are not included in the construction of this curve. These factors are considered now to identify the preferred admissible rescheduling schemes by the creditor and the debtor.

From the creditor's perspective, there is a trade-off between risk of non-payment and impatience along the downward-sloping side of the 'admissable rescheduling curve'. That is, the costs of a shorter period of debt repayment is the increase in the level of risk bearing as the recontracted annual payment rises. If the creditor's decision was not affected by time preference, a risk-averse creditor would prefer rescheduling scheme A over any other scheme, regardless of his or her intensity of risk aversion, in order to minimize the variance of the total repayment for the given amount of expected total repayment. However, impatience shifts the creditor's choice downward along the 'admissible rescheduling curve' toward C. Schemes along the upward-sloping side of the curve may be considered by the creditor if he or she is either risk neutral or risk lover. In general, the creditor's choice of an admissible rescheduling scheme is indicated by one of the nine possible cells defined by attitude toward risk and time preference and displayed by Table 15.1. The schemes chosen by the nine types of creditors are indicated on the 'admissible rescheduling curve' in Figure 15.2 by A, B, C, D, E, F and G.

Similarly, from the debtor's point of view there is a trade-off between risking current domestic stability and altruism toward future generations along the downward-sloping side of the 'admissible rescheduling curve'. That is, the costs of alleviating the current burden of the external debt by negotiating a small annual repayment and avoiding painful measures that might lead to social and political instability is the forgone consumption of future generations imposed by spreading the debt repayment over a long

Table 15.1
The creditor's choice of an admissible rescheduling scheme

Time preference	Attitude toward risk of nonpayment: Aversion	Neutrality	Love
Strong (Impatience)	C	D	E
Average	B	D	F
Weak (Patience)	A	A or G	G

Table 15.2
The debtor's choice of an admissible rescheduling scheme

Time preference	Attitude toward risking domestic stability: Aversion	Neutrality	Love
Strong (Egoism & myopia)	A	A or G	G
Average	B	C	F
Weak (Altruism)	C	D	E

period. Schemes along the upward-sloping side of the curve may be considered by the indebted sovereign if he or she is either risk neutral or risk lover and ready to face the social unrest and the political risk stemming from a large annual repayment and believes that the high domestic pressure would lead to frequent and excusable non-payment. In general, the choice of an admissible rescheduling scheme falls into one of the nine categories defined by the sovereign's attitude toward risk and time preference as displayed in Table 15.2. For simplicity, the rescheduling schemes chosen by the nine types of debtors are also illustrated by A, B, C, D, E, F and G on the 'admissible rescheduling curve' in Figure 15.2. More generally, the chosen schemes are rather likely to be in the vicinity of these points.

15.5 Creditor-debtor combinations of agreement and disagreement

The possible combinations of creditors and debtors, their choices and the degree of similarity or difference between their choices are summarized by Table 15.3. In each cell of this table, the upper entry indicates the creditor's choice and the lower the debtor's choice. The degree of similarity between these choices is indicated by = in the case of consensus, ≈ in the case of a strong similarity, ~ in the case of a weak similarity, ≠ in the case of a substantial difference, and # in the case of a large difference. The combinations of creditor and debtor yielding consensus or similarity are further highlighted by shading. These combinations are located in the top-left, bottom-right, centre and centre-left regions of the table in which there is, in most cases, a similarity between the creditor's and debtor's attitude toward risk. In contrast, strong disagreement exists when one of the sides is risk averse while the other is risk lover as their choices lie on opposite sides of the 'admissible rescheduling curve' and the 'debt-Laffer curve'.

15.6 Conclusion

This chapter proposed that the set of admissible rescheduling schemes of a sovereign debt can be depicted by a U-shaped curve in the plane spanned by the renegotiated annual debt repayment and

Table 15.3
Combinations of types of creditors and debtors and their choices

CREDITOR

DEBTOR	Risk Averse/Impatient	Risk Averse/Average	Risk Averse/Patient	Risk Neutral/Impatient	Risk Neutral/Average	Risk Neutral/Patient	Risk Lover/Impatient	Risk Lover/Average	Risk Lover/Patient
Risk Averse/Myopic	C ~ A	B ≈ A	A = A	D # A	D # A	A/G =/# A	E # A	F # A	G # A
Risk Averse/Average	C ≈ B	B = B	A ≈ B	D ≠ B	D ≠ B	A/G ≈/# B	E # B	F # B	G # B
Risk Averse/Altruist	C = C	B ≈ C	A ~ C	D ≈ C	D ≈ C	A/G ~/# C	E ≠ C	F # C	G # C
Risk Neutral/Myopic	C ~/# A/G	B ≈/# A/G	A =/# A/G	D # A/G	D # A/G	A/G =or# A/G	E #/~ A/G	F #/≈ A/G	G #/= A/G
Risk Neutral/Average	C = C	B ≈ C	A ~ C	D ≈ C	D ≈ C	A/G ~/# C	E ≠ C	F # C	G # C
Risk Neutral/Altruist	C ≈ D	B ≠ D	A # D	D = D	D = D	A/G # D	E ≈ D	F ≠ D	G # D
Risk Lover/Myopic	C # G	B # G	A # G	D # G	D # G	A/G #/= G	E ~ G	F ≈ G	G = G
Risk Lover/Average	C # F	B # F	A # F	D ≠ F	D ≠ F	A/G #/≈ F	E ≈ F	F = F	G ≈ F
Risk Lover/Altruist	C ≠ E	B # E	A # E	D ≈ E	D ≈ E	A/G #/~ E	E = E	F ≈ E	G ~ E

the renegotiated repayment period. The classification of creditors and debtors by risk and time preference led to eighty-one distinct combinations. Consensus and good prospects for quickly reaching an agreement may be obtained in the following cases.

If both the creditor and debtor are risk averse and if the creditor is patient whereas the debtor is myopic, they would both prefer the rescheduling scheme A with the smallest annual repayment and the longest period of repayment.

If both the creditor and debtor are risk averse and if the creditor is impatient whereas the debtor is altruist, they would both prefer the rescheduling scheme C.

If both the creditor and debtor are risk averse and having average rate of time preference, they would both prefer rescheduling scheme B with a relatively small annual repayment over a long period.

If both the creditor and debtor are risk averse and if the creditor has an average rate of time preference and the debtor is altruist, they are likely to reach an agreement about a rescheduling scheme between B and C with a relatively small annual repayment over a considerably long period.

If the debtor is risk averse and altruist and the creditor is risk neutral and not very patient, or if the creditor is risk averse and impatient and the debtor is risk neutral and altruist, they are likely to reach an agreement about a rescheduling scheme between C and D with a substantial annual repayment over a short period.

If both the creditor and debtor are risk neutral and if the creditor is not patient and the debtor is altruist, they would both prefer scheme D with the shortest period of debt repayment and a substantial annual repayment.

If both the creditor and debtor are risk lover and if the creditor is patient whereas the debtor is myopic, they would both prefer scheme G with the largest annual repayment and a considerably long repayment period.

If both the creditor and debtor are risk lover and if the creditor is impatient whereas the debtor is altruist, they would both prefer scheme E with a substantial annual repayment over a relatively short period.

If both the creditor and debtor are risk lover and have an average rate of time preference, they would both prefer scheme F with a very large annual repayment over a substantially long period.

If both the creditor and debtor are risk lover and the creditor is patient (or has an average rate of time preference) whereas the debtor has an average rate of time preference (or is myopic), they are likely to reach an agreement on a scheme between F and G with a high annual payment over a long period.

If both the creditor and debtor are risk lover and the creditor is impatient (or has an average rate of time preference) whereas the debtor has an average rate of time preference (or is altruist), they are likely to reach an agreement on a scheme between E and F with a large annual payment over a medium-length period of repayment.

If the creditor is risk neutral and not very patient and the debtor is risk lover and altruist, they are likely to reach an agreement on a scheme with a short repayment period and a substantially large annual repayment between D and E. Such a rescheduling scheme is also likely to be chosen if the debtor is risk neutral and altruist and the creditor is risk lover and impatient.

If the debtor is risk neutral and altruist and the creditor is risk averse and impatient, they are likely to reach an agreement on a scheme with a short repayment period and a substantial annual repayment between C and D.

Finally, when it is unclear which of the extreme schemes A and G is preferred by either the creditor, debtor, or both, there is scope for consensus, but there is also a possibility of strong disagreement. The rest of the combinations reveal a high degree of disagreement about an admissible rescheduling scheme. In such cases, a substantial level of mediation is required.

Notes

1 Following Berg and Sachs (1988), it can be argued that α is affected by the indebted country's social, political and economic structure.

2 For tests of the debt-overhang hypothesis see Chapters 8 and 9 and Cohen (1993).

3 The nature of the analysis will not be substantially changed by replacing the assumption of a complete default by a partial default, i.e., an actual annual repayment of γM dollars ($0 < \gamma < 1$) with probability p.

4 Alternatively, one may incorporate, for example, an anticipation

of economic growth, or economic slowdown, into the analysis by multiplying ($\bar{Y}$ - δM) by a shift factor g^t, where g is a positive scalar equal to one plus the anticipated growth rate.

5 If the assumption of common knowledge is replaced by asymmetric information, it is likely that the debtor would claim that the probability of default is lower than that perceived by the creditor, for any given annual debt repayment, in order to obtain a repayment period shorter than that required by the creditor. In this case, the rescheduling curve considered by the debtor lies below the rescheduling curve considered by the creditor.

Appendix

Proof of the U-shaped admissible rescheduling curve's proposition

Equation 14 can be rewritten as

$$EADR(M)B(T) = D_0 \tag{A.1}$$

where EADR(M) is explicitly given by equation 9 and

$$B(T) = \beta(1-\beta^T)/(1-\beta). \tag{A.2}$$

By totally differentiating equation A.1

$$\left.\frac{dT}{dM}\right| D_0 = \text{const.} = \frac{-\,\partial EADR/\partial M}{\partial B/\partial T}. \tag{A.3}$$

Since $\partial B/\partial T > 0$,

$$\text{sign}\left\{\left.\frac{dT}{dM}\right| D_0 = \text{const.}\right\} = -\,\text{sign}\left\{\frac{\partial EADR(M)}{\partial M}\right\} \tag{A.4}$$

and in recalling equation 10,

$$\frac{dT}{dM} \Big| D_0 = \text{const.} \begin{cases} < 0 \text{ for} & M_{min} \leq M < \tilde{M} \\ = 0 \text{ for} & M = \tilde{M} \\ > 0 \text{ for} & \tilde{M} < M < M_{max} \,.\, \textit{QED} \end{cases} \tag{A.5}$$

References

Berg, A. and Sachs, J. (1988), 'The Debt Crisis: Structural Explanation of Country Performance,' *Journal of Development Economics*, vol. 29, pp. 271–306.

Boyce, J. K. (1992), 'The Revolving Door? External Debt and Capital Flight: A Philippine Case Study,' *World Development*, vol. 20, no. 3, pp. 335–49.

Bulow, J. and Rogoff, K. (1990), 'Cleaning up Third World Debt Without Getting Taken to the Cleaners,' *Journal of Economic Perspectives*, vol. 4, pp. 31–42.

Cohen, D. (1993), 'Low Investment and Large LDC Debt in the 1980's,' *American Economic Review*, vol. 83, pp. 437–49.

Dooley, M.P. and Helpman, E. (1992), 'Tax Credits for Debt Reduction,' *Journal of International Economics*, vol. 32, pp. 165–77.

Helpman, E. (1989), 'Voluntary Debt Reduction: Incentives and Welfare,' in Frenkel, J.A., Dooley, M.P. and Wickham, P. (eds.), *Analytical Issues in Debt*, International Monetary Fund, Washington DC, pp. 279–310.

Kenen, P. (1990), 'Organizing Debt Relief: The Need for a New Institution,' *Journal of Economic Perspectives*, vol. 4, pp. 7–18.

Krugman, P. (1988), 'Financing vs. Forgiving a Debt Overhang,' *Journal of Development Economics*, vol. 29, pp. 253–68.

—— (1989), 'Market-Based Debt-Reduction Schemes,' in Frenkel, Jacob A., Dooley, M.P. and Wickham, P. (eds.), *Analytical Issues in Debt*, International Monetary Fund, Washington DC, pp. 258–78.

Sachs, J. (1990), 'A Strategy for Efficient Debt Reduction,' *Journal of Economic Perspectives*, vol. 4, pp. 19–30.

Appendix A7

Table A7.1
Pooled cross section-time series estimates of land allocation in summers between rice and maize without money illusion for Punjab 1966–86

Rice land regression equation

Explanatory variable	Estimated coefficients, t-ratios and elasticities				
	β=0.1	β=0.2	β=0.3	β=0.4	β=0.5
P^e_{rice}	-6975.4	3180.6	5969.3	5558.8	3507.7
	(0.2374)	(0.1266)	(0.2866)	(0.3210)	(0.2408)
	-0.689	0.3142	0.5896	0.5491	0.3465
P^e_{maize}	7528.6	-312.92	1292.7	3124.6	4256.6
	(0.1387)	(0.0122)	(0.0810)	(0.2781)	(0.5026)
	0.8232	-0.0342	0.1413	0.3416	0.4654
$\bar{y}_{rice}$	15.662	17.851	19.83	21.58	23.044
	(2.7428)	(2.9441)	(3.1406)	(3.3341)	(3.522)
	0.0623	0.071	0.0789	0.0859	0.0917
$\bar{y}_{maize}$	-16.39	-17.744	-19.225	-20.711	-21.883
	(3.8111)	(3.8850)	(4.0477)	(4.1910)	(4.2312)
	-0.0503	-0.0545	-0.0591	-0.0636	-0.0672
σ^2_{rice}	-0.0083	-0.0125	-0.0141	-0.0143	-0.0138
	(0.6709)	(1.015)	(1.1624)	(1.1946)	(1.1713)
	-0.0008	-0.0012	-0.0013	-0.0014	-0.0013

Table A7.1 (continued)

Rice land regression equation

Explanatory variable	Estimated coefficients, t-ratios and elasticities				
	$\beta=0.6$	$\beta=0.7$	$\beta=0.8$	$\beta=0.9$	$\beta=1.0$
P^e_{rice}	759.60	-2040.7	-4691.7	-7004.3	-7943.0
	(0.0608)	(0.1845)	(0.4590)	(0.7157)	(0.8484)
	0.075	-0.2016	-0.4634	-0.6919	-0.7847
P^e_{maize}	4743.1	4719.3	4159.2	2909.7	1024.7
	(0.7061)	(0.8399)	(0.8311)	(0.6207)	(0.2326)
	0.5186	0.5160	0.4548	0.3181	0.112
$\bar{y}_{rice}$	24.222	25.543	28.001	32.331	35.874
	(3.6995)	(3.9215)	(4.3637)	(5.2893)	(6.349)
	0.0964	0.1016	0.1114	0.1286	0.1427
$\bar{y}_{maize}$	-22.329	-21.528	-18.401	-12.272	-6.8821
	(4.0856)	(3.6773)	(2.9073)	(1.829)	(1.025)
	-0.0686	-0.0661	-0.0565	-0.0377	-0.0211
σ^2_{rice}	-0.0129	-0.0116	-0.0094	-0.0061	-0.003
	(1.1123)	(1.0011)	(0.7857)	(0.4772)	(0.273)
	-0.0012	-0.0011	-0.0009	-0.0006	-0.0003

Table A7.1 (continued)

Explanatory variable	Rice land regression equation: Estimated coefficients, t-ratios and elasticities				
	β=0.1	β=0.2	β=0.3	β=0.4	β=0.5
σ^2_{maize}	0.0347	0.0322	0.0321	0.0325	0.0333
	(2.9438)	(2.7310)	(2.7263)	(2.7473)	(2.7781)
	0.0015	0.0014	0.0014	0.0014	0.0014
$\sigma_{rice,maize}$	0.0743	0.0751	0.0750	0.0748	0.0746
	(4.1623)	(4.308)	(4.3816)	(4.3936)	(4.3672)
	0.0005	0.0005	0.0005	0.0005	0.0005
w^e_1	-50400	-18614	-9429.1	-6255	-4978.4
	(1.5880)	(1.0583)	(0.7661)	(0.6699)	(0.6726)
	-10.877	-4.0171	-2.0349	-1.3499	-1.0744
w^e_2	56050	24900	14080	9193.2	6254.4
	(2.3754)	(1.6965)	(1.2836)	(1.0645)	(0.8919)
	14.8688	6.6054	3.7351	2.4387	1.6591
Constant	7395.5	11806	16245	21117	26747
	(1.0805)	(1.3594)	(1.5826)	(1.826)	(2.0971)
BUSE R^2	0.2673	0.2767	0.2820	0.2865	0.2907
FPE	0.5541	0.5508	0.5461	0.5401	0.5335

Table A7.1 (continued)

Rice land regression equation

Explanatory variable	**Estimated coefficients, t-ratios and elasticities**				
	β=0.6	**β=0.7**	**β=0.8**	**β=0.9**	**β=1.0**
σ^2_{maize}	0.0342	0.0354	0.0369	0.0384	0.04
	(2.8237)	(2.8834)	(2.9417)	(2.9917)	(3.086)
	0.0015	0.0015	0.0016	0.0017	0.0017
$\sigma_{rice,maize}$	0.0744	0.0741	0.0739	0.0733	0.0717
	(4.3037)	(4.1823)	(3.9791)	(3.7228)	(3.501)
	0.0005	0.0005	0.0005	0.0005	0.0005
w^e_1	-4487.6	-4454.1	-4809.1	-5377.4	-5594.9
	(0.7418)	(0.8736)	(1.087)	(1.389)	(-1.633)
	-0.9685	-0.9612	-1.0378	-1.1605	-1.2074
w^e_2	4203.5	2744.2	1677.4	856.21	437.53
	(0.7208)	(0.5505)	(0.3809)	(0.2159)	(0.121)
	1.1151	0.7280	0.4450	0.2271	0.1161
Constant	32831	38173	40283	36386	32082
	(2.3381)	(2.4486)	(2.3187)	(1.9323)	(1.641)
BUSE R^2	0.2933	0.2931	0.2933	0.3140	0.354
FPE	0.5271	0.5220	0.5205	0.5256	0.5323

Table A7.1 (continued)

Maize Land Regression Equation

Explanatory variable	Estimated coefficients, t-ratios and elasticities				
	β=0.1	**β=0.2**	**β=0.3**	**β=0.4**	**β=0.5**
P^e_{rice}	-7514.8 (0.4195) -1.0921	-3867 (0.2308) -0.562	-5725.7 (0.3804) -0.8321	-9371 (0.702) -1.3619	-12286 (1.0465) -1.7855
P^e_{maize}	9302.2 (0.2811) 1.4964	6373.4 (0.3784) 1.0252	7026.6 (0.6116) 1.1303	7228.1 (0.8344) 1.1627	7455.4 (1.0863) 1.1993
$\bar{y}_{rice}$	-5.5146 (1.7225) -0.0323	-5.8246 (1.7844) -0.0341	-5.6649 (1.7001) -0.0332	-5.6448 (1.6963) -0.033	-5.5981 (1.7043) -0.0328
$\bar{y}_{maize}$	5.9059 (2.2351) 0.0267	5.5878 (2.0351) 0.0253	5.6862 (1.9659) 0.0257	6.3534 (2.0598) 0.0287	7.5176 (2.238) 0.034

Table A7.1 (continued)

Maize Land Regression Equation

Explanatory variable	Estimated coefficients, t-ratios and elasticities				
	β=0.6	β=0.7	β=0.8	β=0.9	β=1.0
P^e_{rice}	-13302 (1.3015) -1.9332	-12513 (1.4137) -1.8185	-10742 (1.3944) -1.5611	-8741.2 (1.2852) -1.2704	-6946.1 (1.1359) -1.0095
P^e_{maize}	7593.9 (1.3605) 1.2216	7280.9 (1.5798) 1.1712	6517.5 (1.6893) 1.0484	5560.9 (1.6914) 0.8945	4712.3 (1.6436) 0.758
$\bar{y}_{rice}$	-5.5474 (1.7051) -0.0325	-5.6158 (1.7262) -0.0329	-5.8115 (1.7752) -0.034	-6.0618 (1.8427) -0.0355	-6.2616 (1.913) -0.0367
$\bar{y}_{maize}$	8.9929 (2.4363) 0.0406	10.326 (2.5629) 0.0467	11.057 (2.5588) 0.05	10.875 (2.4257) 0.0491	9.8659 (2.2192) 0.0446

Table A7.1 (continued)

Explanatory variable	Maize Land Regression Equation Estimated coefficients, t-ratios and elasticities				
	β=0.1	β=0.2	β=0.3	β=0.4	β=0.5
σ^2_{rice}	0.01 (1.4354) 0.0014	0.0083 (1.1498) 0.0012	0.0084 (1.1241) 0.0012	0.0093 (1.2186) 0.0013	0.0106 (1.3657) 0.0015
σ^2_{maize}	0.0179 (2.3918) 0.0011	0.0254 (3.4951) 0.0016	0.0282 (3.8715) 0.0018	0.0283 (3.8166) 0.0018	0.0273 (3.6016) 0.0017
$\sigma_{rice\ maize}$	0.0048 (0.4381) 0.00005	0.0059 (0.5240) 0.00006	0.0047 (0.4087) 0.00005	0.0027 (0.2278) 0.00003	0.0003 (0.0276) 0.000003
w^e_1	13757 (0.7891) 4.368	14308 (1.4848) 4.5429	10878 (1.5511) 3.4539	7893 (1.3954) 2.5061	5893.4 (1.2254) 1.8712
w^e_2	-35459 (3.6418) -13.8393	-21468 (3.484) -8.3788	-15663 (3.0589) -6.1131	-12702 (2.813) -4.9575	-11026 (2.6914) -4.3033
Constant	10842 (2.788)	14821 (3.0709)	19981 (3.4436)	26261 (3.9373)	32282 (4.3596)
BUSE R^2	0.3147	0.3266	0.3173	0.3026	0.2861
FPE	0.5649	0.5630	0.5570	0.5524	0.5490

Table A7.1 (continued)

Maize Land Regression Equation

Explanatory variable	Estimated coefficients, t-ratios and elasticities				
	β=0.6	β=0.7	β=0.8	β=0.9	β=1.0
σ^2_{rice}	0.0116 (1.4979) 0.0016	0.0124 (1.6091) 0.0017	0.0132 (1.7429) 0.0018	0.0145 (1.9353) 0.002	0.0163 (2.1932) 0.0023
σ^2_{maize}	0.0262 (3.4036) 0.0017	0.0255 (3.2559) 0.0016	0.0244 (3.0718) 0.0016	0.0224 (2.7577) 0.0014	0.019 (2.288) 0.0012
$\sigma_{rice\ maize}$	-0.0019 (0.1589) -0.00002	-0.0036 (0.2973) -0.00004	-0.0046 (0.3822) -0.00005	-0.0051 (0.4232) -0.00005	-0.0051 (0.43) -0.00005
w^e_1	4715.7 (1.1297) 1.4973	4011.7 (1.1015) 1.2738	3485.6 (1.0892) 1.1067	3042.1 (1.0696) 0.9659	2704 (1.0591) 0.8585
w^e_2	-9789.9 (2.5989) -3.8209	-8522.7 (2.4680) -3.3263	-7114.9 (2.2659) -2.7769	-5689.4 (1.9996) -2.2205	-4428 (1.7136) -1.7282
Constant	36860 (4.5878)	39929 (4.6133)	42296 (4.5136)	44975 (4.4386)	48429 (4.5002)
BUSE R^2	0.2714	0.2573	0.2388	0.2140	0.1872
FPE	0.5471	0.5476	0.5502	0.5538	0.5573

Table A7.2
Pooled cross section-time series estimates of land allocation in summers between rice and maize with money illusion for Punjab 1966–86

Rice Land Regression Equation

Explanatory variable	Estimated coefficients, t-ratios and elasticities				
	β=0.1	β=0.2	β=0.3	β=0.4	β=0.5
P^e_{rice}	229.35 (1.2496) 0.0348	316.60 (2.1458) 0.048	297.27 (2.5156) 0.0451	248.55 (2.5634) 0.0377	201.33 (2.4897) 0.0305
P^e_{maize}	315.50 (0.9072) 0.0538	56.026 (0.3517) 0.0096	14.643 (0.1455) 0.0025	16.430 (0.2269) 0.0028	23.139 (0.4155) 0.0039
$\bar{y}_{rice}$	18.115 (3.2956) 0.0721	18.023 (3.1554) 0.0717	18.126 (3.0978) 0.0721	18.688 (3.1368) 0.0744	19.229 (3.1699) 0.0765
$\bar{y}_{maize}$	-15.919 (3.9153) -0.0489	-15.418 (3.6373) -0.0474	-15.766 (3.5917) -0.0484	-17.084 (3.7253) -0.0525	-18.78 (3.8654) -0.0577
σ^2_{rice}	-0.01102 (0.9119) -0.001	-0.0161 (1.3181) -0.0015	-0.0162 (1.3064) -0.0015	-0.0138 (1.1007) -0.0013	-0.0104 (0.8315) -0.001
σ^2_{maize}	0.0330 (3.0454) 0.0014	0.0292 (2.7825) 0.0013	0.0290 (2.7585) 0.0013	0.0299 (2.7825) 0.0013	0.0311 (2.8188) 0.0014

Table A7.2 (continued)

Rice Land Regression Equation

Explanatory variable	Estimated coefficients, t-ratios and elasticities				
	β=0.6	β=0.7	β=0.8	β=0.9	β=1.0
P^e_{rice}	164.94	139.61	123.09	112.91	106.05
	(2.4142)	(2.3823)	(2.3987)	(2.4467)	(2.4954)
	0.025	0.0212	0.0187	0.0171	0.0161
P^e_{maize}	26.942	28.132	27.705	25.834	22.812
	(0.6028)	(0.7579)	(0.8684)	(0.9044)	(0.8607)
	0.0046	0.0048	0.0047	0.0044	0.0039
$\bar{y}_{rice}$	19.405	19.264	19.196	19.854	21.289
	(3.1294)	(3.0331)	(2.968)	(3.0633)	(3.3568)
	0.0772	0.0767	0.0764	0.079	0.0847
$\bar{y}_{maize}$	-20.281	-21.281	-21.556	-20.636	-18.78
	(3.8817)	(3.7477)	(3.497)	(3.1499)	(2.8123)
	-0.0623	-0.0654	-0.0662	-0.0634	-0.0577
σ^2_{rice}	-0.0068	-0.0032	-0.00006	0.0023	0.0040
	(0.5448)	(0.2618)	(0.0053)	(0.1945)	(0.3300)
	-0.0006	-0.0003	-5E-6	0.0002	0.0004
σ^2_{maize}	0.0321	0.0328	0.0331	0.0332	0.03313
	(2.8529)	(2.8726)	(2.8734)	(2.8525)	(2.8116)
	0.0014	0.0014	0.0014	0.0014	0.0014

Table A7.2 (continued)

Rice Land Regression Equation

Explanatory variable	Estimated coefficients, t-ratios and elasticities				
	$\beta=0.1$	$\beta=0.2$	$\beta=0.3$	$\beta=0.4$	$\beta=0.5$
	0.0742	0.0759	0.0772	0.0783	0.0793
$\sigma_{\text{rice maize}}$	(4.2389)	(4.454)	(4.5179)	(4.5323)	(4.5294)
	0.0005	0.0005	0.0005	0.0005	0.0005
	224.73	145.61	77.656	30.550	0.3047
w_1^e	(0.5593)	(0.7536)	(0.6159)	(0.3199)	(0.0039)
	0.0662	0.0429	0.0229	0.009	0.00009
	140.74	122.80	134.47	145.23	151.89
w_2^e	(0.5549)	(0.9142)	(1.4105)	(1.9016)	(2.3171)
	0.0550	0.048	0.0526	0.0568	0.0594
Constant	-1717.6	-312.91	2430.7	6435.4	11453
	(0.5549)	(0.0654)	(0.4315)	(0.9901)	(1.5147)
BUSE R^2	0.3569	0.3979	0.4201	0.4390	0.4492
FPE	0.5628	0.5636	0.5625	0.5606	0.5576

Table A7.2 (continued)

Rice Land Regression Equation

Explanatory variable	Estimated coefficients, t-ratios and elasticities				
	β=0.6	β=0.7	β=0.8	β=0.9	β=1.0
$\sigma_{rice\ maize}$	0.0797	0.0794	0.0782	0.0763	0.0735
	(4.4962)	(4.4165)	(4.279)	(4.0683)	(3.8096)
	0.0005	0.0005	0.0005	0.0005	0.0005
w_1^e	-18.564	-30.250	-37.313	-41.681	-45.175
	(0.2739)	(0.5051)	(0.6922)	(0.8438)	(0.980)
	-0.0055	-0.0089	-0.011	-0.0123	-0.0133
w_2^e	153.62	151.14	146.11	139.08	131.04
	(2.6107)	(2.7805)	(2.8579)	(2.8579)	(2.8073)
	0.06	0.0591	0.0571	0.0544	0.0512
Constant	17218	23281	28796	32346	33918
	(1.9222)	(2.1827)	(2.3094)	(2.3099)	(2.2628)
BUSE R^2	0.4461	0.4345	0.4222	0.4139	0.4114
FPE	0.5520	0.5475	0.5422	0.5382	0.5360

Table A7.2 (continued)

Maize Land Regression Equation

Explanatory variable	Estimated coefficients, t-ratios and elasticities				
	β=0.1	β=0.2	β=0.3	β=0.4	β=0.5
P^e_{rice}	-48.547	52.606	76.664	71.412	58.599
	(0.3981)	(0.4778)	(0.8447)	(0.9441)	(0.9211)
	-0.0108	0.0117	0.0171	0.0159	0.0131
P^e_{maize}	160.35	107.45	93.326	75.387	64.945
	(0.6768)	(0.9021)	(1.1739)	(1.2664)	(1.3719)
	0.0402	0.027	0.0234	0.0189	0.0163
$\bar{y}_{rice}$	-7.2017	-6.5547	-5.5084	-4.8732	-4.0895
	(2.278)	(2.056)	(1.6965)	(1.4872)	(1.2366)
	-0.0422	-0.0384	-0.0322	-0.0285	-0.0239
$\bar{y}_{maize}$	6.1311	5.8095	5.7166	6.2936	7.7321
	(2.3767)	(2.1237)	(1.9761)	(2.0393)	(2.2971)
	0.0277	0.0263	0.0258	0.0284	0.0349
σ^2_{rice}	0.0146	0.0117	0.0112	0.0119	0.0131
	(2.0208)	(1.5403)	(1.4230)	(1.4816)	(1.6167)
	0.002	0.0016	0.0016	0.0017	0.0018

Table A7.2 (continued)

Maize Land Regression Equation

Explanatory variable	Estimated coefficients, t-ratios and elasticities				
	β=0.6	β=0.7	β=0.8	β=0.9	β=1.0
P^e_{rice}	44.434 (0.8276) 0.0099	31.490 (0.6962) 0.007	19.594 (0.5127) 0.0044	8.0042 (0.2444) 0.0018	-3.7785 (0.1307) -0.0008
P^e_{maize}	61.198 (1.5843) 0.0154	58.763 (1.8515) 0.0147	54.916 (2.0964) 0.0138	48.903 (2.2371) 0.0123	40.615 (2.1625) 0.0102
$\bar{y}_{rice}$	-2.9744 (0.8874) -0.0174	-1.7712 (0.5199) -0.0104	-0.6470 (0.1877) -0.0038	0.2447 (0.0713) 0.0014	0.3970 (0.1172) 0.0023
$\bar{y}_{maize}$	10.092 (2.7448) 0.0456	12.889 (3.2614) 0.0582	15.715 (3.7563) 0.071	18.160 (4.1857) 0.0821	18.736 (4.3244) 0.0847
σ^2_{rice}	0.0142 (1.7372) 0.002	0.0148 (1.8106) 0.0021	0.0150 (1.8695) 0.0021	0.0152 (1.9512) 0.0021	0.0155 (2.051) 0.0022

Table A7.2 (continued)

Maize Land Regression Equation

Explanatory variable	Estimated coefficients, t-ratios and elasticities				
	β=0.1	β=0.2	β=0.3	β=0.4	β=0.5
σ^2_{maize}	0.0174	0.0241	0.0266	0.0257	0.0233
	(2.2554)	(3.2381)	(3.6097)	(3.427)	(3.0071)
	0.0011	0.0015	0.0017	0.0016	0.0015
$\sigma_{rice\ maize}$	0.00083	0.0039	0.0044	0.0038	0.0023
	(0.0725)	(0.3255)	(0.3591)	(0.3073)	(0.1825)
	0.00001	0.00004	0.00004	0.00004	0.00002
w^e_1	-156.74	71.094	89.716	81.983	70.810
	(0.6308)	(0.5552)	(1.0365)	(1.2173)	(1.2385)
	-0.068	0.0308	0.0389	0.0355	0.0307
w^e_2	-112.22	-175.17	-163.9	-143.25	-127.99
	(0.6967)	(2.0252)	(2.7045)	(2.9667)	(3.0871)
	-0.0645	-0.1007	-0.0942	-0.0824	-0.0736
Constant	9307.4	12394	15995	20062	23485
	(4.2929)	(4.7012)	(5.2482)	(5.7294)	(5.7559)
BUSE R^2	0.3240	0.3213	0.3277	0.3177	0.3009
FPE	0.5688	0.5658	0.5584	0.5509	0.5437

Table A7.2 (continued)

Maize Land Regression Equation

Explanatory variable	**Estimated coefficients, t-ratios and elasticities**				
	β=0.6	**β=0.7**	**β=0.8**	**β=0.9**	**β=1.0**
σ^2_{maize}	0.0213 (2.6901) 0.0014	0.0208 (2.6362) 0.0013	0.02156 (2.7698) 0.0014	0.0218 (2.8466) 0.0014	0.0196 (2.5374) 0.0013
$\sigma_{rice\ maize}$	0.0004 (0.0286) 0.000004	-0.0010 (0.081) -0.00001	-0.0017 (0.1343) -0.00002	-0.0021 (0.1703) -0.00002	-0.0032 (0.2611) -0.00003
w^e_1	57.106 (1.1505) 0.0248	42.898 (1.0192) 0.0186	31.384 (0.9015) 0.0136	23.786 (0.8226) 0.0103	19.242 (0.7647) 0.0083
w^e_2	-118.06 (3.2207) -0.0679	-111.66 (3.4416) -0.0642	-108.12 (3.7581) -0.0622	-105.57 (4.0738) -0.0607	-98.567 (4.0821) -0.0567
Constant	25605 (5.3826)	26722 (4.8812)	27381 (4.3969)	28357 (4.0889)	32104 (4.338)
BUSE R^2	0.2945	0.3054	0.3281	0.3501	0.3456
FPE	0.5385	0.5364	0.5355	0.5360	0.5397

Table A7.3
Pooled cross section-time series estimates of land allocation in winters between wheat and gram without money illusion for Punjab 1966–86

Wheat Land Regression Equation

Explanatory variable	Estimated coefficients, t-ratios and elasticities				
	β=0.1	β=0.2	β=0.3	β=0.4	β=0.5
	-13262	-18867	-22937	-24498	-25930
P^e_{wheat}	(2.2426)	(3.1758)	(3.9252)	(4.292)	(3.9717)
	-0.6174	-0.8784	-1.0679	-1.1405	-1.2072
	-807.93	714.11	290.88	51.179	-2088.5
P^e_{gram}	(0.0764)	(0.1128)	(0.0631)	(0.0146)	(0.7028)
	-0.0578	0.0511	0.0208	0.0037	-0.1495
	16.381	22.373	28.207	33.932	54.33
$\bar{y}_{wheat}$	(4.2554)	(5.5516)	(6.6252)	(7.5258)	(7.9238)
	0.0257	0.0351	0.0442	0.0532	0.0851
	-4.205	-4.5588	-4.6082	-4.5306	-5.7851
$\bar{y}_{gram}$	(1.8578)	(1.8134)	(1.7466)	(1.7236)	(3.8533)
	-0.0025	-0.0027	-0.0027	-0.0027	-0.0034
	0.0468	0.0382	0.0360	0.0365	-0.0379
σ^2_{wheat}	(2.7332)	(2.1575)	(1.9615)	(1.9387)	(1.6230)
	0.0014	0.0011	0.0010	0.0011	-0.0011

Table A7.3 (continued)

Wheat Land Regression Equation

Explanatory variable	Estimated coefficients, t-ratios and elasticities				
	β=0.6	β=0.7	β=0.8	β=0.9	β=1.0
P^e_{wheat}	-20145	-15349	-10044	-5224.1	-1663.1
	(3.73)	(2.9210)	(1.9258)	(0.9796)	(0.2974)
	-0.9379	-0.7146	-0.4676	-0.2432	-0.0774
P^e_{gram}	-155.89	-155.75	-145.67	-200.00	-335.66
	(0.0714)	(0.0878)	(0.0978)	(0.1530)	(0.2787)
	-0.0112	-0.0112	-0.0104	-0.0143	-0.0240
$\bar{y}_{wheat}$	43.889	47.441	49.743	50.817	50.544
	(8.436)	(8.5156)	(8.5757)	(8.7469)	(8.9665)
	0.0688	0.0743	0.0779	0.0796	0.0792
$\bar{y}_{gram}$	-4.2344	-4.2416	-4.2889	-4.3021	-4.2767
	(1.7100)	(1.7929)	(1.8974)	(1.9703)	(1.9928)
	-0.0025	-0.0025	-0.0025	-0.0025	-0.0025
σ^2_{wheat}	0.0389	0.0404	0.04198	0.0440	0.04617
	(2.0495)	(2.1422)	(2.2302)	(2.3174)	(2.3785)
	0.0011	0.0012	0.0012	0.0013	0.0013

Table A7.3 (continued)

Explanatory variable	Wheat Land Regression Equation Estimated coefficients, t-ratios and elasticities				
	β=0.1	β=0.2	β=0.3	β=0.4	β=0.5
σ^2_{gram}	0.00038 (1.3423) 0.00001	0.00038 (1.2905) 0.00001	0.00037 (1.2526) 0.00001	0.00036 (1.2597) 0.00001	0.00036 (2.331) 0.00001
$\sigma_{wheat\ gram}$	-0.0033 (0.3508) -0.00001	-0.0034 (0.3489) -0.00001	-0.0020 (0.2048) -4.2 E -6	-0.00057 (0.0591) -1.2E-6	0.00486 (0.0475) 0.00001
w_1^e	91855 (2.6790) 8.7223	53020 (2.8246) 5.0347	34111 (2.6346) 3.2391	22608 (2.311) 2.1468	12640 (1.273) 1.2003
w_2^e	-17781 (1.0672) -2.1007	-2899.2 (0.2693) -0.3425	-916.77 (0.1.30) -0.1083	-1456.8 (0.1873) -0.1721	-7098.3 (0.9161) -0.8386
Constant	12842 (2.7522)	24740 (4.2790)	39002 (5.644)	52857 (6.669)	61057 (6.3736)
BUSE R^2	0.2293	0.3287	0.3890	0.4326	0.4411
FPE	0.5461	0.5391	0.5332	0.5293	0.4978

Table A7.3 (continued)

Wheat Land Regression Equation

Explanatory variable	Estimated coefficients, t-ratios and elasticities				
	β=0.6	β=0.7	β=0.8	β=0.9	β=1.0
σ^2_{gram}	0.00033	0.00031	0.00027	0.00022	0.00019
	(1.2134)	(1.1573)	(1.0360)	(0.8640)	(0.7162)
	0.00001	0.00001	0.00001	4.5E-6	3.9E-6
$\sigma_{wheat\ gram}$	0.0023	0.0037	0.0054	0.0072	0.0090
	(0.2516)	(0.4125)	(0.5939)	(0.7884)	(0.9588)
	4.8E6	0.00001	0.00001	0.00002	0.00002
w^e_1	11625	9696.9	8975.9	8713.1	8303.4
	(1.9105)	(1.9816)	(2.2037)	(2.4453)	(2.5253)
	1.1039	0.9208	0.8523	0.8274	0.7885
w^e_2	-4404.3	-5002.0	-4695.5	-3792.2	-2502.7
	(0.7247)	(0.9507)	(1.029)	(0.9376)	(0.6733)
	-0.5203	-0.5909	-0.5547	-0.4480	-0.2957
Constant	74422	81299	86556	91832	99085
	(7.5448)	(7.4376)	(7.1271)	(6.8473)	(6.756)
BUSE R^2	0.4733	0.4812	0.4912	0.5071	0.5230
FPE	0.5281	0.5306	0.5333	0.5366	0.5406

Table A7.3 (continued)

Gram Land Regression Equation

Explanatory variable	Estimated coefficients, t-ratios and elasticities				
	β=0.1	β=0.2	β=0.3	β=0.4	β=0.5
P^e_{wheat}	3296.0	4060.6	4020.9	3054.9	2089.6
	(2.6078)	(2.8763)	(2.4622)	(1.7558)	(1.2444)
	1.3639	1.6804	1.6639	1.2642	0.8647
P^e_{gram}	-3289.9	-4635.6	-4725	-4231.8	-3218
	(1.8430)	(4.6144)	(5.7509)	(5.6887)	(4.8032)
	-2.0932	-2.9494	-3.0063	-2.6925	-2.0475
$\bar{y}_{wheat}$	-2.3836	-4.0202	-5.4797	-6.7504	-7.466
	(2.2614)	(3.4280)	(4.8968)	(5.802)	(3.9383)
	-0.0332	-0.0560	-0.0763	-0.0940	-0.1040
$\bar{y}_{gram}$	0.7279	0.4190	0.2322	0.2567	0.2932
	(1.8020)	(0.9738)	(0.4650)	(0.4554)	(0.6249)
	0.0038	0.0022	0.0012	0.0013	0.0015
σ^2_{wheat}	-0.0125	-0.0115	-0.0109	-0.0105	-0.0049
	(2.567)	(1.9284)	(1.6763)	(1.5216)	(0.6605)
	-0.0032	-0.0029	-0.0028	-0.0027	-0.0013

Table A7.3 (continued)

Gram Land Regression Equation

Explanatory variable	Estimated coefficients, t-ratios and elasticities				
	β=0.6	**β=0.7**	**β=0.8**	**β=0.9**	**β=1.0**
P^e_{wheat}	1086.9	439.95	-86.438	-521.78	-861.12
	(0.6225)	(0.2589)	(0.0523)	(0.3152)	(0.50297)
	0.4498	0.1821	-0.0358	0.2159	-0.3563
P^e_{gram}	-2757.3	-2080.8	-1512.6	-1078.9	-781.33
	(4.6203)	(4.0024)	(3.3468)	(2.6860)	(2.1066)
	-1.7543	-1.3239	-0.9624	-0.6865	-0.4971
$\bar{y}_{wheat}$	-9.8332	-11.344	-12.375	-12.653	-12.193
	(6.8533)	(7.1542)	(7.2022)	(7.0987)	(6.9613)
	-0.1370	-0.1580	-0.1724	-0.1762	-0.1698
$\bar{y}_{gram}$	0.2999	0.2908	0.2883	0.2976	0.30237
	(0.4934)	(0.4929)	(0.5132)	(0.5512)	(0.5694)
	0.0016	0.0015	0.0015	0.0015	0.0016
σ^2_{wheat}	-0.0111	-0.0120	-0.0134	-0.0148	-0.01617
	(1.5477)	(1.7041)	(1.9328)	(2.1994)	(2.4791)
	-0.0028	-0.0031	-0.0034	-0.0038	-0.0041

Table A7.3 (continued)

Gram Land Regression Equation

Explanatory variable	Estimated coefficients, t-ratios and elasticities				
	β=0.1	β=0.2	β=0.3	β=0.4	β=0.5
σ^2_{gram}	-0.00013	-0.0002	-0.00018	-0.00018	-0.00007
	(2.5513)	(2.8412)	(2.8528)	(2.6279)	(1.4035)
	-0.00002	-0.00004	-0.00003	-0.00003	-0.00001
$\sigma_{wheat\ gram}$	0.0018	0.0039	0.0054	0.0055	0.00087
	(0.8034)	(1.4996)	(1.7328)	(1.6279)	(0.3327)
	0.0003	0.00007	0.0001	0.0001	0.00002
w^e_1	23781	12421	9587.4	7260	6140.5
	(2.8236)	(2.2132)	(2.2605)	(2.1823)	(2.497)
	20.0721	10.4838	8.0921	6.1277	5.1828
w^e_2	-14560	-12929	-11936	-10542	-9312.7
	(3.6701)	(4.7108)	(5.3677)	(5.3248)	(4.7394)
	-15.29	-13.5768	-12.534	-11.0702	-9.7793
Constant	12.626	5072.5	10317	15828	19965
	(0.0117)	(3.7581)	(6.6842)	(8.9655)	(0.7775)
BUSE R^2	0.2466	0.4065	0.5518	0.5896	0.5246
FPE	0.5255	0.5277	0.5369	0.5397	0.5292

Table A7.3 (continued)

Gram Land Regression Equation

Explanatory variable	Estimated coefficients, t-ratios and elasticities				
	β=0.6	β=0.7	β=0.8	β=0.9	β=1.0
σ^2_{gram}	-0.00014 (1.9873) -0.00003	-0.00011 (1.7171) -0.00002	-0.000094 (1.4620) -0.00002	-0.00076 (1.2092) -0.000014	-0.000063 (0.9891) -0.00001
$\sigma_{wheat\ gram}$	0.0049 (1.4877) 0.0001	0.0044 (1.4284) 0.0001	0.0038 (1.3012) 0.0001	0.0031 (1.0912) 0.0001	0.00249 (0.8581) 0.00005
w_1^e	3677.8 (1.5235) 3.1042	2400.1 (1.1252) 2.0258	1517.1 (0.8150) 1.2805	1082.0 (0.6673) 0.9132	968.22 (0.6682) 0.8172
w_2^e	-6952.8 (3.516) -7.3012	-4938.3 (2.5038) -5.1857	-3331.3 (1.7788) -3.4982	-2487.2 (1.4476) -2.6118	-2310.2 (1.4670) -2.4259
Constant	27201 (10.783)	32359 (10.558)	36881 (10.074)	40668 (9.6134)	43660 (9.2849)
BUSE R^2	0.5290	0.4891	0.4560	0.4334	0.4190
FPE	0.5351	0.5314	0.5263	0.5197	0.5136

Table A7.4
Pooled cross section-time series estimates of land allocation between wheat and gram with money illusion for Punjab 1966–86

Wheat Land Regression Equation

Explanatory variable	Estimated coefficients, t-ratios and elasticities				
	β=0.1	β=0.2	β=0.3	β=0.4	β=0.5
P^e_{wheat}	-124.79	-119.66	-115.17	-109.45	-96.244
	(2.1195)	(2.0185)	(1.9781)	(1.9127)	(1.7284)
	-0.0086	-0.0082	-0.0079	-0.0075	-0.0066
P^e_{gram}	-97.507	-31.897	-12.457	-4.0225	0.6616
	(1.1622)	(0.6374)	(0.3446)	(0.1474)	(0.0312)
	-0.0121	-0.004	-0.0016	-0.0005	0.00008
$\bar{y}_{wheat}$	17.180	22.117	26.571	31.144	36.117
	(4.6603)	(5.8190)	(6.5428)	(7.1580)	(7.7371)
	0.0269	0.0347	0.0416	0.0488	0.0566
$\bar{y}_{gram}$	-4.9726	-5.7449	-5.8554	-5.6911	-5.3573
	(2.1837)	(2.3388)	(2.2888)	(2.2512)	(2.1886)
	-0.0029	-0.0034	-0.0034	-0.0033	-0.0031
σ^2_{wheat}	0.0396	0.02737	0.0235	0.0236	0.0249
	(2.269)	(1.5638)	(1.3402)	(1.3268)	(0.3860)
	0.0011	0.0008	0.0007	0.0007	0.0007
σ^2_{gram}	0.00052	0.0005	0.00047	0.00044	0.00038
	(1.8371)	(1.7974)	(1.6723)	(1.5712)	(1.4301)
	0.00001	0.00001	0.00001	0.00001	0.00001

Table A7.4 (continued)

Explanatory variable	Wheat Land Regression Equation Estimated coefficients, t-ratios and elasticities				
	β=0.6	β=0.7	β=0.8	β=0.9	β=1.0
	-76.005	-53.491	-35.021	-24.722	-20.400
P^e_{wheat}	(1.4298)	(1.0679)	(0.7290)	(0.5132)	(0.4124)
	-0.0052	-0.0037	-0.0024	-0.0017	-0.0014
	2.4421	1.2665	-2.2161	-5.8505	-7.8319
P^e_{gram}	(0.1462)	(0.0947)	(0.1984)	(0.5835)	(0.8240)
	0.0003	0.0002	-0.0003	-0.0007	-0.0010
	40.982	45.243	47.887	48.015	46.099
$\bar{y}_{wheat}$	(8.1405)	(8.4073)	(8.5616)	(8.5058)	(8.3350)
	0.0642	0.0709	0.075	0.0752	0.0722
	-4.9897	-4.7873	-4.7402	-4.667	-4.5163
$\bar{y}_{gram}$	(2.1228)	(2.1347)	(2.1992)	(2.2057)	(2.1587)
	-0.0029	-0.0028	-0.0028	-0.0027	-0.0026
	0.0264	0.0286	0.0327	0.0390	0.0442
σ^2_{wheat}	(1.4786)	(1.614)	(1.8336)	(2.1302)	(2.3277)
	0.0008	0.0008	0.0009	0.0011	0.0013
	0.00033	0.00028	0.00025	0.00023	0.00023
σ^2_{gram}	(1.2537)	(1.1044)	(1.0039)	(0.9402)	(0.9101)
	0.00001	0.00001	0.00001	4.7E-6	4.7E-6

Table A7.4 (continued)

Wheat Land Regression Equation

Explanatory variable	Estimated coefficients, t-ratios and elasticities				
	β=0.1	β=0.2	β=0.3	β=0.4	β=0.5
	-0.0047	-0.0026	0.00006	0.0017	0.0031
$\sigma_{\text{wheat gram}}$	(0.4947)	(0.2769)	(0.0065)	(0.1823)	(0.3407)
	-0.00001	-0.00001	1.3E-7	3.6E6	0.00001
	820.52	563.01	401.62	288.35	212.64
w_1^e	(2.5423)	(3.2)	(3.3930)	(3.2808)	(3.1253)
	0.0856	0.0587	0.0419	0.0301	0.0222
	-187.66	-89.738	-31.78	2.9070	15.531
w_2^e	(0.9456)	(0.8025)	(0.3998)	(0.0463)	(0.2969)
	-0.0260	-0.0124	-0.0044	0.0004	0.0022
Constant	15996	26447	36981	46925	55347
	(5.5237)	(7.0737)	(7.91863)	(8.4008)	(8.5656)
BUSE R^2	0.2213	0.3320	0.3973	0.4440	0.4817
FPE	0.5393	0.5309	0.568	0.5234	0.5211

Table A7.4 (continued)

Explanatory variable	Wheat Land Regression Equation Estimated coefficients, t-ratios and elasticities				
	β=0.6	β=0.7	β=0.8	β=0.9	β=1.0
	0.0043	0.0053	0.0061	0.0067	0.0072
$\sigma_{\text{wheat gram}}$	(0.4903)	(0.6206)	(0.7094)	(0.7505)	(0.7731)
	0.00001	0.00001	0.00001	0.00001	0.00002
	162.71	130.84	110.24	95.54	83.284
w_1^e	(3.0667)	(3.1413)	(3.2288)	(3.1459)	(2.8902)
	0.0170	0.0136	0.0115	0.010	0.0087
	13.678	5.9174	1.254	4.2844	13.372
w_2^e	(0.3065)	(0.1534)	(0.0366)	(0.1344)	(0.4736)
	0.0019	0.0008	0.0002	0.0006	0.0019
Constant	62469	69073	76774	87259	100540
	(8.5295)	(8.4606)	(8.5202)	(8.7879)	(9.3073)
BUSE R^2	0.5083	0.5300	0.5468	0.5509	0.5469
FPE	0.5205	0.5215	0.5223	0.5223	0.5227

Table A7.4 (continued)

Gram Land Regression Equation

Explanatory variable	**Estimated coefficients, t-ratios and elasticities**				
	β=0.1	**β=0.2**	**β=0.3**	**β=0.4**	**β=0.5**
P^e_{wheat}	27.379	30.187	28.428	19.802	10.185
	(2.1026)	(1.9627)	(1.6368)	(1.1187)	(0.5933)
	0.0167	0.0184	0.0173	0.0121	0.0062
P^e_{gram}	-21.823	-29.310	-30.614	-25.865	-19.483
	(1.4824)	(3.469)	(4.4232)	(4.2528)	(3.7199)
	-0.0241	-0.0324	-0.0339	-0.0286	-0.0215
$\bar{y}_{wheat}$	-2.0388	-3.9222	-5.5494	-6.7875	-7.8383
	(1.9842)	(3.275)	(4.8383)	(5.7661)	(6.0799)
	-0.0284	-0.0546	-0.0773	-0.0945	-0.1092
$\bar{y}_{gram}$	0.6510	0.4270	0.1656	0.0824	0.0603
	(1.5587)	(0.9719)	(0.3354)	(0.1535)	(0.10896)
	0.0034	0.0022	0.0009	0.0004	0.0003
σ^2_{wheat}	-0.0123	-0.0109	-0.01037	-0.0101	-0.0105
	(2.4824)	(1.7086)	(1.4938)	(1.4247)	(1.4996)
	-0.0031	-0.0028	-0.0026	-0.0026	-0.0027

Table A7.4 (continued)

Gram Land Regression Equation

Explanatory variable	Estimated coefficients, t-ratios and elasticities				
	β=0.6	β=0.7	β=0.8	β=0.9	β=1.0
P^e_{wheat}	3.0697	-1.5011	-4.0346	-5.3223	-6.2126
	(0.1868)	(0.0955)	(0.2681)	(0.3649)	(0.4305)
	0.0019	-0.0009	-0.0025	-0.0032	-0.0038
P^e_{gram}	-14.212	-10.274	-7.3263	-5.1888	-3.7741
	(3.2251)	(2.7818)	(2.3382)	(1.895)	(1.5119)
	-0.0157	-0.0114	-0.0081	-0.0057	-0.0042
$\bar{y}_{wheat}$	-8.8175	-9.6640	-10.209	-10.268	-9.7767
	(6.1356)	(6.0495)	(5.8517)	(5.6035)	(5.3447)
	-0.1228	-0.1346	-0.1422	-0.143	-0.1362
$\bar{y}_{gram}$	0.0601	0.0866	0.13003	0.1717	0.1968
	(0.1101)	(0.1655)	(0.2630)	(0.3660)	(0.4339)
	0.0003	0.0005	0.0007	0.0009	0.001
σ^2_{wheat}	-0.0111	-0.0118	-0.0128	-0.0139	-0.0148
	(1.6284)	(1.7852)	(1.9807)	(2.1986)	(2.398)
	-0.0028	-0.003	-0.0033	-0.0036	-0.0038

Table A7.4 (continued)

Gram Land Regression Equation

Explanatory variable	Estimated coefficients, t-ratios and elasticities				
	β=0.1	β=0.2	β=0.3	β=0.4	β=0.5
σ^2_{gram}	-0.00011	-0.00013	-0.00015	-0.00015	-0.00013
	(2.0712)	(2.3165)	(2.4447)	(2.3469)	(2.0396)
	-0.00002	-0.00002	-0.00003	-0.00003	-0.00002
$\sigma_{wheat\ gram}$	0.0010	0.0028	0.0047	0.0053	0.0051
	(0.4637)	(1.0516)	(1.5359)	(1.6739)	(1.6511)
	1.8E-5	0.0001	0.0001	0.0001	0.0001
w^e_1	223.78	97.867	63.409	48.915	37.487
	(2.8940)	(1.7582)	(1.4390)	(1.4144)	(1.3599)
	0.2074	0.0907	0.0588	0.0453	0.0348
w^e_2	-134.62	-81.028	-62.707	-54.401	-47.938
	(2.9822)	(2.5023)	(2.4233)	(2.5982)	(2.7169)
	-0.1656	-0.0996	-0.0771	-0.0669	-0.059
Constant	-177.37	4054.6	8935.4	13958	19181
	(0.2510)	(4.1101)	(7.6777)	(10.408)	(12.016)
BUSE R^2	0.1913	0.2977	0.4525	0.5180	0.5177
FPE	0.5186	0.5198	0.5269	0.5286	0.5266

Table A7.4 (continued)

Gram Land Regression Equation

Explanatory variable	**Estimated coefficients, t-ratios and elasticities**				
	β=0.6	**β=0.7**	**β=0.8**	**β=0.9**	**β=1.0**
	-0.00011	-0.00009	-0.000075	-0.000064	-0.00006
σ^2_{gram}	(1.7406)	(1.5111)	(1.3347)	(1.1824)	(1.0514)
	-0.00002	-0.00002	-0.00001	-0.00001	-0.00001
	0.0046	0.0041	0.0034	0.0028	0.0023
$\sigma_{wheat\ gram}$	(1.5931)	(1.4834)	(1.3177)	(1.1113)	(0.9087)
	0.0001	0.0001	0.0001	0.0001	0.00001
	28.007	20.256	14.550	11.163	9.8160
w^e_1	(1.2320)	(1.0478)	(0.8704)	(0.7625)	(0.7486)
	0.026	0.0188	0.0135	0.0103	0.0091
	-41.556	-35.019	-29.241	-25.66	-25.019
w^e_2	(2.6459)	(2.4052)	(2.134)	(1.9870)	(2.0527)
	-0.511	-0.0431	-0.036	-0.0316	-0.0308
Constant	24457	29478	33866	37398	40100
	(12.496)	(12.166)	(11.513)	(10.979)	(10.732)
BUSE R^2	0.4935	0.4629	0.4350	0.4159	0.4054
FPE	0.5257	0.5250	0.5227	0.5838	0.5148

List of authors

Index

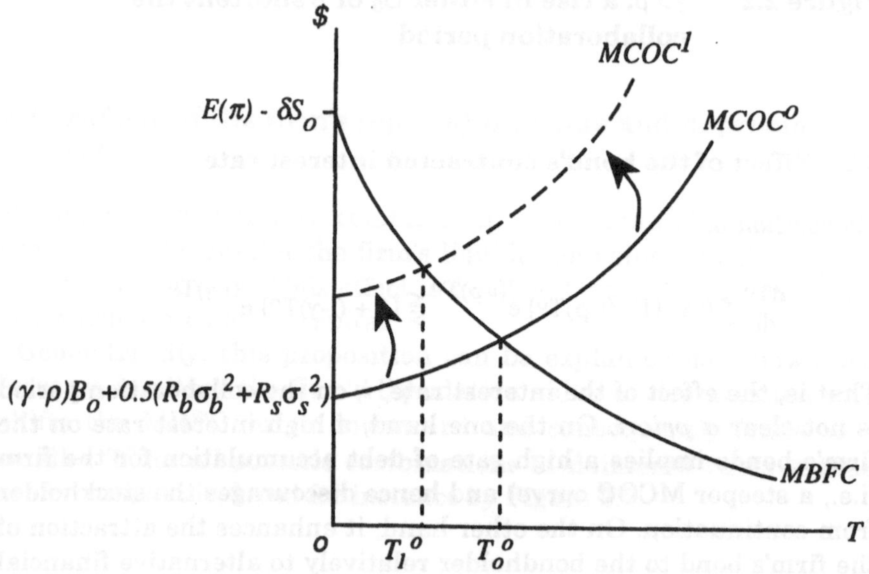

suggested that an increase in σ_2^2 would most likely increase L_1 when the growing and market conditions are less favourable for cereal 1.

Proposition 4: (The yields covariance effect)

$$\frac{\partial L_1^*}{\partial \sigma_{12}} \gtreqless 0 \text{ as } [P_1^e \bar{y}_1 - c_1(w^e)] - [P_2^e \bar{y}_2 - c_2(w^e)] \gtreqless R(P_1^{e^2} \sigma_1^2 - P_2^{e^2} \sigma_2^2) .$$

This proposition indicates that if the risk-adjusted marginal expected return on cereal 1 is greater (smaller) than that on cereal 2, the larger (smaller) the per-hectare yield covariance the larger (smaller) the area under cereal 1.

By symmetry, propositions 1 to 4 also describe the properties of the optimal allocation of land to cereal 2. However, it might be that under certain circumstances farm land is fully allocated for growing only one of the cereals. In terms of the model, such a corner solution evolved when the combination of growing conditions (e.g., land fertility and yield variation) and market conditions (e.g., perceived output and input prices) is more favourable for one of the crops, irrespective of the scale of operation.

7.3 Estimation procedure and data

For estimating the effects of the determinants of land allocation between the major cereals, a first-order Taylor's approximation of equation 15 is considered:

$$\begin{aligned} L_{1t} = a_0 + a_1 P_{1t}^e + a_2 P_{2t}^e + a_3\bar{y}_{1t} + a_4\bar{y}_{2t} + a_5\sigma_{1t}^2 \\ + a_6\sigma_{2t}^2 + a_7\sigma_{12t} + a_8 w_{1t}^e + a_9 w_{2t}^e + \eta_{1t} \end{aligned} \qquad (17)$$

and by symmetry

$$\begin{aligned} L_{2t} = b_0 + b_1 P_{1t}^e + b_2 P_{2t}^e + b_3\bar{y}_{1t} + b_4\bar{y}_{2t} + b_5\sigma_{1t}^2 \\ + b_6\sigma_{2t}^2 + b_7\sigma_{12t} + b_8 w_{1t}^e + b_9 w_{2t}^e + \eta_{2t} \end{aligned} \qquad (18)$$

Table 9.3
Long-term rates, causality test's results and long-term effects for countries in Sub-Saharan Africa

Country	*Long-Term Rates of* GNP growth*	*Long-Term Rates of* debt accumulation*	*Reject at 1% Level of Significance* H_1	*Reject at 1% Level of Significance* H_2	*Long-Term Effects of* x on y	*Long-Term Effects of* y on x
Cote d'Ivoire	0.03307	0.16291	Yes**	Yes**	0.158	-0.843
	(3.995)	(6.663)				
	0.935	0.977				
Ethiopia	0.02240	0.10065	No	Yes	0.203	—
	(11.196)	(24.395)				
	0.939	0.990				
Ghana	0.00560	0.03654	Yes*	Yes	0.141	—
	(1.097)	(3.834)				
	0.359	0.800				
Kenya	0.05293	0.09016	No	No	0.452	0.137
	(13.349)	(5.555)				
	0.970	0.959				
Nigeria	0.02151	0.18119	Yes	No	—	5.507
	(2.373)	(19.234)				
	0.809	0.940				
Sudan	0.02850	0.14125	No	Yes**	-2.271	1.979
	(3.722)	(5.911)				
	0.849	0.977				
Tanzania	0.02253	0.10104	No	Yes**	0.290	2.779
	(7.102)	(5.156)				
	0.965	0.974				
Zaire	0.00407	0.12366	Yes**	Yes	0.018	—
	(1.166)	(3.880)				
	0.341	0.949				

* The numbers in the parentheses are t-ratios and the numbers below the t-ratios indicate the determination coefficients (R^2).

** The opposite conclusion is obtained at the 5 per cent level of significance.

Table A7.1 (continued)

Maize Land Regression Equation

Explanatory variable	Estimated coefficients, t-ratios and elasticities				
	β=0.1	β=0.2	β=0.3	β=0.4	β=0.5
P^e_{rice}	-7514.8	-3867	-5725.7	-9371	-12286
	(0.4195)	(0.2308)	(0.3804)	(0.702)	(1.0465)
	-1.0921	-0.562	-0.8321	-1.3619	-1.7855
P^e_{maize}	9302.2	6373.4	7026.6	7228.1	7455.4
	(0.2811)	(0.3784)	(0.6116)	(0.8344)	(1.0863)
	1.4964	1.0252	1.1303	1.1627	1.1993
$\bar{y}_{rice}$	-5.5146	-5.8246	-5.6649	-5.6448	-5.5981
	(1.7225)	(1.7844)	(1.7001)	(1.6963)	(1.7043)
	-0.0323	-0.0341	-0.0332	-0.033	-0.0328
$\bar{y}_{maize}$	5.9059	5.5878	5.6862	6.3534	7.5176
	(2.2351)	(2.0351)	(1.9659)	(2.0598)	(2.238)
	0.0267	0.0253	0.0257	0.0287	0.034

Table A7.1 (continued)

Maize Land Regression Equation

Explanatory variable	Estimated coefficients, t-ratios and elasticities				
	β=0.6	β=0.7	β=0.8	β=0.9	β=1.0
	-13302	-12513	-10742	-8741.2	-6946.1
P^e_{rice}	(1.3015)	(1.4137)	(1.3944)	(1.2852)	(1.1359)
	-1.9332	-1.8185	-1.5611	-1.2704	-1.0095
	7593.9	7280.9	6517.5	5560.9	4712.3
P^e_{maize}	(1.3605)	(1.5798)	(1.6893)	(1.6914)	(1.6436)
	1.2216	1.1712	1.0484	0.8945	0.758
	-5.5474	-5.6158	-5.8115	-6.0618	-6.2616
$\bar{y}_{rice}$	(1.7051)	(1.7262)	(1.7752)	(1.8427)	(1.913)
	-0.0325	-0.0329	-0.034	-0.0355	-0.0367
	8.9929	10.326	11.057	10.875	9.8659
$\bar{y}_{maize}$	(2.4363)	(2.5629)	(2.5588)	(2.4257)	(2.2192)
	0.0406	0.0467	0.05	0.0491	0.0446

Table A7.1 (continued)

Maize Land Regression Equation

Explanatory variable	Estimated coefficients, t-ratios and elasticities				
	β=0.6	β=0.7	β=0.8	β=0.9	β=1.0
	0.0116	0.0124	0.0132	0.0145	0.0163
σ^2_{rice}	(1.4979)	(1.6091)	(1.7429)	(1.9353)	(2.1932)
	0.0016	0.0017	0.0018	0.002	0.0023
	0.0262	0.0255	0.0244	0.0224	0.019
σ^2_{maize}	(3.4036)	(3.2559)	(3.0718)	(2.7577)	(2.288)
	0.0017	0.0016	0.0016	0.0014	0.0012
	-0.0019	-0.0036	-0.0046	-0.0051	-0.0051
$\sigma_{rice\ maize}$	(0.1589)	(0.2973)	(0.3822)	(0.4232)	(0.43)
	-0.00002	-0.00004	-0.00005	-0.00005	-0.00005
	4715.7	4011.7	3485.6	3042.1	2704
w^e_1	(1.1297)	(1.1015)	(1.0892)	(1.0696)	(1.0591)
	1.4973	1.2738	1.1067	0.9659	0.8585
	-9789.9	-8522.7	-7114.9	-5689.4	-4428
w^e_2	(2.5989)	(2.4680)	(2.2659)	(1.9996)	(1.7136)
	-3.8209	-3.3263	-2.7769	-2.2205	-1.7282
Constant	36860	39929	42296	44975	48429
	(4.5878)	(4.6133)	(4.5136)	(4.4386)	(4.5002)
BUSE R^2	0.2714	0.2573	0.2388	0.2140	0.1872
FPE	0.5471	0.5476	0.5502	0.5538	0.5573

Table A7.2
Pooled cross section-time series estimates of land allocation in summers between rice and maize with money illusion for Punjab 1966–86

Rice Land Regression Equation

Explanatory variable	Estimated coefficients, t-ratios and elasticities				
	β=0.1	β=0.2	β=0.3	β=0.4	β=0.5
P^e_{rice}	229.35	316.60	297.27	248.55	201.33
	(1.2496)	(2.1458)	(2.5156)	(2.5634)	(2.4897)
	0.0348	0.048	0.0451	0.0377	0.0305
P^e_{maize}	315.50	56.026	14.643	16.430	23.139
	(0.9072)	(0.3517)	(0.1455)	(0.2269)	(0.4155)
	0.0538	0.0096	0.0025	0.0028	0.0039
$\bar{y}_{rice}$	18.115	18.023	18.126	18.688	19.229
	(3.2956)	(3.1554)	(3.0978)	(3.1368)	(3.1699)
	0.0721	0.0717	0.0721	0.0744	0.0765
$\bar{y}_{maize}$	-15.919	-15.418	-15.766	-17.084	-18.78
	(3.9153)	(3.6373)	(3.5917)	(3.7253)	(3.8654)
	-0.0489	-0.0474	-0.0484	-0.0525	-0.0577
σ^2_{rice}	-0.01102	-0.0161	-0.0162	-0.0138	-0.0104
	(0.9119)	(1.3181)	(1.3064)	(1.1007)	(0.8315)
	-0.001	-0.0015	-0.0015	-0.0013	-0.001
σ^2_{maize}	0.0330	0.0292	0.0290	0.0299	0.0311
	(3.0454)	(2.7825)	(2.7585)	(2.7825)	(2.8188)
	0.0014	0.0013	0.0013	0.0013	0.0014

Table A7.2 (continued)

Rice Land Regression Equation

Explanatory variable	Estimated coefficients, t-ratios and elasticities				
	β=0.6	β=0.7	β=0.8	β=0.9	β=1.0
P^e_{rice}	164.94 (2.4142) 0.025	139.61 (2.3823) 0.0212	123.09 (2.3987) 0.0187	112.91 (2.4467) 0.0171	106.05 (2.4954) 0.0161
P^e_{maize}	26.942 (0.6028) 0.0046	28.132 (0.7579) 0.0048	27.705 (0.8684) 0.0047	25.834 (0.9044) 0.0044	22.812 (0.8607) 0.0039
$\bar{y}_{rice}$	19.405 (3.1294) 0.0772	19.264 (3.0331) 0.0767	19.196 (2.968) 0.0764	19.854 (3.0633) 0.079	21.289 (3.3568) 0.0847
$\bar{y}_{maize}$	-20.281 (3.8817) -0.0623	-21.281 (3.7477) -0.0654	-21.556 (3.497) -0.0662	-20.636 (3.1499) -0.0634	-18.78 (2.8123) -0.0577
σ^2_{rice}	-0.0068 (0.5448) -0.0006	-0.0032 (0.2618) -0.0003	-0.00006 (0.0053) -5E-6	0.0023 (0.1945) 0.0002	0.0040 (0.3300) 0.0004
σ^2_{maize}	0.0321 (2.8529) 0.0014	0.0328 (2.8726) 0.0014	0.0331 (2.8734) 0.0014	0.0332 (2.8525) 0.0014	0.03313 (2.8116) 0.0014

Table A7.2 (continued)

Maize Land Regression Equation

Explanatory variable	Estimated coefficients, t-ratios and elasticities				
	β=0.1	β=0.2	β=0.3	β=0.4	β=0.5
	-48.547	52.606	76.664	71.412	58.599
P^e_{rice}	(0.3981)	(0.4778)	(0.8447)	(0.9441)	(0.9211)
	-0.0108	0.0117	0.0171	0.0159	0.0131
	160.35	107.45	93.326	75.387	64.945
P^e_{maize}	(0.6768)	(0.9021)	(1.1739)	(1.2664)	(1.3719)
	0.0402	0.027	0.0234	0.0189	0.0163
	-7.2017	-6.5547	-5.5084	-4.8732	-4.0895
$\bar{y}_{rice}$	(2.278)	(2.056)	(1.6965)	(1.4872)	(1.2366)
	-0.0422	-0.0384	-0.0322	-0.0285	-0.0239
	6.1311	5.8095	5.7166	6.2936	7.7321
$\bar{y}_{maize}$	(2.3767)	(2.1237)	(1.9761)	(2.0393)	(2.2971)
	0.0277	0.0263	0.0258	0.0284	0.0349
	0.0146	0.0117	0.0112	0.0119	0.0131
σ^2_{rice}	(2.0208)	(1.5403)	(1.4230)	(1.4816)	(1.6167)
	0.002	0.0016	0.0016	0.0017	0.0018

Table A7.2 (continued)

Maize Land Regression Equation

Explanatory variable	Estimated coefficients, t-ratios and elasticities				
	β=0.6	β=0.7	β=0.8	β=0.9	β=1.0
P^e_{rice}	44.434	31.490	19.594	8.0042	-3.7785
	(0.8276)	(0.6962)	(0.5127)	(0.2444)	(0.1307)
	0.0099	0.007	0.0044	0.0018	-0.0008
P^e_{maize}	61.198	58.763	54.916	48.903	40.615
	(1.5843)	(1.8515)	(2.0964)	(2.2371)	(2.1625)
	0.0154	0.0147	0.0138	0.0123	0.0102
$\bar{y}_{rice}$	-2.9744	-1.7712	-0.6470	0.2447	0.3970
	(0.8874)	(0.5199)	(0.1877)	(0.0713)	(0.1172)
	-0.0174	-0.0104	-0.0038	0.0014	0.0023
$\bar{y}_{maize}$	10.092	12.889	15.715	18.160	18.736
	(2.7448)	(3.2614)	(3.7563)	(4.1857)	(4.3244)
	0.0456	0.0582	0.071	0.0821	0.0847
σ^2_{rice}	0.0142	0.0148	0.0150	0.0152	0.0155
	(1.7372)	(1.8106)	(1.8695)	(1.9512)	(2.051)
	0.002	0.0021	0.0021	0.0021	0.0022

Table A7.2 (continued)

Maize Land Regression Equation

Explanatory variable	Estimated coefficients, t-ratios and elasticities				
	β=0.6	β=0.7	β=0.8	β=0.9	β=1.0
	0.0213	0.0208	0.02156	0.0218	0.0196
σ^2_{maize}	(2.6901)	(2.6362)	(2.7698)	(2.8466)	(2.5374)
	0.0014	0.0013	0.0014	0.0014	0.0013
	0.0004	-0.0010	-0.0017	-0.0021	-0.0032
$\sigma_{rice\ maize}$	(0.0286)	(0.081)	(0.1343)	(0.1703)	(0.2611)
	0.000004	-0.00001	-0.00002	-0.00002	-0.00003
	57.106	42.898	31.384	23.786	19.242
w^e_1	(1.1505)	(1.0192)	(0.9015)	(0.8226)	(0.7647)
	0.0248	0.0186	0.0136	0.0103	0.0083
	-118.06	-111.66	-108.12	-105.57	-98.567
w^e_2	(3.2207)	(3.4416)	(3.7581)	(4.0738)	(4.0821)
	-0.0679	-0.0642	-0.0622	-0.0607	-0.0567
Constant	25605	26722	27381	28357	32104
	(5.3826)	(4.8812)	(4.3969)	(4.0889)	(4.338)
BUSE R^2	0.2945	0.3054	0.3281	0.3501	0.3456
FPE	0.5385	0.5364	0.5355	0.5360	0.5397

Table A7.3 (continued)

Explanatory variable	Wheat Land Regression Equation: Estimated coefficients, t-ratios and elasticities				
	β=0.1	β=0.2	β=0.3	β=0.4	β=0.5
σ^2_{gram}	0.00038	0.00038	0.00037	0.00036	0.00036
	(1.3423)	(1.2905)	(1.2526)	(1.2597)	(2.331)
	0.00001	0.00001	0.00001	0.00001	0.00001
$\sigma_{wheat\ gram}$	-0.0033	-0.0034	-0.0020	-0.00057	0.00486
	(0.3508)	(0.3489)	(0.2048)	(0.0591)	(0.0475)
	-0.00001	-0.00001	-4.2 E -6	-1.2E-6	0.00001
w^e_1	91855	53020	34111	22608	12640
	(2.6790)	(2.8246)	(2.6346)	(2.311)	(1.273)
	8.7223	5.0347	3.2391	2.1468	1.2003
w^e_2	-17781	-2899.2	-916.77	-1456.8	-7098.3
	(1.0672)	(0.2693)	(0.1.30)	(0.1873)	(0.9161)
	-2.1007	-0.3425	-0.1083	-0.1721	-0.8386
Constant	12842	24740	39002	52857	61057
	(2.7522)	(4.2790)	(5.644)	(6.669)	(6.3736)
BUSE R^2	0.2293	0.3287	0.3890	0.4326	0.4411
FPE	0.5461	0.5391	0.5332	0.5293	0.4978

Table A7.3 (continued)

Gram Land Regression Equation

Explanatory variable	Estimated coefficients, t-ratios and elasticities				
	β=0.1	β=0.2	β=0.3	β=0.4	β=0.5
P^e_{wheat}	3296.0 (2.6078) 1.3639	4060.6 (2.8763) 1.6804	4020.9 (2.4622) 1.6639	3054.9 (1.7558) 1.2642	2089.6 (1.2444) 0.8647
P^e_{gram}	-3289.9 (1.8430) -2.0932	-4635.6 (4.6144) -2.9494	-4725 (5.7509) -3.0063	-4231.8 (5.6887) -2.6925	-3218 (4.8032) -2.0475
$\bar{y}_{wheat}$	-2.3836 (2.2614) -0.0332	-4.0202 (3.4280) -0.0560	-5.4797 (4.8968) -0.0763	-6.7504 (5.802) -0.0940	-7.466 (3.9383) -0.1040
$\bar{y}_{gram}$	0.7279 (1.8020) 0.0038	0.4190 (0.9738) 0.0022	0.2322 (0.4650) 0.0012	0.2567 (0.4554) 0.0013	0.2932 (0.6249) 0.0015
σ^2_{wheat}	-0.0125 (2.567) -0.0032	-0.0115 (1.9284) -0.0029	-0.0109 (1.6763) -0.0028	-0.0105 (1.5216) -0.0027	-0.0049 (0.6605) -0.0013

Table A7.4 (continued)

Wheat Land Regression Equation

Explanatory variable	Estimated coefficients, t-ratios and elasticities				
	β=0.1	β=0.2	β=0.3	β=0.4	β=0.5
$\sigma_{\text{wheat gram}}$	-0.0047 (0.4947) -0.00001	-0.0026 (0.2769) -0.00001	0.00006 (0.0065) 1.3E-7	0.0017 (0.1823) 3.6E6	0.0031 (0.3407) 0.00001
w_1^e	820.52 (2.5423) 0.0856	563.01 (3.2) 0.0587	401.62 (3.3930) 0.0419	288.35 (3.2808) 0.0301	212.64 (3.1253) 0.0222
w_2^e	-187.66 (0.9456) -0.0260	-89.738 (0.8025) -0.0124	-31.78 (0.3998) -0.0044	2.9070 (0.0463) 0.0004	15.531 (0.2969) 0.0022
Constant	15996 (5.5237)	26447 (7.0737)	36981 (7.91863)	46925 (8.4008)	55347 (8.5656)
BUSE R^2	0.2213	0.3320	0.3973	0.4440	0.4817
FPE	0.5393	0.5309	0.568	0.5234	0.5211

Index

Table 4.6

3SLS estimates of the building & construction industry and the transport, storage & communication industry bankruptcy rates equation system*

Explanatory Variables	Nation-wide Time-Series Observations				Pooled Cross-States Time-Series Observations				Pooled and Weighted Cross-State Time-Series Observations			
	MODEL 1		MODEL 2		MODEL 1		MODEL 2		MODEL 1		MODEL 2	
	$IBR4_t$	$IBR5_t$	$IBR4_t$	$IBR5_t$	$IBR4_t$	$IBR5_t$	$IBR4_t$	$IBR5_t$	$IBR4_t$	$IBR5_t$	$IBR4_t$	$IBR5_t$
Constant	0.002 (1.372)	-0.008 (-0.622)	0.001 (0.419)	0.001 (0.880)	0.003 (0.619)	0.010 (1.585)	0.003 (0.404)	0.007 (2.949)	3.89E-04 (2.299)	-6.69E-05 (-0.222)	1.39E-04 (1.337)	1.42E-04 (1.560)
$IBR4_t$		2.630 (1.147)		1.329 (2.595)		1.243 (2.455)		1.293 (2.722)		1.432 (5.992)		1.372 (6.711)
$IBR5_t$	0.667 (1.046)		-0.123 (-0.1102)		0.058 (0.176)		-0.152 (-0.203)		0.111 (0.667)		-0.004 (-0.020)	
$IBR4_{t-1}$	-0.304 (-0.294)		0.977 (0.538)		0.697 (0.384)		0.939 (1.080)		0.615 (2.166)		0.811 (2.347)	
$IBR5_{t-1}$		-0.222 (-0.242)		0.310 (1.551)		0.124 (0.666)		0.100 (0.581)		0.287 (3.061)		0.312 (3.903)
Interest $Rate_{t-1}$	-2.78E-04 (-1.773)	0.001 (0.730)			-2.04E-04 (-1.029)	-3.79E-04 (-0.532)			-2.61E-05 (-1.967)	1.82E-05 (0.752)		

Estimation Results with (spanning header over all three observation groups)

The t-ratios are indicated in the parentheses.

added delay before the moshav's current capital costs are known to the farmer.

5 See discussion in Freund (1956) and recent applications by Yassour, Zilberman and Rausser (1981) and Collender and Zilberman (1985). As regards the generality of this framework Hammond (1974) has argued that the easy-to-analyze utility curve of constant absolute risk aversion can be used in place of non-constant absolute risk aversion when the rival choices in any pair-wise comparison yield uncertain payoffs that are either simply-intertwined or one stochastically dominates the other. In our particular case the former condition holds: our assumptions about ε_i implies that for any pair of chosen values of the decision variables, d_i and I_i, the cumulative distribution functions of the random payoffs $(c_i + \rho_i S_i)$ cross only once.

6 The model indicates under-investment given a level of borrowing, but as there may well be over-borrowing (see below in the text) investment levels may also exceed the joint-optimum level of investment. Of course this is only a partial analysis of optimal investment in agricultural capacity. Naive price expectations are a common reason for suboptimal investment levels.

7 We also simulate debt, capital and leverage trajectories using the estimated reduced form in which the moshav dummies are omitted. The simulations obtained also exhibit a large decline in capital and debt, and strongly indicate the more cautious behaviour of moshav members of type G2 and G3.

8 The state-transition matrix is

$$A = \begin{pmatrix} 1 - 0.018067 & - 0.001336 \\ - 0.315270 & 1 - 0.130267 \end{pmatrix}$$

and its characteristic roots are found by $\lambda_{1,2} = 0.5[tr\, A \pm (tr\, A - 4det\, A)^{0.5}]$. They are within the unit circle, and so the solution to the homogeneous part of the difference equation system 11, $c_1\lambda_1^t + c_2\lambda_2^1$, converges to zero as t goes to infinity; and the trajectories of D and K approach their trend curves.

Table A7.3 (continued)

Wheat Land Regression Equation

Explanatory variable	Estimated coefficients, t-ratios and elasticities				
	β=0.6	β=0.7	β=0.8	β=0.9	β=1.0
σ^2_{gram}	0.00033 (1.2134) 0.00001	0.00031 (1.1573) 0.00001	0.00027 (1.0360) 0.00001	0.00022 (0.8640) 4.5E-6	0.00019 (0.7162) 3.9E-6
$\sigma_{wheat\ gram}$	0.0023 (0.2516) 4.8E6	0.0037 (0.4125) 0.00001	0.0054 (0.5939) 0.00001	0.0072 (0.7884) 0.00002	0.0090 (0.9588) 0.00002
w^e_1	11625 (1.9105) 1.1039	9696.9 (1.9816) 0.9208	8975.9 (2.2037) 0.8523	8713.1 (2.4453) 0.8274	8303.4 (2.5253) 0.7885
w^e_2	-4404.3 (0.7247) -0.5203	-5002.0 (0.9507) -0.5909	-4695.5 (1.029) -0.5547	-3792.2 (0.9376) -0.4480	-2502.7 (0.6733) -0.2957
Constant	74422 (7.5448)	81299 (7.4376)	86556 (7.1271)	91832 (6.8473)	99085 (6.756)
BUSE R^2	0.4733	0.4812	0.4912	0.5071	0.5230
FPE	0.5281	0.5306	0.5333	0.5366	0.5406

Table A7.4
Pooled cross section-time series estimates of land allocation between wheat and gram with money illusion for Punjab 1966–86

Wheat Land Regression Equation

Explanatory variable	Estimated coefficients, t-ratios and elasticities				
	β=0.1	β=0.2	β=0.3	β=0.4	β=0.5
P^e_{wheat}	-124.79 (2.1195) -0.0086	-119.66 (2.0185) -0.0082	-115.17 (1.9781) -0.0079	-109.45 (1.9127) -0.0075	-96.244 (1.7284) -0.0066
P^e_{gram}	-97.507 (1.1622) -0.0121	-31.897 (0.6374) -0.004	-12.457 (0.3446) -0.0016	-4.0225 (0.1474) -0.0005	0.6616 (0.0312) 0.00008
$\bar{y}_{wheat}$	17.180 (4.6603) 0.0269	22.117 (5.8190) 0.0347	26.571 (6.5428) 0.0416	31.144 (7.1580) 0.0488	36.117 (7.7371) 0.0566
$\bar{y}_{gram}$	-4.9726 (2.1837) -0.0029	-5.7449 (2.3388) -0.0034	-5.8554 (2.2888) -0.0034	-5.6911 (2.2512) -0.0033	-5.3573 (2.1886) -0.0031
σ^2_{wheat}	0.0396 (2.269) 0.0011	0.02737 (1.5638) 0.0008	0.0235 (1.3402) 0.0007	0.0236 (1.3268) 0.0007	0.0249 (0.3860) 0.0007
σ^2_{gram}	0.00052 (1.8371) 0.00001	0.0005 (1.7974) 0.00001	0.00047 (1.6723) 0.00001	0.00044 (1.5712) 0.00001	0.00038 (1.4301) 0.00001

Table A7.4 (continued)

Explanatory variable	Wheat Land Regression Equation Estimated coefficients, t-ratios and elasticities				
	β=0.6	β=0.7	β=0.8	β=0.9	β=1.0
$\sigma_{wheat\ gram}$	0.0043 (0.4903) 0.00001	0.0053 (0.6206) 0.00001	0.0061 (0.7094) 0.00001	0.0067 (0.7505) 0.00001	0.0072 (0.7731) 0.00002
w_1^e	162.71 (3.0667) 0.0170	130.84 (3.1413) 0.0136	110.24 (3.2288) 0.0115	95.54 (3.1459) 0.010	83.284 (2.8902) 0.0087
w_2^e	13.678 (0.3065) 0.0019	5.9174 (0.1534) 0.0008	1.254 (0.0366) 0.0002	4.2844 (0.1344) 0.0006	13.372 (0.4736) 0.0019
Constant	62469 (8.5295)	69073 (8.4606)	76774 (8.5202)	87259 (8.7879)	100540 (9.3073)
BUSE R^2	0.5083	0.5300	0.5468	0.5509	0.5469
FPE	0.5205	0.5215	0.5223	0.5223	0.5227

Index

It is postulated that the firms' expected profit-maximization problem is

$$\max_{q_n} E\{[p(Q, Y, P) - mc]q_n\}$$

subject to

$$Q = \sum_{n'=1}^{N} q_{n'} \; . \qquad (3)$$

The solution of this problem yields the Cournot-Nash expected product price

$$E(p^*) = \frac{1}{1 - 1/\xi N}\{mc - 0.5[\tilde{p}_{YY}Var(Y) + \tilde{p}_{PP}Var(P) + \tilde{p}_{YP}Cov(Y, P)]\} \qquad (4)$$

as is shown in the Appendix.

The firm's expected instantaneous profit is given by

$$E[\pi(t)]_n = E[(p^* - mc)\, q_n^*] \qquad (5)$$

and by recalling equation 4 and that q_n^* is a chosen quantity and all of the firms have an identical production operation, the individual firm's expected instantaneous profit can be expressed further as:

$$E[\pi(t)]_n = \frac{Q^*}{N}[E(p^*)\text{-}mc] = \frac{mcQ^*}{N(\xi N\text{-}1)} - \frac{0.5\xi Q^*}{\xi N\text{-}1}[\tilde{p}_{YY}Var(Y) + \tilde{p}_{PP}Var(P) + \tilde{p}_{YP}Cov(Y, P)] \qquad (6)$$

where Q^* is the industry's volume of sales. *A priori*, the signs of the second derivatives of $\tilde{p}$ and Cov(Y, P) are unknown and hence the effects of uncertainty about the macroeconomic conditions, as well as the effects of the degree of industry concentration and price elasticity, on the firm's expected operating profit are not clear. When the overall effect of aggregate income and consumer price volatility on the industry product price (i.e., $\tilde{p}_{YY}Var(Y)$ + $\tilde{p}_{PP}Var(P)$ +

since $H < 0$.

The Solution to the Firm's Expected Profit-Maximization Problem

Given the second-order Taylor approximation of the inverse demand function, the firm's objective function can be displayed as

$$\max_{q_n} E\{[Q^{-1/\xi} + \tilde{p}_Y(Y - \bar{Y}) + \tilde{p}_P(P - \bar{P}) + 0.5\,\tilde{p}_{YY}(Y - \bar{Y})^2$$

$$+ 0.5\,\tilde{p}_{PP}(P - \bar{P})^2 + 0.5\,\tilde{p}_{YP}(Y - \bar{Y})(P - \bar{P}) - mc]\,q_n\}.$$

Taking the expectation of the objective function and recalling that the choice variable q_n is deterministic and that $E(Y-\bar{Y})=0=E(P-\bar{P})$, the objective function can be expressed further as

$$\max_{q_n} \{Q^{-1/\xi} q_n + 0.5[\,\tilde{p}_{YY}\mathrm{Var}(Y) + \tilde{p}_{PP}\mathrm{Var}(P) +$$

$$\tilde{p}_{YP}\mathrm{Cov}(Y,P)]q_n - mc\,q_n\}.$$

The first-order condition for maximum is

$$-(1/\xi)Q^{*-1/\xi}\,q_n^*/Q^* + Q^{*-1/\xi} - mc + 0.5[\tilde{p}_{YY}\mathrm{Var}(Y) + \tilde{p}_{YY}\mathrm{Var}(P) + \tilde{p}_{YP}\mathrm{Cov}(Y,P)] = 0$$

and since $Q^{*-1/\xi} = E(p^*)$ and $q_n^*/Q^* = 1/N$ (all firms have identical production operation)

$$E(p^*) = \frac{1}{1 - 1/\xi N}\{mc - 0.5[\tilde{p}_{YY}\mathrm{Var}(Y) + \tilde{p}_{PP}\mathrm{Var}(P) + \tilde{p}_{YP}\mathrm{Cov}(Y,P)]\}.$$

Proof of Proposition 6: By virtue of proposition 5 and equation 6

$$\frac{dT^o}{d\mathrm{Var}(Y)} = \frac{dT^o}{dE(\pi)}\frac{dE(\pi)}{d\mathrm{Var}(Y)} = -\frac{0.5\xi Q^*}{\xi N - 1}\frac{dT^o}{dE(\pi)}\tilde{p}_{YY} \gtreqless 0 \text{ as } \tilde{p}_{YY} \lesseqgtr 0,$$

Table 9.1 (continued)

Country	GNP growth*	debt accumulation*	H_1	H_2	x on y	y on x
Brazil	0.05126 (5.960) 0.966	0.11368 (4.394) 0.968	No	No	-2.768	0.497
Chile	0.01813 (2.758) 0.693	0.05955 (4.476) 0.957	No	No	0.273	-8.446
Colombia	0.04335 (12.555) 0.992	0.08046 (16.591) 0.961	No	No	0.158	1.125
Costa Rica	0.03299 (5.437) 0.938	0.10393 (5.025) 0.980	No	Yes**	0.331	2.811
Ecuador	0.05814 (5.343) 0.956	0.15529 (4.368) 0.957	No	No	0.109	1.967
Jamaica	-0.01347 (3.093) 0.799	0.02542 (2.668) 0.792	No	No	-0.714	-2.631
Mexico	0.03821 (5.216) 0.970	0.10035 (4.772) 0.977	Yes	Yes	—	—
Peru	0.02114 (5.388) 0.825	0.04930 (4.464) 0.906	No	no	-0.007	-2.939
Uruguay	0.01432 (2.329) 0.805	0.09242 (13.023) 0.952	No	No	0.359	-1.707
Venezuela	0.0200 (3.059) 0.895	0.14902 (3.185) 0.921	No	Yes	-0.755	—

* The numbers in the parentheses are t-ratios and the numbers below the t-ratios indicate the determination coefficients (R^2).

** The opposite conclusion is obtained at the 5 per cent level of significance.

Table 9.4
Long-term rates, causality test's results and long-term effects for countries in South Europe and the Mediterranean Basin

	Long-Term Rates of		*Reject at 1% Level of Significance*		*Long-Term Effects of*	
Country	GNP growth*	debt accumulation*	H_1	H_2	x on y	y on x
Greece	0.02814	0.10328	Yes	No	—	9.146
	(5.040)	(17.303)				
	0.957	0.978				
Morocco	0.04423	0.12723	Yes	Yes	—	—
	(27.247)	(5.416)				
	0.984	0.971				
Portugal	0.03117	0.12014	Yes	Yes	—	—
	(9.373)	(4.317)				
	0.954	0.965				
Yugoslavia	0.03212	0.07209	No	Yes	0.324	—
	(4.218)	(3.291)				
	0.959	0.950				

* The numbers in the parentheses are t-ratios and the numbers below the t-ratios indicate the determination coefficients (R^2).
** The opposite conclusion is obtained at the 5 per cent level of significance.

the rate of growth of GNP and the external debt accumulation rate are traced in the cases of Morocco and Portugal.

9.4 Conclusion

The statistical tests of causal relationships between the GNP growth rate and the external debt accumulation rate and the computed long-term effects of the GNP growth rate on the external

Table 10.1
3SLS estimation results for Latin-America*

Explanatory Variables	GNP	CAPITAL	EDPUB	EDPRIV
	Dependent variables			
Endogenous				
GNP	—	2.0084	0.1214	0.0216
		(10.302)	(14.824)	(7.4589)
CAPITAL	0.7360	—	—	—
	(11.6950)			
EDPUB	-1.2378	2.5063	—	—
	(6.8979)	(12.419)		
EDPRIV	1.5378	-4.4637	—	—
	(3.4459)	(3.8420)		
Predetermined				
LEDPUB	—	—	0.5539	—
			(18.441)	
LEDPRIV	—	—	—	0.7035
				(18.368)
LCAPITAL	—	0.0167	—	—
		(1.1538)		
LABOR	341.86	—	—	—
	(0.2662)			
CAPITALSQ	-5.0E-07	—	—	—
	(2.5993)			
LABORSQ	141.690	—	—	—
	(2.0748)			
PLFAG	-36.733	254.60	-48.680	-2.9730
	(0.6188)	(2.1152)	(2.0577)	(0.5771)
TOT	—	—	-71.354	0.3478
			(7.3833)	(0.1689)
POP	—	-914.67	—	—
		(4.1129)		
INSH40	—	162.89	79.930	—
		(1.1382)	(0.8523)	
CONSTANT	957.90	-10754.0	8101.1	63.044
	(0.3804)	(2.0596)	(4.3728)	(0.2013)

* The t-ratios are indicated in the parentheses.

Table A7.2 (continued)

Explanatory variable	Maize Land Regression Equation Estimated coefficients, t-ratios and elasticities				
	β=0.1	β=0.2	β=0.3	β=0.4	β=0.5
σ^2_{maize}	0.0174 (2.2554) 0.0011	0.0241 (3.2381) 0.0015	0.0266 (3.6097) 0.0017	0.0257 (3.427) 0.0016	0.0233 (3.0071) 0.0015
$\sigma_{rice\ maize}$	0.00083 (0.0725) 0.00001	0.0039 (0.3255) 0.00004	0.0044 (0.3591) 0.00004	0.0038 (0.3073) 0.00004	0.0023 (0.1825) 0.00002
w^e_1	-156.74 (0.6308) -0.068	71.094 (0.5552) 0.0308	89.716 (1.0365) 0.0389	81.983 (1.2173) 0.0355	70.810 (1.2385) 0.0307
w^e_2	-112.22 (0.6967) -0.0645	-175.17 (2.0252) -0.1007	-163.9 (2.7045) -0.0942	-143.25 (2.9667) -0.0824	-127.99 (3.0871) -0.0736
Constant	9307.4 (4.2929)	12394 (4.7012)	15995 (5.2482)	20062 (5.7294)	23485 (5.7559)
BUSE R^2	0.3240	0.3213	0.3277	0.3177	0.3009
FPE	0.5688	0.5658	0.5584	0.5509	0.5437

Table A7.3 (continued)

Gram Land Regression Equation

Explanatory variable	Estimated coefficients, t-ratios and elasticities				
	β=0.6	**β=0.7**	**β=0.8**	**β=0.9**	**β=1.0**
σ^2_{gram}	-0.00014	-0.00011	-0.000094	-0.00076	-0.000063
	(1.9873)	(1.7171)	(1.4620)	(1.2092)	(0.9891)
	-0.00003	-0.00002	-0.00002	-0.000014	-0.00001
$\sigma_{wheat\ gram}$	0.0049	0.0044	0.0038	0.0031	0.00249
	(1.4877)	(1.4284)	(1.3012)	(1.0912)	(0.8581)
	0.0001	0.0001	0.0001	0.0001	0.00005
w^e_1	3677.8	2400.1	1517.1	1082.0	968.22
	(1.5235)	(1.1252)	(0.8150)	(0.6673)	(0.6682)
	3.1042	2.0258	1.2805	0.9132	0.8172
w^e_2	-6952.8	-4938.3	-3331.3	-2487.2	-2310.2
	(3.516)	(2.5038)	(1.7788)	(1.4476)	(1.4670)
	-7.3012	-5.1857	-3.4982	-2.6118	-2.4259
Constant	27201	32359	36881	40668	43660
	(10.783)	(10.558)	(10.074)	(9.6134)	(9.2849)
BUSE R^2	0.5290	0.4891	0.4560	0.4334	0.4190
FPE	0.5351	0.5314	0.5263	0.5197	0.5136

Index